T0271749

Will Sergeant is best known as the founding member and lead guitarist of Echo & the Bunnymen. By inventing his own experimental style of playing, he has explored the outer edges of what can be achieved by the electric guitar in the limited realm of rock music.

ECHOES

A Memoir Continued . . .

Will Sergeant

CONSTABLE

CONSTABLE

First published in Great Britain in 2023 by Constable
This paperback edition published in 2024 by Constable

1 3 5 7 9 10 8 6 4 2

A CIP catalogue record for this book
is available from the British Library.

ISBN: 978-1-40871-931-2

Typeset in Bembo by Hewer Text UK Ltd, Edinburgh
Printed and bound in Great Britain by Clays Ltd, Elcograf, S.p.A.

Papers used by Constable are from well-managed
forests and other responsible sources

Constable
An imprint of
Little, Brown Book Group
Carmelite House
50 Victoria Embankment
London EC4Y 0DZ

An Hachette UK Company

www.hachette.co.uk

www.littlebrown.co.uk

To my girls: Paula, Alice and Greta

Contents

CHAPTER 1

Mini Gets the Boot

'You're Gonna Miss Me' – 13th Floor Elevators

Bunnymen three piece, 1979

It's 15 September 1979. It's a slow news day. Monty Python's new film *The Life of Brian* is causing sour God-botherers the world over to develop the hump; somehow, Python's Brian is getting confused with some far-out hippie bloke called Jesus.

As you may or may not know, my favourite war is the Cold War. The frosty relations between East and West are as strong as ever. And over in an East German forest clearing, two families are frantically inflating a homemade hot-air balloon. The gas burner's flames heat the air of a vast home-sewn nylon sack. It billows as the air expands and tightly plumps up the membrane. The balloon starts to rise slowly and then tilts in a sudden gust of wind. The nylon skin catches the burners; it's now on fire. These Ossi are quick thinkers and soon extinguish the flames without much damage. It's a close shave, but there's no turning back now. They all clamber into the makeshift gondolier, anchor lines are cut and upwards they float to catch the westerly wind and softly drift towards the border.

Onto even more joyous news of 15 September. My new favourite band, Manchester's Joy Division, are on the telly tonight. Granada TV has just started a new show for the youth made by the youth called *Something Else*. But for me, Ian McCulloch and Les Pattinson, that night of the fifteenth is a pivotal day in the story of the Bunnymen. We play at our spiritual home, Eric's Club in Liverpool, alongside The Teardrop Explodes. Gigs have been picking up of late after John Peel from BBC Radio 1 played our Zoo Records single 'The Pictures on My Wall'.

The London-based music press have pricked up their ears, and they sense something happening up north. They turn their dopey gaze towards the Mersey and the bands that are sprouting up all over the city – bands with one tenuous link that binds them, as all have ridiculous and vaguely psychedelic/avant-garde-sounding names. In the desperate haze of the punk-rock comedown, that's enough to call it a scene. And just like Jesus's lookalike Brian in the Python film, we are starting to collect disciples whether we want them or not. We, of course, do want disciples; we are glad to bring them along and expand our grass-roots devotees. Some will remain fans for their whole lives, and

I am grateful for that, as it has prevented me from doing a proper job until this very day. So far, so good.

That August, we had played at London's YMCA. American record boss Seymour Stein, the head honcho of Sire Records, was in attendance. After our show, he let it be known to our management, Big Bill Drummond, that he was interested in signing us to his incredibly hip New York label, with only one condition. 'They get a drummer.'

Factory flyer

Bill Drummond told me recently, 'I was worried that you would say no to this idea and tell Sire and me to fuck right off. Or worse still, not say anything,' and in Bill's words, 'drift into one of your ominous moods.'

I admit I could be a funny bugger back then and keep a gob on me for weeks. I was legendary for not saying hello to Macul for months on end if he had pissed me off somehow; the icy silence was my weapon of choice, my very own little Cold War.

I was very precious of our sound and the format of the band. Bill must have thought that having a drummer would take a little of my control away. It was my drum machine that was looking at life on the scrap heap, after all.

A few days later, Bill Drummond finally plucked up the nerve to give us the news Seymour wanted to sign us, and the proviso that we retired the drum machine (known as Echo) and employed a real drummer. To Bill's delight and shock, we all agreed sharpish (even me). He was expecting me to be dead against this drastic move, as I was generally the band member quick to get a shitty on with all the cheesy crap you are expected to do to become a successful pop group, plus I was the drum machine's operator.

On this occasion, I was not so stupid or stubborn as not to realise that the band, the songs and the live gigs would be better with a drummer, plus it would take the pressure off me at the gigs, with the constant worry that the drum machine would stop or, worse, I would perform some sort of fuck-up with my cobbled-together footswitch system. It was always touch and go; often, a desperate cry would go out from me:

'Shit! Nothing's working.'

I would occasionally miss-hit the footswitch, my count one, two, three, four would be greeted by silence, and a stumbled start would make us all look like a bunch of dicks. It was easy to slip when guiding the slender sole of a painfully fashionable winklepicker onto the tiny footswitch button on a darkened stage.

The truth is that we had outgrown the limited repertoire of our electronic beatbox. We wouldn't conquer the world with the anaemic tick-tock of the only two settings on the drum machine we found useful, namely Rock 1 and Rock 2. Our songs were now demanding a more dynamic and powerful rhythm.

It was just like when the Fab Four's early drummer Pete Best got the Beatle-boot up the arse to be replaced by Ringo. As all you Beatles fans know, this was done for the benefit of moving the recording of the song and groove up a notch. (Believe that and you'll believe anything.) This had nothing to do with Pete Best's stubborn quiff haircut that didn't quite fit in with the other lovable mop-tops' locks.

We follow suit, and the Mini Pops junior drum machine aka Echo is the first casualty of this new post-punk war; Echo gets the elbow for the greater good.

Behind the scenes, our manager Big Bill Drummond is still unsure of my acceptance of the group having a real live human member. Even so, Bill and Dave Balfe, who founded Zoo Records together and are both involved in looking after the Bunnymen and The Teardrop Explodes, leap into action and set about trying to find the band a drummer. It is a challenging task to fish out a loose drummer in the small pond that is Liverpool. There is a defiant cockiness that comes ready installed in the scouse breed. Most Liverpudlian muso types have a bravado welded onto their egos. They think of themselves as singers or guitarists, even if they are, like me, not that competent. Most scousers don't want to be drummers destined to be stuck at the back of the stage. Hence in Liverpool, drummers are very thin on the ground.

Luckily, up steps Dave Balfe's younger brother Kieran. Kieran attended a posh boarding school near Bath in Somerset, Downside. Quite an apt name for this school; the downside, in my view, is the fact that Benedictine monks run it. The school and Pete's life couldn't be further away from what I and the rest of us are used to.

Kieran tells Dave, 'There is a lad from our school who is a drummer; his name is Pete de Freitas.'

And just like that, Big Bill and Dave Balfe decide to go and meet this kid who used to go to the posho school. They are on a trip down south anyway, on their way to collect pressings of the latest Zoo Records release, then drop the product off in London at Rough Trade Records, Small Wonder in Walthamstow, Beggars Banquet in Wandsworth and various other indie record shops. It was all very cottage industry in those days. Bill and Dave were storming up and down the motorways with a car full of boxes of seven-inch singles. Soon the country's indie record shops would be chock-a-block with Zoo Records products.

Consequently, it's no big detour to head off to a flat in Stamford Hill, north London, that Pete shares with Kieran Balfe and another bloke called Percy Penrose. When Bill and Dave arrive, they head for the local pub to get acquainted with Pete and his mates. After a few pints, some chit chat, and, like these things do, pub closing time fast approaches; they head off via a chippy, and with fish and chips warming their hands, it's all back to the flat where they are treated to a jokey musical performance with guitar, bass and drums.

I give Dave Balfe a call, and he tells me, 'It was rubbish, but the drummer stood out,' and both he and Bill think he's brilliant.

★ ★ ★

A few days later, Pete's invited to Liverpool to meet us. I can't remember if I had much worry or thoughts about this; I guess I was taking these developments with a pinch of salt. Coincidentally, Pete was in the audience at the YMCA gig in London in August. And later said in an interview, 'I thought they were not particularly good . . . They were weird and weird-looking.'

That sounds like a plus to me; who doesn't like things weird? I know I do.

After the Eric's gig, we are all chatting with Pete; he's a very quiet lad and happy to observe. He's surrounded by these loud scouse punks, with his posh accent and polite manners, a fish out of water. Underneath the posh exterior, it's clear that he's a cool kid and he's getting on with everyone. He's being viewed as some fascinating exotic animal, but from the start, Pete is open and friendly, without the slightest hint of any snobbery. I feel a bit protective towards him and am keen for this weird situation to work. I am trying my best to keep him entertained. I bring a steady stream of the girls that I know over for him to say hello. OK, that's a slight exaggeration. I only know about three girls, and them only vaguely; even so, they all seem to like him and are chatting with him happily.

He tells me he thought the gig was good (obviously better than the one at the YMCA). After a couple of bottles of Eric's Pilsner and more random chat about music, the clocks tick forward to closing time. The lights are unceremoniously flicked on; it's kicking out time, 2 a.m. When any lifting or carrying is on the cards, Macul does his usual disappearing act, so Les and I are loading our scant equipment up the back stairs of Eric's and into Les's rust-pocked Ford Transit, which is parked on Mathew Street's cobbles.

7

At this exact moment over in Germany, the do-it-yourself balloon is getting dragged along the ploughed soil of a Bavarian spud field. The two families on this night-time ride scramble out of the balloon's basket, get themselves together on the solid earth and gaze up at freedom's clouds. They have made it. Oh dear, someone in the Stasi has dropped a bollock, and no doubt it will be the East German equivalent of the Gulag for them.

Unlike those poor sods fleeing the East for a better life in the West, Pete is escaping his already better life in the South. With a posh upbringing, a lovely family house in Goring-on-Thames and a place at Oxford University, Pete is likely to be giving all that up in exchange for an uncertain future with a trio of northerners in the Bolshevik heartland that is Liverpool. It's a brave thing to do, and I still wonder, *Why?* But I'm so glad he did.

It is decided that the next day, Sunday, we are all to head to our practice room or, in the slang we use, praccy room. By the way, for some reason we always called it going to praccy or practice, not rehearsals, back then – I think most of the bands did. I can still see in my mind's eye Gary Dwyer, the drummer from The Teardrop Explodes, sitting in the Armadillo Tea Rooms as he drains the last few dregs of cold tea he has been nursing for ages, saying, 'We're off to praccy at Yorkie's ma's basement.' Yorkie's ma being the amazing Gladys.

It must have been a Liverpool thing. Or maybe another punk-rock hangover. 'Rehearsals' sounded a little too old school, a touch too much like professional terminology for the likes of us Johnny-come-latelys, the reserve of bands that know what they are doing. So praccy is good enough for us young upstarts.

Yorkie's basement today

Yorkie's real name is Dave Palmer, who's persuaded his mum Gladys to let bands use her basement. Dave is the apple of Gladys's eye and he is indulged by his mum, even if this means suffering a gang of scruffs making an unholy racket radiating from the basement, thundering up the wooden stairs and through the flimsy cellar door into her kitchen on a regular basis. Yorkie is a few years younger than us. He is an interesting character, to say the least. Some of his clothes made our over-coats and oversized dead men's suits, with a touch of charity-shop shit that we thought Mark E. Smith of the Fall might wear, look mainstream. The teenage Yorkie was often seen about town in a Second World War tin hat, jodhpurs, highly polished black leather Canadian motorcycle dispatch riders' boots and

9

gaiters, all this topped off by a severe Richard III haircut. Yorkie told me he would get our friendly neighbourhood barber Victor to cut his hair in this rather unusual way.

'As long as you don't tell anyone where you got it cut, will ya, lad?'

As a sixteen-year-old, it must have taken balls of steel to be seen wandering the streets of Kenny (Kensington), not the most accepting area of Liverpool, to put it mildly. As his style developed, he could be spotted trotting up and down the city centre's nearest thing to a bohemian or groovy street, Bold Street, in a thick hooded First World War nurse's cloak with a ceremonial scabbard, covered with ornate metallic flourishes and housing a full-size sword, clattering around on his belt.

He had been questioned about this by an inquisitive member of our post-punk gang, a chap called Justin, he himself obsessed with all things from the 1930s and 1940s, and dressing accordingly in demob suits, silk ties, highly polished brogues and a collection of Roy Fox, Lou Stone and Cab Calloway records stacked up in his radiogram.

'Hey, Yorkie, don't you ever get into bother with the scals around your way walking about looking like that?'

'No, not really,' Yorkie said softly in his slightly more rounded, song-like Liverpool accent.

A quick note on Liverpool accents. Now, this is just my opinion, so no actual scientific study has been made, but I generally feel that for dwellers in the south end of the city their accent is a little smoother and the words are delivered a bit slower. The city's northern parts have a more complex and faster, abrasive edge, with a lot more of the phlegm-inducing back-of-throat growl. I have always felt the southern

Liverpudlian accent sounded posher. More like George from the Fab Four.

So back to the question.

'Don't you get your head kicked in or at least legged by those beastly young Kensington scallywags?'

Then it struck me: he was armed with a fucking massive sword in a scabbard at his side. And he looked like a mental hospital escapee. No offence, Dave, but you looked fucking nuts. And I'm glad you did, so well done. We need more Yorkies in this world. People that just say, 'I like it, so get fucked, you fuckers.' As far as I know, zero swashbuckling shenanigans were ever engaged in, and the sword was never drawn in anger.

Back in Yorkie's basement, our plan is to run through some of the songs with Pete on drums and see if it works.

Les sets off from his house in Aughton in his Transit van and picks me up from my dad's house in Melling, then on we go to get Macul from his flat. It's a short journey across the backside of Liverpool's suburbs. We chug past Anfield, Liverpool FC's ground, then we climb up to the foothills of Everton Valley. We can see the city spread out before us. The two contrasting cathedrals, ancient and modern, reach skywards, both magnificent beacons shrouded grey in the misty city swirl. This haze softens the hard Liverpudlian streets below. In the distance, the broad Mersey shines like a mercury ribbon. It's our city. Never mind that I'm from a few miles out of the town, a 'wool', I am a Bunnyman, and it's our city now.

We continue to Breck Road then along Sheil Road traversing the outskirts till we arrive at Yorkie's Victorian house in Prospect Vale, just a stone's throw away from the Silver Blades ice rink, where I used to go with my secondary school for free-choice skating fun. I would slither around and around with the grace of a larupped ostrich while the Supremes' 'Baby Love' was blasted out of the tinny speakers.

Yorkie meets us at the Prospect Vale basement and lets us in the room. It's a little damp; it's always cold. The walls are lined with cardboard and eggboxes, as is the ceiling. It's a vain attempt to quell the sound.

As Macul attends to the vital task of smoking fags, me and Les have our equipment out of the van and set up and ready in no time. We nervously wait like we are on some sort of weird date. A couple of cups of tea later, Pete arrives with Bill Drummond and Dave Balfe in tow. Bill and Dave decide to bail out and let us get to know Pete on our own, without much interference from them. Yorkie brings us yet more tea in his strange *Eraserhead*-ish garb; it doesn't seem to be freaking out Pete in the slightest. But he is used to being taught algebra by celibate geezers in hooded robes. It's not surprising that Yorkie's clobber strikes him as no weirder.

While we make small talk, Pete works on the drum setup. He is using Gary Dwyer of The Teardrop Explodes' kit, recently bought off Deaf School drummer, artist and Gary's hero Tim Whittaker; the drums are already set up inside the basement's hopeful cardboard-lined walls. We will soon learn that no amount of eggboxes will quell Pete's din.

Pete takes the whole matter of drumming very seriously; he is tweaking the drums just how he likes them. Drums are like clothes: they must fit and be comfortable. He is wearing a percussive made-to-measure suit, but it's been fitted for Gary Dwyer, not Pete. Every part of the kit is positioned precisely, and comfortably. This kit needs major alterations. I have observed this ritual many times over the years. Each drummer has their own way of it feeling just right. This is a very personal and precise requirement for drummers to play at their best. We stand around awkwardly. We are used to plugging in the drum machine and testing the volume, and that's it, drum check over. Pete is fucking around bashing the drums and turning a little chromium key used to tighten or loosen the drum skins, all done to tune them up. I never even knew you had to tune drums. Pete continues bash-tweak-bash. This seems to go on for hours. Suddenly I'm thinking having a drummer appears a bit of a faff. Eventually, Pete has a final run around the kit to check that the drum tones sound good together.

We are ready.

Yorkie's mum, the marvellous Gladys, sits upstairs with her feet up. All dusting is done. She is taking five. She's dressed in the standard 1970s mum's uniform of floral-patterned tabard and fluffy slippers, with a tight curly perm sitting above large-framed glasses. She's holding a cup of tea as the oven slowly crisps the King Edward's spuds and crackles golden her signature dish of honey-roast pork. It's going to be a fantastic Sunday lunch. Down in the basement, and as Jethro Tull say in their song 'Wond'ring Aloud', I'm tasting the smell. The wonderful aromas are wafting down the steep stairway and straight up my oversized hooter. I am hoping we get a taster. After what is to come, it's doubtful. She is expecting the usual din from below but nothing like what is coming.

We go through the song at roughly the right tempo so that Pete has an idea of speed.

Pete counts in 'One-two-three-four' in the time-honoured

tradition of the rock drummer. We launch into 'Villiers Terrace'. Macul is sharply chugging away at the chords; I am making a stab at my best Tom Verlaine impression. Les is pummelling the bass like a heavy punchbag at a boxing gym. The drums are loud, thunderous, made even louder by the confined space of the small cellar. There is only one thing for it, we all turn up our amplifiers to compete with Pete's heavy-metal thunder. Pete is the loudest thing I've ever heard since the Pink Fairies blew my mind out at the Liverpool Stadium gig in 1972. He seems to want to punish the shit out of the drum skins. It's no wonder he had to spend ages tightening Gary's flabby skins. The windows in the street are beginning to rattle as is, just above us, the glazing in Gladys's large, amber, plastic-framed glasses. Any distressed shouts from up in the kitchen go unheard by us. We are riding out on the adrenaline of this whole new scene when, in midflow, the basement door is flung open.

There stands Gladys. She's not happy. She rushes over to Pete and is all up in his grill, as the kids say nowadays. She growls at him with high-pitched, intense, sarcastic venom: 'Can't you play those fucking drums any louder?' adding, 'Turn them fucking down!'

And the funny thing is, as we learn over the coming years, yes, he could play those drums a fuck of a lot louder if he wanted to.

Pete jolts up to attention at Gladys's furious screech and shits himself (not really; at least, I don't think so). Young Peter has not been used to or even been in the same room as someone like Gladys. He stops playing immediately. The shock on his face is portrayed in an ashen grimace. He is white with fear. We are all glad her spleen is not being vented at us. Far from being scared, we all look on at Pete's terror. This is very amusing to us. We know Gladys's bark is worse than her bite, as we have been on the other side of her acerbic tongue on many occasions. A cheeky smile from Macul is usually enough to diffuse any anger when she storms into the basement. Gladys has a soft spot for Macul.

We never had this problem with the drum machine, but we could turn that down. Turn Pete de Freitas down? That seems unlikely, and why the hell would you want to?

Pete's terror is downgraded to the bemused look of a frightened puppy.

Gladys breaks into a smile, her bright eyes enlarged by her glasses. She softens her face and says, 'Just turn those sodding drums down, will ya?'

Gladys heads back upstairs and then returns a little later with tea and biscuits. We try a few more songs, and Pete does try his hardest to turn it down, slightly.

I'm no expert on drums (especially back then). Of course, I love Keith Moon from the Who, Charlie Watts of the Stones, John Bonham of Zeppelin, Clive Bunker, Barriemore Barlow from the aforementioned Jethro Tull, and the jazz vibes of Robert Wyatt from the Soft Machine and John Densmore from the Doors, and numerous others. I can even tell the styles of such giants, but technically I'm no drum aficionado. So, I have no idea that we have just found one of the world's most inventive, influential and musical drummers. He will be cited as an influence by countless world-class drummers in the future. Back in the cellar at the arse end of 1979, all I know or understand is that he sounded brilliant. POWERFUL is the best word to use. The butterflies flapping about in my stomach seem

15

to agree. All of us are smiling; Macul and Pete spark up a fag in celebration.

Pete's easy-going personality is a joy to be around. We manage to get him laughing a lot on that first day. Bill and Dave Balfe return, and we set about playing a couple of tunes for them. Bill is grinning excitedly and is flailing his arms around like he's playing the drums in the way that an air guitarist would play, well you know, air guitar. We can see that he and Dave are liking what they are hearing. We are complete now, and fortune has smiled on us yet again. As a band, we have increased our power by several shed-loads. Let's hope he decides to bin off all that Oxford University nonsense and stay up north.

CHAPTER 2

Punch-up Near Slowcoach's Secret Garden

'Fire' – The Crazy World of Arthur Brown

Me, up to arty self-timer photography in the back parlour

Back at the Sergeants', life is relatively stable; the old man and I are getting along just fine. Not much in the way of arguments echo around 15 Station Road any more. We hardly ever see each other, so maybe that's why. I'm either out on my seaside-salvaged motorbike (it's a long story) razzing along in the night air as the slow flakes of rust start to gain a foothold and are gradually blistering the paint off the frame; or I'm at work as a commis chef. In the evenings and days off, I usually find myself in the back parlour listening to records or dicking about with my tape-recording machines.

You will find me at the punk club, Eric's, or practising with my band when the weekend comes. My mates in Melling are still going to the pubs around the area, but I'm not a massive fan of the pub, probably because my dad is the pub's biggest fan: he's in there every night, and I don't want to be like him. My mates Davo and the gang are still into music, but not the same stuff I listen to now. We all still love the Ramones and the Buzzcocks, but I am drawn to the more out-there records. The Residents are my band now. And I delight in playing them to mates I know won't understand them and even hate them.

As happens with friends, you grow up, things change, and your interests are no longer the same as your mates' interests. Even though it is only eight miles away, being in Liverpool shapes my view of the horizon, and I'm contemplating moving out of my dad's house. Paul Simpson, my friend and ex-bandmate who was on keyboards in The Teardrop Explodes for a while, has a flat, and I can see his freedom. Besides, all the action is in Liverpool now.

Returning to sleepy Melling has become a touch bland. It's all got a little stagnant in my tiny Melling and Station Road bubble.

Occasionally I team up with the old gang, but they are moving on too. They have bought more enormous motorbikes, beasts that I would have no way of keeping up with. I go with them sometimes on the pillion, mainly with Davo on the back of his Suzuki GS1000. It goes like stink, and I am clinging on to the back like my life depends on it, and guess what, it does depend

Liverpool, early 1980s

on it. We go to the Bootle Arms in an area called the Melling Rocks, so-called because this is where the red sandstone rock was quarried and used to build Melling church. It's out of the way of the semi-detached housing estates and the people living there. The Rocks are a slightly more well-to-do area of Melling, and the Sergeant brothers who didn't spend all their money down the boozer could afford to buy houses up there. Two of my uncles live at the Rocks. The Bootle Arms is only a ten-minute walk, up past my junior school, along an old sandy path known as the pads. Pads? I've been told 'pads' is short for paddocks; it only took me sixty-odd years to figure that out. As kids, we never thought it could mean something. It was just part of the linguistic landscape of our youth.

There's a small shop up at the Rocks. As kids, it was exciting to venture up to Makin's Shop. Mrs Makin would always give you a couple of extra sweets. White mice were the ultimate expensive treat at a halfpenny each. The Bootle Arms solid-stone pub must have been a farm at some point. Maybe it was one of those stop-off places to rest horses as you travelled from town to town. Or, more than likely, somewhere that the people from the nearby canal barges could get some food and beer. With the arrival of cars and the demise of canal transport, the barn and stables were no longer needed and are now part of the pub. Random long oak tables with mismatched chairs provide the seating. It's quaintly rustic with a hard-worked stone floor and whitewashed and fire-soot-stained walls. The décor, like all pubs then, has been tarnished by decades of pipe and cigarette smoke. The sticky ceiling above has a coated dark, raw sienna sheen. It looks like it hasn't changed for centuries.

In the sixties, my mum was a cleaner in the Bootle Arms. She claimed she saw a ghost in the upstairs living quarters while cleaning the bar. Mum was beckoned from the stairs by a woman in old-fashioned clothing, including a white linen mop hat. Initially, she thought it was the woman who ran the pub, Nora Blundell, in fancy dress. She followed her up the stairs and into a bedroom, where she found the entity looking out of the window, beckoning to someone over in the fields. As she tried to make sense of this scene, the apparition faded, and my mum realised this wasn't Nora. She ran down the stairs screaming. My mum said she asked the vicar, Dr Hayes, about this, and he said someone was killed in the fields by the Roundhead soldiers of Oliver Cromwell's New Model Army. After winning the civil war, Cromwell's parliamentarians had Charles I executed in 1649, so when the monarchy was reinstated, his son Charles II insisted Cromwell be dug up and executed even though he was already a long time dead. His head was stuck on a spike, only for it to fall off the next stormy night. It's unclear where it is now. Those royals – you couldn't make it up, all proper nutjobs. They make the Sergeant clan seem normal.

Very occasionally, my mate Davo and I go to the pub in the centre of the village, the Horse and Jockey: the name is due to the proximity of the Aintree racecourse, home of the Grand National. Sometimes I see my dad in the bar area. Back then, pubs were segregated between the bar and the lounge, with the bar for workers with dirty overalls and even dirtier mouths. Generally, women, though not strictly banned, were discouraged from going into the bar areas. It was somewhere that blokes could swear and be rowdy.

I see my dad being the life and soul of the party and telling jokes with all the regulars. He's a totally different fellow in the pub. The alcohol changes him. But by kicking-out time, the reality of his life floods back, and the dark mood returns, but all in all, things are not too bad after my mum has jumped ship. And we could watch some early evening TV shows together like *Star Trek* and the bargain basement BBC sci-fi show *Blake's Seven*. He likes science fiction, which is not what I would expect from someone with such a closed mind.

But I know what you are thinking: *Hold on; we never signed up for happy families; conflict is what we want!*

OK, what about this one? Not quite as out there as Charlie and Ollie's seventeenth-century right royal religious capers, but somewhat odd, so read on.

Thursday is my day off from work; I lazily lie in my tiny, freezing bed. I am gleaning and storing all the possible body heat I can muster. My army blanket and the fully unzipped nylon sleeping bag that has been promoted to the rank of eiderdown are trying their best to warm me. I am like a lizard on a rock waiting for the rising sun to bring me to a slow simmer and back into life. I'm still chilled; my pink snout poking out of the covering is nearly dropping off with the cold. The freezing room is causing my breath to be visible; grey plumes of vapour are puffed out like fag smoke. I don't want to face the icy day just yet. I laze there, and my mind occupies that creepy little region of consciousness between sleep and waking. I drift nonchalantly along the astral plane. My thoughts are sliding back to the mid-sixties and recalling something that still shocks me.

I am about eight years old; it's sunny, so I presume it was in the summer holidays. I reckon about 1966. I am playing in the yard at the Sergeants' woodworking business, which everyone in the family called the works. I am clambering among the stacks of wood and general detritus of a woodyard, with only the occasional forklift truck or heavy wagon whizzing about the yard. I am crawling over and under precariously stacked rows of planks waiting to be made into packing cases. Sergeants' Woodyard is owned and operated by my dad and five of his brothers, Frankie, Johnny, Tommy, David and Harold.

I am mooching around near what was known as the big shed; that's right, it's a great big shed with massive metal sliding doors at either end of the structure. The sliding doors are daubed with pink rust-resisting paint. It's big enough for the firm's Bedford flatbed lorry to drive through comfortably. The shed is clad in corrugated asbestos sheeting, grey and crumbling with the odd jagged hole where a rogue plank or sacked worker's boot have made their mark. Asbestos was used everywhere in those days.

My dad told me that he and his brothers had constructed the shed shortly after the war. They were slicing the massive asbestos sheets with the big circular bench saw. He said the dust clouds from the sawing made it almost impossible to see what they were doing. Asbestos particles billowed all around. This shit is best not to be breathed in as it lodges in your lungs and can take years to start to cause problems. Back in the 1950s, no one knew how dangerous asbestos fibres were; luckily, I don't think any of the uncles died of asbestosis; by all accounts, not the nicest way to go.

The big shed's massive sliding metal doors are wide open. I can hear raised voices increasing in volume; I become attracted to a commotion at the entrance. Two of my uncles are shouting and scuffling with each other. I only have a vague memory of which of my uncles were fighting. I don't want to name them anyway. I'll call them uncle one and uncle two. They are swearing and pushing one another. And the argument is escalating as they jostle in the doorway. The shoving now becomes punching. And wrestling.

By their feet is a dirty tin tray of machine parts. Bits and bobs from the big machines, submerged and soaking in an oily liquid, most likely diesel fuel. Poking out of the black goop are cogs, random nuts, bolts and broken bits of woodworking machinery – to put it simply, a shitload of widgets. Uncle one, on the right, grabs for the tin and flings it at uncle two on the left. The heavy cogs and mechanical components hit uncle two square in the chest. The liquid drenches him; his dirty blue overalls now glisten with the oily liquid. I am amused and slightly excited by this in the same way I am when it all kicks off in my house between my mum and dad. I thought this hostility was expected – everyday normality in the grown-up world. Witnessing the violence of life back home gave me some weird nervous thrill. Like when you are getting told off at school, but you can't help but plaster a grin on your stupid mush . . . And then you get told, 'What are you smirking at, laddie?'

My reactions to conflict are all messed up. I look on, now transfixed, and then uncle one wants to finish the job. He reaches into his overall pockets, quickly brings out a box of Swan Vestas, and instantly begins to strike and throw the lit matches at oil-drenched uncle two. The matches are extinguished well before hitting their target; they only leave little smoke trails in the afternoon sunshine streaming through the sliding door. I'm almost sure that uncle one never intended to set uncle two ablaze and burn him to death; I believe now it was just for show.

The scrap fizzles out like the Vestas bouncing off the concrete floor. After a little more shoving and swearing they slink back to opposite areas of the shed, still spitting insults over their shoulders: 'Fucking gobshite!' 'Fucking bastard!' 'Fucking arsehole,' and the good old, 'Why don't you fuck off, big mouth?' Not forgetting one of my dad's all-time favourites from back in the day, the rather quaintly old-school, 'You're a fucking yard dog!'

There had been no attempt to stop the fight by any of the other brothers. My dad Alf was nowhere to be seen. There is no suggestion that this display should not have happened before the eyes of a little sun-bleached blond eight-year-old lad. I'm sure uncle one understood the matches would be extinguished before reaching their objective. And I am also certain you are all well aware that the flammable properties of diesel oil need immense compression and heat for ignition. Therefore, I don't consider this a serious attempt at murder. In hindsight, it was merely an ordinary act of absolute hatred from one Sergeant brother to another. Normal.

The fun is over, and without a word or any embarrassment I can remember from any of the uncles, I'm ignored, so off I trot and return to play, this time around the back of the big shed. It's another world around there. It's like Narnia, though I had never heard of Narnia back then. So more likely, somewhere like the magical and forbidden part of the garden that Bill and Ben the Flowerpot Men sneak into on occasion. Those plant potheads slink into this forbidden zone via a ragged hole in the fence. In this mysterious and secluded garden, they encounter my favourite supporting puppet character of BBC's most out-there kids' TV show, under the catchall moniker of *Watch with Mother*. However, the Woodentops and Andy Pandy are all, let's face it, out-there too. Yes, you've guessed it, Slowcoach the tortoise, who, now that I think back, had an exceedingly Zen demeanour and was a welcome addition to this children's TV show. He is a soft, contemplative foil to Bill and Ben's constant frantic blame game. Slowcoach never gets troubled by anything, always calm; of course, as we all know, the tortoise is the most chilled of all the reptiles. He lives in the moment; nothing worries old Slowcoach. He never develops the hump or gets in a mood and certainly never seems to mind if Bill (or is it Ben?) clambers uninvited on top of his shell and is now getting a free ride. Not sure if I would have put up with it myself, with their uncomfortable clattering flowerpot legs all over the shop. But old Slowcoach is happy to trudge deliberately along, giving them a lift. As usual Little Weed back at the house is saying nowt. She may be a weed, but she's not a grass.

Behind the big shed is my secret playground. It extends to the banks of the Leeds and Liverpool Canal. I love exploring this boggy uncharted territory in the shadow of the significant asbestos shed that looks down on me, glowing white in the sun. I spend school holidays making dens, jumping ditches and constructing bridges with old spare planks. I'm getting covered in mud and shite and watching the numerous frogs hopping about. It's common to turn over a discarded piece of corrugated asbestos to find the occasional grass snake chilling and snoozing.

Sadly, I've never seen one since those sun-drenched days.

Peppered among the long grass, ferns, brambles and nettles, giant exotic opium poppies glow pink and red. The tiny poppy seeds must have hitched a ride with a shipment of wood from some decimated rainforest in the Far East. After all the argy-bargy between my uncles, this serene and secret place has a calming effect on me. This is not anything to do with the narcotic nature of the poppy seed pods; no, I'm only eight, after all. It feels quiet and peaceful lying on flattened grass, with spiders, hoverflies and beetles keeping me company. I'm looking up at the cloud formations interspersed with swallows swooping and scooping up flies by the ounce. I could spend hours there. There's something entrancing about lying in long grass out of earshot of the authorities, namely parents and teachers, and quietly out of sight. I am a kid just soaking it all in. Not sure kids today would understand this. They hardly ever look up from their phones to see life as it is.

In my bedroom, or as I like to think of it now, *Ice Station Zebra*, I unwillingly slide away from past lazy summers and back into consciousness, and with the fortitude of a dead-end-street Shackleton, I decide to brave the cold of the house. I am visualising a cup of piping hot tea. I throw on my clothes and head for the electric kettle my dad has recently invested his substantial hoard of Green Shield stamps in.

Soon, clutching my comforting steaming mug of tea, I head into the back parlour, which I have adopted and adapted as my music room. The gas fire is lit. I plonk an LP on the deck of my Pioneer PL-12D. *Another Green World* by Brian Eno: track one, side two, 'Sombre Reptiles', wondering if Eno was thinking about our reptilian mate, the highly chilled Slowcoach. When he clicks the drum machine's start button this is unlikely; anyway, Slowcoach is seldom sombre, always happy, like I said, Zen-like. Eno's rhythmic chug of the electronic beat machine is ticking away on a samba, or was it a mambo setting? Then it all floods back, the practice with Pete on Sunday. And the possibility of having a real live drummer. This is such an exciting prospect, and Pete, though we haven't known him long, we could already tell he was such a nice, chilled bloke. His demeanour is not too dissimilar to the easy-going, Zen Slowcoach. Unlike Slowcoach, though, when it comes to drumming, he is a thunderous force of muscle, precision and speed. Poor old Slowcoach, the tortoise, could only ever dream of beating the shit out of a drumkit.

CHAPTER 3

Goodbye, Flared-sleeved Tank Top

**'Sanctus' from *Missa Luba* – composed
by Father Guido Haazen**

Will meets Pete Erics, 1979

I had never considered anything about the life that Pete would be leaving behind. I had yet to learn how middle-class people lived. Life outside my tiny pond was a mystery to me. I ate with my knife and fork the wrong way round. I had never drunk wine, I'd not been abroad or had meals in restaurants.

I know what you are thinking. *Hold a minute, Will, your dad and his brothers own a factory, so you must be posh or at least middle class.*

If you had seen the woodyard and the state of our house, you would not doubt our social standing in the class system. I considered people in the new estates surrounding Station Road to be posh, but they were not. To my way of thinking back then, you were posh if you still had an intact teapot lid or handles on your cups.

The naivety I had as a kid was incredible; I almost thought the royal family were gods and that the streets of London were paved with gold.

We wait a few days after the try-out in the basement and, eventually, the word comes back to us. We are to get our drummer. Pete has decided to give it a go. He will travel with his drum kit to Liverpool. Pete had already been part of two bands with his schoolmates back at Downside. First was a punk outfit; with all the punk anger that switched-on public schoolboys could muster, they called this band the relatively tame sounding 'The Grot'. Not sure if they got this name from the TV show *The Fall and Rise of Reginald Perrin*, where Reg's shop in the show was christened Grot and sold all kinds of shite that could be categorised as grotty. Pete's second effort and, by all accounts, slightly more together band were Rigor Mortis and the Gravediggers. I love the name. It sits alongside Manchester's early punks Slaughter and the Dogs or even Echo and the Bunnymen. Rigor Mortis even played a gig at their school. They featured Pete's mate Percy Penrose on guitar and Pete on drums and vocals.

I have done some investigations about the arrival of Pete in

Liverpool. On coming north, he stayed with his friend from school, Kieran Balfe, who lived with his mum and dad in that mysterious and wonderful part of England that divides us from the Welsh, the little peninsula that sprouts out into Liverpool Bay called the Wirral. After a few days with Kieran, it was time for Les's mum and dad to play host to the polite and well-spoken teen, no doubt feeding him up with all the ace baked goods Les's mum could provide. Pete loves his grub but annoyingly never puts on an ounce of fat. I'm sure Pete's folks back in Goring-on-Thames were unhappy about the situation. It was a big decision for an eighteen-year-old just out of school. Pete's dad Denis was a Performing Rights Society solicitor, so I imagine he was not too keen on his son throwing away a place at Oxford and heading to the north.

Steps down into Yorkie's basement

About a week later, we all gather in Yorkie's musty basement. Bill Drummond and Dave Balfe have come along too. They are worried that Pete is feeling intimidated by us. And indeed, he would have been. We only had two quality measures at the time, good or crap, and no in-between or compromise. We could all be highly abrasive in our own way. I was the worst for the sarcastic comment and quick to put the verbal boot in if the song was heading in the wrong direction. I was very blunt back then, I expect as a product of living with the old man back in Melling, who was as direct as they come. If something was not to my liking, I would say, 'That's shit, that is; it sounds crap,' especially if it reminded me of some band we all hated, and that usually saw the back of it. Macul and Les would also occasionally employ this tactic, and I would abandon some cheesy riff – or maybe it was good, who knows? So many rules to be cool. I never gave much consideration to diplomacy or feelings.

After a couple of months at Les's mum and dad's place, Dave Balfe let Pete crash at his Liverpool flat in Grove Park, Toxteth. This was a lot more convenient for him. It was easy to hang out with us in town, where he could sign on the dole and get to practice quickly.

After kipping on Dave's couch for a month, Pete eventually got a flat just walking distance to Yorkie's basement, our practice room. I can remember when Pete moved in. It was a horrible, dark, dank, damp, freezing flat; the old couch and grubby floral furnishings could have been in situ since the thirties. The furniture was probably in better condition than the shit at my dad's house; I felt right at home. It was freezing in that flat. Most cheapo flats were converted from poorly insulated Victorian houses.

Les had swiped an electric heater from his dad's garage, and we took it to Pete's dingy apartment in Kensington. Pete gratefully accepted. He had been used to a comfortable life in Goring; I'm certain conditions at the Roman Catholic Downside boarding school were not considered five-star accommodation, but not as bad as this dump. The boarding-school education had likely toughened him enough to live in such squalid conditions. And gave him the courage to leave his home and friends in Goring. I'm not sure I would have had the guts to make such a move at eighteen. The only point of reference of boarding-school life I had seen was watching Lindsay Anderson's 1968 film *If . . .*, which got shown on BBC Two quite regularly back then. The film features a significant amount of bullying, homoerotism, and toffs acting jolly beastly to one another. It culminates in a pre-Drooged-up Malcolm McDowell and his followers shooting up the place from a vantage point on the roof of a college house, in symbolic destruction of the establishment, church and authority. It also features a beautiful 'Sanctus' sung in the pure Congolese style, off the *Missa Luba* album. A few years later, we came on stage with that beautiful recording.

Whether his folks liked it or not, Pete never complained about much and selflessly greeted each day with a sense of wonder and exploration.

Back in the basement for our first praccy, he brings power to the songs; this is quite apparent from the start, breathtakingly creating crescendos where needed and then effortlessly slipping into delicate lulls. Bill Drummond can't contain himself. He is exploding around the tiny cellar. Over the coming weeks, the songs will become more structured. Pete's drums are signalling changes, and I adapt to them quickly. No one had to instruct

Pete what to do, though he did receive some guidance from Dave Balfe. Dave had the strange idea that he knew better than us how we wanted our songs to sound.

Big Bill Drummond's book of contacts

The dynamics of the songs are changing. They are punctuated by Pete's steady thump of the drums. Our simple songs start to feel more complex, not like prog rock, you understand; I had hung up my flared-sleeved tank top a good few years back. We are developing our signature sound to be more worked out and interesting. We are avoiding all rock 'n' roll clichés. Pete is smoothly interpreting our chord sequences in a natural and flowing manner. Les's style of bass playing fits in beautifully. Our work with the drum box's unwavering tempo helped with his instinctive tightness. He adheres to the drums like shit to a blanket. This is an essential part of any rock band. The tightness between the bass and drums gives a solid foundation.

We start to extend bits that we feel are working well and cut parts that we, in our infinite twenty-year-old wisdom, do not think are working well. We were still very new to the dark art of song arranging. A lot of the time, we are working things out instrumentally, and Macul's lyrics are fitted in once we have the music together. We sometimes extend or shorten parts of the songs to accommodate the lines. The ups and downs that build and flourish make a tune more interesting. There are only twelve notes on a musical scale. It's pretty easy to slip into some-one else's territory without even realising those few chords you have just put together and think are unique have been used many times. This is fine if it reminds you of something you consider cool but, if it's uncool, it soon gets the elbow.

We are all in control of what we are adding to the songs. It's a very socialistic approach and all the better for that. Four different minds coming together from differing angles create a unique sound. If one person were dictating it all, it would be predictable, boring and dull. Given the amount of guitar music that has been around since the birth of rock 'n' roll, repetition is inevitable, so any way of trying to expand the format can only be good. Many bands that stand out from the same old crap do it this way.

The power of Les and Pete can carry everything along, and we are all going with it for the ride. 'Villiers Terrace' and 'Going Up' are among the first tracks to get the Pete treatment. A new element is being added: space, space to breathe. This leaves Macul to fit his dark poetic vocals in with a rock-solid background, and it gives me room to drift about within the parameters of the tune during the parts that are not strictly formulated.

Over the coming weeks, we will work on the setlist and get seven or eight gelling tunes. When we come to creating 'All That Jazz', the drums and bass can carry the song with a determined stomping beat. We forgo a chorus and instead allow my heavy guitar riff to take the place of a vocal hook.

The way I play, I am living in the moment. The Buddhists will know the Zen practice is to do just that. Can you only live for the now? When you are in a band and need to keep remembering stuff you came up with just yesterday, your mind is already racing ahead. I have a low boredom threshold, and as soon as I have thought of something, er, like a guitar riff, chord sequence or some other musical part, if I don't hammer it home by repetition or record it, it will be lost. Having a real-live drummer helps with this. It's almost like a signpost or map. Listening to the drums leads you along the right track; this reminds you that just a little further on is a turn or fork in the road, a crash of a cymbal or slight change in the emphasis in the rhythmic map. Turn left for the stabbing guitar, then second right to follow the road to the improvised solo. And remember, it starts on the D string. At the time, none of this was even thought about. It was all a kind of instinctive part of our music. When you play so much and listen to so much music, eventually, it is just in you.

One of these early practice days, Yorkie appears in the doorway and says rather excitedly, 'Quick, turn the keyboards on. The cops are here.'

Bemused, we stop playing, and Yorkie gets behind The Teardrop Explodes' Vox Jaguar organ.

Yorkie explains, 'The police have been coming around when Teardrops have been rehearsing. Now you lot have Pete drumming, your volume has gone up, and some old cow called Kelly from across the street keeps moaning.' He continues, 'We can't be seen as a rehearsal room; if I pretend I'm the keyboard player, the cops will think it's just my mates and me fucking around.'

In hindsight, I don't think the coppers were in the slightest bit bothered that Yorkie and his ma might have been making a few bob from us budding bands practising in his dismal basement. It would have been pretty low on the list of criminal activities that the city hosted.

Yorkie in his casual day wear

Just then several world-weary uniformed coppers blunder into the cellar. They've been here before at the behest of Old Ma Kelly. We are instructed to play a song, which we do at about half the volume we usually play. The cops head into the garden and quickly return. They are not too concerned with the volume outside the basement and go away with a 'Don't get any louder than that, will ya, eh lads?'

We all nod and nervously say, 'Nah, we won't.'

The cops could see that Yorkie had done his best to keep the noise in the basement. Loads of cardboard boxes had been deconstructed and nailed to the wall, along with the old favourite of the budget sound-deadening architect, the egg tray. Add to this heavy-duty charity-shop curtains pinned up here and there. All these modifications would at least soften the reflective sound of the hard brick walls.

After the coppers have gone, Yorkie's mum, Gladys, who is, as you know, quick to complain about the noise, rather weirdly sets off around to the house of the woman she suspects of being the complainant. If anyone tells us off for the noise, it will be her.

'So, keep your fucking busy pimp nose out!'

Gladys bangs on the door of the disgruntled neighbour. The woman shuffles up to the door, slippers on, rollers in, with her top lip covered by her hand. Under Mrs Kelly's hand, Immac hair remover slowly dissolves the bristles on her top lip.

She mumbles through her fingers, 'What do you want?'

Gladys barks, 'I'll tell you what I effing want. We know you're the bitch that keeps calling the police on us.' The woman is now petrified as Gladys continues, 'Why didn't you just come around and tell me it was too loud not to go to the bleeding coppers?'

The woman, shaken, replies, 'It wasn't me that called the police, Gladys.'

But Gladys is no fool; she knows.

'I wasn't born yesterday. You are a fucking liar. It's all right for you hiding your fucking moustache; you're a snitching cow.'

'It's all right for you' is a common precursor to an insult or statement in Liverpool. Not sure why, but 'It's all right for you' works with most insults.

'It's all right for you and your fucking fat arse.'

'It's all right for you and your Ken Dodd teeth.'

'It's all right for you and your huge nose.'

'It's all right for you and your bug eyes,' etc., etc.

Why not try it for yourself?

'It's all right for you and your . . .'

OK, stop it now.

'It's all right for you and your . . .'

Shut it!

Back to the story . . .

With that, Gladys sets off back to the basement and tells us once more to 'Turn those fucking drums down.'

We never hear another thing from Old Ma Kelly from over the road.

CHAPTER 4

Pete's First Gig Madness

'Vicious' – Lou Reed

Madness poster

I'm looking at the dates for when Pete de Freitas joined and for the date of his first gig with the Bunnymen. Pete agreed to join the band quickly after meeting with us on 15 September 1979. Our next gig wasn't until about a month later, on 12 October 1979. And it was the infamous Electric Ballroom gig in London. This would have given us plenty of time to amalgamate Pete into the setup and the songs, of which we didn't have that many at the time, around seven or eight. I remember this gig well and don't recall being shackled by my headphones and operating the drum machine. Which tells me Pete must have been drumming for us by then.

The promotor of the gig (Straight Music) had the bright idea to mix up the genres. After the punk revolution, it seemed like anything was possible now. So much new music was popping up all over the land. Influenced by electronic music, psyche, garage and reggae, it seemed like punk had reminded everyone that there was more to music out there than just prog and pop.

The meeting at Straight Music Promotions might have sounded something like this.

'Hmm, what's the maddest bill we can put together, for a laugh?'

'Did you say saddest?'

'No deaf lugs, maddest.'

'Oh, maddest. Well, er . . . let's see. I know, what about Madness?'

'I like it, but what else is mad?'

'What about that mob Bad Manners? Their singer Buster is very eccentric.'

'True, but in the same vein as Madness, ska music and all that.'

'OK, what's the furthest thing from Ska that's happening right now?'

'I don't know, maybe that weird stuff coming out of Liverpool.'

'What d'ya mean? The bands with whacky names?'

'Yes, well, whacky is another word for mad, isn't it?'

'Yes, that's true.'

'I know the number of the manager of one of those scouse bands.'

'Is it the manager of Ancestorial Man Hoovers in the Park or Gecko and His Funnymen?'

'The Funnymen, ha-ha, good one, boss; I actually think it is Bunnymen, though.'

'They all sound as mad as march hares.'

'Boss, ha-ha, I see what you did there.'

'I like it. Make them an offer they can't refuse.'

'Will do, boss.'

Straight Music springs into action.

'Get me psychedelic impresario and ley-line botherer Big Bill Drummond, the Bunnymen's manager, on the blower.'

The offer we can't refuse is £1,500, by far the most cash we have been paid for a gig. We usually loaded the van and applied shitloads of hairspray for as little as a few hundred quid.

Later, Bill broaches the idea, and we are not that concerned, as far as I can remember. We had seen Madness with the Specials at Eric's that July. It was a great night with no aggro to speak of. I bought a single from the Specials, and I still have it.

Only a month later, Madness are back at Eric's. Their loyal and growing skinhead following is in tow. Most seemed to be from other areas rather than Liverpool. Quite a lot of southern accents were in that night. When Madness was on, there was some scuffling when a pork-pie hat that blocked the crowd's view of Suggs and the other nutty boys had been knocked off. A disgruntled skinhead (aren't they all?) had kicked off a bit. I have found some info about this online, and some claim there was a riot. Er, don't think so; a minor fracas at best. I think back to the days of gigs at the Liverpool Stadium. This so-called 'Eric's riot' was chicken feed compared to any gig in the boxing arena. AC/DC's *Lock Up Your Daughters* tour in 1976 was bedlam. I recall Bon Scott climbing on top of the left PA stack as a very young Angus Young followed suit and scaled to the top of the right speaker stack. A roadie passed up his Gibson SG; schoolboy Angus launched into the blistering riff fest that nearly had the PA tumbling down onto the crowd. They both survived, and we did too – the seats, maybe not. Luckily no pork-pie hats were injured during the making of that show.

The day of the Electric Ballroom gig comes, and we set off down the M6 and then onto the M1 into the horrendous London-bound traffic.

The atmosphere in Camden's Electric Ballroom is, you guessed it . . . electric. Yes, this venue does precisely what it says on the tin. There is a fizz of testosterone crackling in the air. This is Madness's home crowd, and the skins have turned out in droves. I feel like an away supporter that has been plonked in the home team's end at the footy.

Madness had adopted the style and music of the original skinhead movement, in the spirit of the late sixties. Unfortunately, this had attracted, through no fault of their own, a small contingent of rather unsavoury skins – a hardcore group of right-wing National Front supporters. Somehow the NF had managed to enlist some of the more rabid skins as a menacing ragtag army. This is a fucked-up situation; the skinheads turned to racism while at the same time idolising the reggae, soul and ska culture that was born in the hearts of black men and women whom they supposedly hated. The whole concept of the 2 Tone record label was for black and white to unite, so it baffles me that they don't get it. It will never make sense to me.

Bad Manners are up first, and the Nazi skins are hurling racial abuse and the occasional bottle at the stage. The football-style chants are mainly directed at the band's black drummer, Brian Tuitt. It's hard to imagine how he must have felt with these idiots baying for blood while he was playing in a band whose musical roots pay homage to the Jamaican originators of ska.

Eventually, our turn comes; we trundle on stage and begin our set with the song that has become our regular opener, 'Going Up'. I'm peering from behind my fringe. I can see hundreds of shaven heads like eggs in a tray through a crack in my haystack hair. It seems the skins are not too keen on this new psychedelic outfit emanating from the grim and grimy north. As soon as we start, the chants begin: 'Off, off, OFF!

Then a few bright sparks in the crowd begin to flick Nazi salutes, and a new mantra becomes audible: 'Sieg Heil, Sieg Heil!' The translation is 'Hail victory'; what are they on about? Victory? Victory for what? Being the champion bell-ends they are? Then the bottles start skidding across the stage. It's the first time something like this has ever happened to us; we are usually greeted by nothing more dangerous than a splattering of awkwardly moody youths in suits raided from Grandad's wardrobe, staring and not doing much but a kind of grumpy swaying motion in time to the music, then the obligatory ripple of clapping at the end of the songs, which is good enough for us. Our following is still tiny at this stage. The number of gigs under our belts has only just reached double figures. We are still squeaky clean, all brand-new and shiny. Though I don't think about this then, this is Pete's first gig. I'm more engaged in dodging bottles and getting angrier and angrier. The stage seems to be a dangerous place where you are exposed, an easy target.

An online account states that Suggs from Madness came on and tried to calm down the angry mob; I can't remember this happening. I do remember grabbing the mic stand away from Macul and shouting, 'Do you want to hear us or not?'

A few sensitive types in long overcoats at the back sheepishly shout yes, while still staring at the ground, but jeers drown them out, and my appeal to the mob is quickly answered with more chucked beer bottles, chanting and Nazi salutes. So that's a definite not, then. We get about three songs into the set before we knock it on the head and abandon the gig. Pete must have thought, *What the hell am I doing? I have given up Oxford for this.*

After the gig and a few drinks later, we soon put it behind us. Big Bill Drummond is not too arsed either; we still got paid the fee, after all. So, we all thought *their loss*; it's a sign of our growing arrogance.

Pete doesn't hang around afterwards and scarpers back to his parents' house in leafy Goring-on-Thames. So, I'm not entirely sure what he thought of his first Bunnymen gig. I expect, like us, he got over it quickly and just thought it would be an exciting story to tell years later, just like I am doing now.

Pete is back for the next gig, by which time it all seemed like ancient history. The subject of the first gig is not even thought about, by me anyway. Things are moving fast, no time to reminisce. For our next gig, we are returning to the Tingle Tangle in Manchester, this time with our mates, The Teardrop Explodes. We do quite a few gigs around this period with the Teardrops. We get on well and help each other with the load out and shared equipment. If they need a backup guitar, we let them borrow ours. And vice versa. It's an excellent period of friendly cooperation.

With Pete playing the drums, we have become more power-ful. We are becoming confident. Big Bill recognises that we are leaving the Teardrops behind, and our growth as a band is becoming unstoppable. The Teardrops are a lot better musicians than us, but they are lacking something that we have in bucket loads. We can exude a genuine attitude. Mac is unquestionably the perfect, charismatic singer and is sharp and as cocky as they come; Mac's stage presence is emulated by many bands' frontmen that come after him. I'm sure you know who they are. As the year went on, with quite a few gigs driven by the power of Pete's drums, we had a growing confidence in our playing, and by 1981 we had increased our stubborn, arrogant attitude. It was sort of like us against them – them being any other band, journalist or music biz type. The Teardrops are trying too hard to be outrageous, and it's coming across as fake. They seem to be playing at being a band. It looks phoney; they are trying too hard to be weird and whacky, a stupid buzzword at the time.

Big Bill thinks back to the Beatles in Hamburg and starts formulating a plan for the Teardrops. He will set up a club in Liverpool, and they can play there several nights a week. It will be an intense training course, a boot camp for rock 'n' roll apprentices. Bung them on a simple stage with nowhere to hide. Very few lights and no smoke to mask the shortfalls. They will have to write songs or learn other bands' songs to keep the sets fresh. Back at the Zoo office, Big Bill finds an old disused club that dates back to the Merseybeat era and creates Club Zoo. In those beat-city days, this club was called the Iron Door. Legend has it that the Beatles played their first gig there with the name the Silver Beatles. Though if you scratch around in Liverpool, just about every pub and club has some claim that the Beatles played there first.

Up a couple of granite steps to a heavy iron door. The surface is pitted and painted in numerous coats of thick glossy black. This is the entrance to this once-a-warehouse building on Temple Street, tucked away down a back jigger in the small-business district. The place had a makeover by the eighties and is now called the Pyramid Club. The interior is decked out in Egyptian hieroglyphs and various other items of cack you may find in a pyramid, including the odd dusty homemade mummy propped up somewhere. It's a maze of a place inside with little stairs up and down, in and around, leading to many areas of the club with small bars dotted about.

When the Club Zoo night is on, only one bar is open. And weirdly, Tim Whittaker, the drummer from the band Deaf School and a future housemate of Les, me, Jake and Pete, is in charge of the kitchens. A cute blonde girl, Laura, who will become my girlfriend by the end of this book, is helping him with the burgers, chips, etc. Liverpool is such a small place, it's just like a village; everyone knows everyone else and has a connection somewhere along the way. All the Zoo bands are issued with a credit card-sized Club Zoo pass made from black plastic with gold lettering. This is the Willy Wonka golden ticket for the underground scene in Liverpool. This will get us in for free whenever these Zoo nights are on. We go, but only because it's somewhere to hang out midweek. After a week or so, the Teardrops have a new support act called the Ravishing Beauties: three rather posh girls from a London music school. Suddenly, going to Club Zoo is worth the ten-minute walk from the far side of town to Temple Street.

Club Zoo logo

Liverpool also has a night started by Nathan McGough, who joins the Pale Fountains and later becomes the Happy Mondays' manager. It's held in an old-style nightclub called Mr Pickwick's situated off London Road, which is fast becoming Liverpool's answer to Skid Row. (It's had a tidy-up and now it's like the rest of Liverpool: student accommodation land.)

The club Nathan picked has had a strange Dickensian make-over to reflect the name. Not exactly Studio 54. The inside is complete with a cobbled lane, old-fashioned street lanterns and fake shops behind windows with those early glass panes, the ones with a circular lumpy bit in the middle, that makes every-thing a bit distorted.

Nathan's night has the gloriously pretentious title of 'Plato's Ballroom', and the large queue down the street is chock-a-block with the gloriously pretentious hip kids of Liverpool and the surrounding area, all attracted by the chance to show off their latest post-punk clobber and prove Nathan's idea is working.

There were no artful dodgers, street urchins or Uriah Heap types in that line-up of pinafore-dressed girls and baggy-trousered creatures of the nightlife. They jostle to hand over their £1.50 to gain entry to Liverpool's premiere Dickensian disco. It's an arty affair with performance artists and old cabaret acts rubbing shoulders in non-existent dressing rooms; cowboys whipping cigarettes out of glamourous fishnet-and-cowboy-booted cowgirls' mouths to gasps of indifference from us.

One act is definitely on the performance art end of the spectrum. A coffin sits in the middle of the dancefloor. It sits there all night; most people take no notice of it and very little dancing goes on. Most prefer to chat and hang near the bars. A few minutes before the band is due to come on, the coffin lid is violently booted off from inside the casket and out pops a shirtless geezer; as expected with these sort of performance art shenanigans, he is covered in some crap or paint. On this occasion, his shit of choice is ash; with the sooty cloud still hanging in the air, he starts to walk off with zero reaction to this sudden and dramatic display of art. These are the days when, above all, you must remain uber-cool and project a demeanour of disinterest in everything at all times. The coffin dodger is expecting us all to be shocked. We aren't. Julian Cope, Paul Simpson and Jake Brockman, who will later play keyboards with the Bunnymen, are huddled together; all have taken acid for the occasion and all have been smeared with eye makeup by one of the girls. Even in their heightened state of consciousness, they never bat an eyelinered eyelid. They are all happy in their own little world and sit on a raised platform by the security of a wrought-iron railing. They are deep in conversation.

We all liked the nights at Plato's. It wasn't on every week, so it seemed special when the gigs came up. It was quite a small club and the Bunnymen could have easily done a bigger venue, but we played there in 1980 simply because we thought it was a cool thing to do. I saw a few good bands coming up and out of the punk scene. New Order played one of their first gigs there. Orange Juice, A Certain Ratio, Cabaret Voltaire and the Pale Fountains all performed at Plato's Ballroom Nights. The Fall had played it way back in 1978 when it was still known as a disco.

There were a few other places besides Eric's to see bands. The Top Rank in St John's Precinct had a makeover; well, they changed its name to Rotter's (unsure whether Johnny Rotten inspired the name). I saw the Ramones and Captain Beefheart there. For years, I had a reel-to-reel tape of the Beefheart gig and have no idea how I came to have it. The overriding memory of the show was someone in the crowd shouting at the Captain about his now absent rhythm guitarist, 'Where's Rockette Morton, ya bastard?'

And Beefheart responded under his breath, 'Oh shiiiiiiit, man.'

We would have somewhere to go almost every night if we had the money: Eric's, Lincoln's Inn, Macmillans. And venturing to the higher reaches of Liverpool, up on Hope Street, at the Everyman Bistro, the bench tables would be packed with real-ale-swilling radicals that saw themselves as budding communist agitators, poets and playwrights. There was the Philharmonic pub and the Casablanca, the Casa as it was called, which was always suitable for cheap curry, good music, dub reggae mainly, and dark corners for copping off in; as you can imagine, I never had any success on that front even though I employed my formidable deluxe standing-around-looking-miserable technique to send the girls wild. It never failed to fail. Zero women were flocking to me.

Paul Simpson, Jake Brockman and Julian Cope take a
trip to Plato's Ballroom

Times were hard; you had to pretend you were students to
get in as they didn't have to pay the fifty-pence entrance fee. On
many occasions, they sussed out I wasn't a student, and they
wouldn't take my ten bob to get in either. I must have looked a
little unsavoury.

Another time, I manage to convince the doormen of my
student credentials, and I slip in to find Les and Paul Simpson are
ensconced in the corner, underneath one of the large black and
white paintings of Humphrey Bogart and Lauren Bacall dotted
around the club's walls. They are acting a little strangely, giggling
away like schoolgirls. This has something to do with the fact that
they have exchanged the contents of a packet of Big D peanuts for
the earthy crunch of dried magic mushrooms. I have never had

shrooms, as the kids call them, but I know they are a mild version of acid. These two space cadets are wolfing them down like they are going out of fashion. In fact, they are coming right into fashion as an LSD alternative to accompany Liverpool's new psychedelic scene. Come September, the fields and parks of Liverpool would be rife with hordes of merry pranksters looking for the little pale fungi faces looking up from the tufts of damp grass.

I leave Les and Paul to it, drift into the darkest corner with a pint of Guinness, and attempt to dance to the dub reggae sounds of the Upsetters, the bass throb of 'Croaking Lizard' rattling the fillings of all who are in there. I had no fillings to rattle, having never been to the dentist since the early sixties when I kicked the dentist in the shins and was gassed for my crime. I deserved it, to be fair. After the club closes, it's all back to Paul's flat. Just a brief stumble down the hill and straight through the black front door of 14 Rodney Street. Cups of tea and a couch-crash till the morning, then trains back to Kirkby and the short walk down Station Road to number 15.

CHAPTER 5

Bugs Bunny Bendy Toy

'Once Bitten Twice Shy' – Ian Hunter
'Dead Parrot Sketch' – *Monty Python's Flying Circus*

At my job in the kitchens, things are starting to be hard for me, the band are getting more bookings now, and I am knackered. I must juggle the band and the day job; it's becoming evident that a nine-to-five and being in a band are incompatible. We are arriving back from gigs at all hours of the day and night, mostly rolling into a deserted Liverpool as the dawn is breaking and the polished copper sheen of the sun begins to seep warmth back into cold grey streets. I fall out of the van and straight into the Binns department store locker-rooms. Swapping rancid, ciggy-smoked post-punk clothes for equally rancid checked trousers and double-breasted chef's jacket, collectively called whites, I then head down through the sub-basement, up in the clattering service lift to the fourth-floor kitchen, or what's left of it. That's all about to change.

After our Zoo single 'The Pictures on My Wall' had received such great reviews, there was an offer for a publishing deal from Warner Music. I was not even sure what that meant. I'm no business head by a long chalk, and I still can't get my head around mechanical royalties or all the legal jargon to do with contracts. Bill and Dave negotiated the deal with the publishers in London. We did make a few trips on the train to meet Warner's publishers in their Berners Street offices. All around the offices were cupboards stocked to the brim with vinyl. I was more interested in which free records I could snaffle from Warner's catalogue. This was the central and only exciting part of going to see the company for me.

We also made a couple of trips to the Sire Records office in Floral Street, Covent Garden. Heading the UK operation for Sire was a lovely chap called Paul McNally. He had more than a passing resemblance to the English actor Cardew Robinson. I realise most of you will now be thinking, eh . . . who the hell is that? Well, that's what the internet is for, no?

Paul had this Bugs Bunny bendy toy, one of those dolls you pull a string out of its back, and it would say things like 'What's up, Doc?' or 'That's all folks' – Bugsy's well-worn catchphrases off the cartoons. You may have to look those up also, as they are seldom on the telly nowadays; too violent for today's sensitive youth, poor lambs.

We are in the office, messing with the doll, pulling the dangling string from Bugs Bunny's back, and all laughing at the catchphrases. Then Bugs says something relevant to the band, something like 'Here are the Bunnymen,' and we are all stunned. Even Cardew Robinson-lookalike Paul exclaims, 'It's never said anything like that before, that's very weird.'

It may be a collective hallucination, us all high on the exuberance of being in the Sire office and the thought of the Ramones and Talking Heads vinyl booty we are going to nab. It had been a great day and we all see Bugs Bunny's interjection as a good omen.

These are the days when gig tickets cost pennies. We are play-ing at tiny places on the punk-rock circuit. Consequently, very small gigs bring in very small money by the time we have paid the fuel costs and crew. Yes, we now have crew. Well, one roadie, Alan, an Eric's stalwart and a lovely fellow. He has a Bee Gees' haircut and neon teeth to match. Not sure he has the falsetto voice, though; this might need some more investigation. If I ever see him in Liverpool, I'll get him to give me a few bars of 'Stayin' Alive'.

Alan does most of the fetching and carrying of the amps now, and he sets up the gear and tunes up the guitars. Me and Les help, though Macul is usually conspicuous by his absence when the load-out time comes.

Mac, Les, Alan Jones and Pam Young go for a stroll

Big Bill Drummond, who is now comfortable in the role of manager, realises that we must start moving the group forward. We need to concentrate on the band and only on the band, give it our full attention. Les and I need to pack in our jobs, or quit the dole in Macul and Pete's case.

Bill's negotiations with the Warner publishers are done now, and we all gather at the Brookhouse pub on Smithdown Road in Liverpool. Here Bill presents us with the publishing contract, and we all happily sign and then have a drink to celebrate. There's an atmosphere of jubilation underneath our too-cool-for-school exterior. It's strange being in a pub in the daylight, and it brings a flashback to Melling's number-one hotspot in the sixties and seventies, the aforementioned Horse and Jockey, and a sunny Sunday afternoon crown green bowls tournament, in which my dad was competing. All the neighbourhood kids were invited in, to demolish like locusts a table straining under the weight of egg or cheese sandwiches, sausage rolls, crisps, creamy trifle and gallons of pop. Out of our minds on all this luxury nosh, we were allowed to go apeshit around the pub gardens. I witnessed my dad after a few pints; like a butterfly emerging from a brown-ale cocoon, he would undergo meta-morphosis and just like magic a smiling genial chap would appear. He became a lot more likeable. This was the face most of the village would see. This magical effect would have vanished by closing time and the gloom would return by the time the key went into the Yale lock. If only he could have been like this without the ale.

Bill suggests we take the looming publishing deal cash, which will be split up equally, and pay ourselves a wage. I see no prob-lem, and it appeals to my left-wing socialist leanings. I'm not keen on people who make a big deal about voting Labour, but then in life basically act like a Tory and are only out for themselves; that's a disgrace. It's worse than voting for Thatcher – at least those fools were honest. Bill Drummond also says he will manage the Bunnymen for 15 per cent rather than the customary 20 per cent management commission. At the time, this act of generosity is not recognised enough by me as I have little understanding of how the music business works. It says a lot about Bill's character and his disregard for money. He will more than prove this later in the 1990s at the height of KLF mania. Big Bill and his partner Jimmy were perched high on a scaffolding tower, throwing their fee to the Ravers below. The Cheesy Quavers, well, the ones who were not too loved up, were scrambling like Hyenas at an all-you-can-eat buffet. These neon boys and girls were pocketing the disco biscuit money raining down from above. And let's not forget later in 1994 with the formation of the K Foundation and the notorious million-quid bonfire caper.

We are all creating our own parts and giving the band our artistic identities. This also gives all four of us, Macul, Les, Pete and me, a loyal incentive to be committed 100 per cent. At the same time, it makes the band attractive and exciting for our young fans. Not one person is calling all the shots. That would fall into a formulaic structure and very soon become stale. We all do the hard work involved, the travelling, the uncomfortable, slow, late-night trips up and down the motor-ways of Britain, the lack of sleep, all the things that you are expected to do to be in a band. We are all in this together so the rewards deserve to be equal. At the time, I was not think-ing too profoundly of any of this. I just felt instinctively it was the proper, fair and honest thing to do. After all, we were doing this for the vibe, kudos and, above all, fun. I was not doing it for any money that might or might not show up. And I am proud that we all did it in this egalitarian way. I also think it made for a stronger band with a bonus of a more interesting take on music creation.

Four minds are coming from different angles in fresh and exciting ways, and this is what makes the Bunnymen *the* Bunnymen. We generate a unique sound. We would expand and jam the riffs or chords, and Les and Pete would drive a pathway through. Les, with his unyielding insistent bass lines, nothing too flowery and wanky, solid as a rock. Pete, in turn, would interpret the tunes in his dynamic and fluid tom-filled way. Macul would be quiet vocally at this stage but is obviously forming the vocal ideas shyly in his head. He would be playing stabbing rhythm guitar, and when the time comes for vocals, he's very quickly fitting in perfectly with the music.

A week or so later, we are back in the Zoo office at number 1 Chicago Buildings, Whitechapel, Liverpool. Outside, it is energetic and busy as ever with shoppers, shop workers and punks. Zoo's ramshackle office is stacked up with boxes of the new Teardrop Explodes seven-inch single, 'Treason (It's Just a Story)', waiting to be delivered to the shops. Bill has news for us from Sire. Now that we have Pete de Freitas drumming and Sire Records' stipulation is fulfilled, Seymour Stein has been as good as his word and offered us a deal.

But another week later, we are back at Zoo again. There is a problem. Immediately after the deal dropped on the table, it disappeared just as fast as it had appeared. I'm not 100 per cent sure why. We get told that Sire Records has used up their budget on various other projects, and now could not afford to fund the recording of our album.

Our publisher at Warner's is a young Rob Dickins. He has

worked his way up through the label from the post room to be the head of Warner publishing at just twenty-six years old. He is now in a position of some power. Rob fancies having a stab at a label. He has a plan and sets up a meeting with Seymour Stein. Warner Bros will fund the record and release it in England. Seymour can put it out in the USA.

At this time, all things independent are taking over from the old-school record companies known as majors. The do-it-yourself ethos of punk is still quite strong. The hip thing is to be on an independent record label, so Rob has a cunning plan: his label will be in the style of indie. It will be in effect a false flag operation, distributed and funded through the Warner network, so it will be a Warner Brothers deal, but will appear to be a lot cooler. He will call his label Korova. I am disappointed that we will no longer be on Sire Records with my heroes, the Ramones and the Talking Heads, but we will still have records coming out on Sire in the USA, so it's not so bad. I do like the idea that Warner is creating a label just for our band. The label name Korova means 'cow' in Russian, but it's very cool due to the Korova milk bar in the everlastingly hip cult-classic film *A Clockwork Orange*. This film's cool status will forever be assured by the simple fact that it was banned not long after it was released. This was due to gangs of disaffected youths taking up the bowler hat and white-overall Droog attire, and emulating the young ruffians in the film by engaging in ultra-violence up and down the land.

Now that we have some money in the Bunny bank, Bill plucks a number out of the air: we will get £35 a week each to live on. That's fine by me. My take-home pay as a commis chef was just £36. It's a big decision for me, but I must now leave my steady job. I feel I have a safety net, my share of the publishing money. I decide to pack in my job in the kitchens, and I go to see the personnel woman at Binns. She is a pleasant lady and even though she's seen as management, she has helped in the kitchens when we're short of staff, so I know her a little and she knows what it is like to graft. She's got that very English jolly-hockey-sticks, roll-your-sleeves-up-and-get-stuck-in kind of personality.

She is taken aback by my talk of the band and quitting the kitchen and says, 'You are being stupid. It will not go anywhere. You have an excellent job here.'

I'm thinking, *Excellent? Are you kidding? I knew it wasn't even a good job, not any more at any rate.*

The department store's restaurant has virtually vanished, and by this point I'm basically working in a greasy-spoon café that's taking the piss out of the toffee-nosed customers with shit food at toffee-nosed prices. It has gone so far down the culinary toilet that you would get the bends getting back up to the surface.

She looks on with a frowning face.

I looking at her and my ego is thinking, *Maybe I will be hard to replace? I am one of the longest-serving commis chefs in the place.* Then reality comes crashing into my self-importance. *Who am I kidding? Millions are on the dole queue, and many would snap at the chance to work in catering with the same hours as a nine-to-five job.*

She is still trying to persuade me to stay. 'You know, not many bands make it big time?'

Big time? Who said anything about big time, and what does that even mean? I'm not in it for the big time. This is pure art we are creating. I'm not here for some pathetic attempt at fame and fortune. She's still waffling on about us failing. Going on about the negative aspects of the group a little too much for my liking. It's starting to annoy me.

I tell her I'm leaving in the old-fashioned way: 'No, I'm going. I'm handing my cards in.'

She reluctantly hands me a form to sign, and I do just that.

I must work for the two-week notice period, then I'm free.

The two weeks whip by very fast, and it's now my last day in the starched-crisp uniform of a commis chef. Mine is crisper with dried baked bean residue. The few staff members we have left have a whip-round to buy me a leaving present and card, as is tradition when someone leaves a place of employment. I pretend to be oblivious to what's going on but, in the confines of a tiny kitchen, it's easy to read the signs. One of the waitresses takes charge and scurries off with a cup to collect the odd bits of slummy people are willing to donate. It's getting near closing time. When I am presented with the cash, the collection has amassed a massive £6.50. For a while, I've had my eye on a Timex watch glistening in the illuminated case in the jewellery department of the store, and I've even dropped a few hints over the last two weeks, knowing a whip-round would be on the cards. The watch is £8.50.

I cheekily say to the waitresses, 'It is not enough, and you need to try harder.'

I'm being a little tongue-in-cheek. There is no way I would have said such a cocky thing a year ago. This is a sign of the growing confidence that being in the band has brought me.

Instead of telling me to fuck right off, which I would have truly deserved, a little later they come back with the watch. I still have it to this day, and it's one of my most prized possessions. That Timex is better than any Rolex to me.

After my final day at work, I am literally dragged to go for a drink on the corner of Sir Thomas Street and Victoria Street. We go to a little bar called the Captain's Cabin under a pub named the New Court (now the Victoria Cross). A few of us would go to this bar after work now and then, though generally I managed to avoid it. We approach the doorway at around six bells, and Ian Hunter's 'Once Bitten Twice Shy' is drifting up the stairs. The steep steps are traversed and into the cellar bar we go. It's dead as a doornail.

Timex

Weirdly for someone heading out on a career in showbiz, I'm not keen on being the centre of attention and I know it's going to end up with me throwing up somewhere. I feel like I'm walking the plank down into the wood-panelled interior of the bar. The walls are peppered with heaps of seafaring shit, securely nailed to the walls to prevent this crap from going walkies and ending up nailed to the walls of dwellings in the area or drunkenly flung into the Mersey. Anchors, lifebelts, a battered wooden helmsman's wheel, many photographs of Liverpool-registered transatlantic liners and tugboats, and various nautical bits and bobs that reflect

Liverpool's glorious bygone age of salty seadoggery. The essential item of the nautical-themed bar, a scabby, moth-eaten stuffed parrot, is nailed to a perch above the bar. All this is topped off by a shiny brass ship's bell hopefully waiting to be rung for last orders. The bar staff can't wait for shore leave and have all these pissed landlubbers disembark the fuck off out of there. I can't remember much else about that night but I'm sure it ended with me talking to God on the great white telephone.

A few weeks later, word gets around town that Binns' Liverpool Church Street branch is closing; all the staff are being made redundant. At the time, I thought to myself, *That was a lucky bit of timing, me bailing out just as the Zeppelin was about to explode.*

After a jolly good muse over the years, I now think the personnel officer was going way beyond the call of duty with all that you're leaving a great job shite and trying to persuade me to stay on. She must have known of the imminent closure of Binns. This information was above top secret at that time, and she couldn't divulge highly sensitive intel to me. I would have spilled the beans and told the rest of the staff, and they would have had a riot on their hands. Well, maybe not a riot, but at least a handful of disgruntled shop workers giving the top-floor brass a few dirty looks in the canteen.

The staff would all receive redundancy pay; a percentage of their wages multiplied by the number of years working at the store. And she knew I would be missing out on getting this cash by leaving. I now realise she was saying all that crap about it being a good job for my best interests. It's funny how things look clearer when you view them from a distance.

CHAPTER 6

Tame the Squealing Feedback

'I Can See for Miles' – The Who

Now we have a little bit of publishing cash in the Bunny bank, we have the means to buy ourselves some reasonable equipment. My catalogue-bought FAL amp will no longer make the grade. Jimmy Page or Pete Townshend wouldn't be seen dead wired up to such an amateur-hour contraption.

It's an average night at Eric's. It could be any night, but I think it may be when Ian Broudie and Steve Allen aka Enrico Cadillac Jnr – the singer from Liverpool's local heroes, the art-college band Deaf School – are debuting their new project, the Original Mirrors. I spot Clive Langer aka Cliff Hanger, the guitarist from Deaf School, so he may have been there as a bit of friendly support for his mate. Les and I sidle up to Clive as he swigs from the Pilsner bottle clutched in his hand. We are after advice.

'All right, Clive?'

I'm pretending I already knew him, in that weird overly familiar way that fans do. Clive looks up, slightly bemused.

'All right.'

I continue, 'We have started a band. Have you got any idea what type of guitar amp I need?' I follow up with 'How many watts and that?'

Clive smiles and replies, 'I dun know – about thirty to fifty watts should do it.'

I nod and look on as though I know what he is on about. A watt is how the volume of an amp is measured. It seems to be the most important question I should ask: basically, how loud? I know very little of this technical stuff, but hi-fi equipment is also measured in watts, and I'm familiar with hi-fis. Beaver Radio's price tags would always include the wattage of the amps on display. The higher the wattage, the higher the price usually.

Clive adds, 'I have a Vox AC30 and, as you would expect, it's thirty watts. It does for me, OK.'

I think back to the sound of the Deaf School song 'Capaldi's Café', one of their rockier songs. It's thick and nasty. I nod and say, 'Thanks, Clive.'

Chat over, we wander off to avoid that awkward overstaying-your-welcome moment when you have cornered a genuine pop star, and they stop looking you in the eye.

In the main room Norman, the DJ, is playing one of our favourites, Subway Sect's 'Ambition', and it all seems very apt.

I had seen an AC30, and it looked a bit too old school for me. I knew immediately I didn't want one of those. I have used them now, or at least tried to use them, I should say. Every studio we have been in seems to have one. They always leave me dissatisfied somehow, or maybe the ones I've tried were a bit crappy. I have never been able to get a sound that I liked, anyway. They seem too woolly, dull and muffled. I know they are great amps, and lots swear by them, but I still have my nonsensical punk-rock aversion to anything too old-school rock 'n' roll and

I want a harsh and crisp sound that cuts like the Fall or the Subway Sect.

A few days later, with Bill Drummond in tow as guardian of the brand-new Bunnymen chequebook, we decide to head over to Manchester to A1 music shop.

All our knowledge has been gleaned from watching bands perform but we still know little of the mechanics. In the heat of a gig, not much time is spent analysing the equipment on the stage. But we have a secret weapon: it's basically the manual 'How to be Cool for Dummies' and it goes by the title *Marquee Moon*. In the unlikely event that you have never heard of this masterpiece, it's an album by New York guitar pre-punk quartet Television. We all love Television. The guitar sounds, the poetic lyrics, the bass playing, and the drumming are a masterclass in feel and technique. What we have been listening to has become a guide. On the inside cover of the LP there is a picture of the band sitting at what appears to be a practice session. Behind the backs of four young kids of just skin and bone is an array of silver-fronted amplifiers, all made by Fender. A couple of Twin Reverb amps are connected to the guitars and at the back on the right is a huge Fender Bassman – yes, you guessed it, it's for the bass guitar's mighty boom. All are sparkling like tinsel in a Christmas window display, beautiful shiny slabs of sound. That's what we must have! The same equipment as Television.

Les has already bought a 1970s black Fender Jazz Bass, but thinking it a bit too mainstream rock he immediately took it to pieces and spraypainted it blue. A few weeks earlier, he had taken one for the team: with the selfless comradery that we had in those days, Les traded in his own short-scale Fender Mustang

Bass at Curly Music in Liverpool to enable Macul to afford a neat salmon-pink Telecaster Thinline he'd had his eye on. Now forever to be known as Pinky.

We head into town to pick up Big Bill. All clamber into the Bunnymobile, Les's battered old Ford Transit van, the unsung hero of just about every band that ever pulled into the car park of Watford Gap service station at three in the morning in search of a bacon-and-egg butty.

We have a leisurely fifty-mph cruise down the M62 – like the Liverpool band It's Immaterial would correctly point out a couple of years later in their song 'Driving Away from Home', Manchester is only thirty-nine miles away. The Transit's Perkins diesel engine is thumping away under the bonnet and relentlessly gobbling up the miles until we arrive at Manchester's musical heart. Hidden down a litter-strewn side lane off Oxford Road, under a dripping brick railway bridge arch, sits the A1 music shop.

The ground floor is packed to the ceiling with guitars of every persuasion. Bill pipes up to the geezer behind the counter in his soft Scottish accent, 'Where are your second-hand amps, please?'

The Mancunian nasal reply follows: 'All old shit is in basement, cocker.'

We don't want brand-new equipment. We want the vintage sound that bands like Television create.

We head down the narrow stairs into a musty room. The flickering fluorescent glow lights our way. The space is crammed with a sea of wooden boxes, mainly dressed in a black textured leatherette called Tolex. These old fellas have been hiding down here, avoiding the Mr Sheen, since Manchester's answer to the

Beatles, er, Freddie and the Dreamers, were saying, 'You Were made for Me'.

How the fuck did that get into the charts? At this point Gerry Marsden shouts down from Heaven 'I Wish I Knew'.

Let's just say several years of dust are encrusted on them. A couple of hundred well-worn amps, speaker cabinets, combo amps, PA amps and all kinds of random band-related shite everywhere. It's a chock-a-block mess of equipment. There is a narrow maze-like corridor that weaves in and around this mountain of gig-battered gear. We split up and go on the rummage for sonic gold.

I don't know if these old amps were as desirable then as they are now; I for one just thought they looked cool. Most bands we knew wanted something reliable. And, generally, that meant a transistor amp. Valve amps were heavy, fragile and prone to problems as the old solder joints become cracked by constantly getting very hot and then cold in the back of vans rattling along the pothole-stippled lanes of the country, shaking the valves loose. Transistor amps were the thing. Nice and light, reliable, they were proving popular.

The amp that seemed to be cropping up on the stage of Eric's at the time was a combo made by H & H called a VS Musician 100. It is a mighty hundred watts. I'm sure the late and fucking great Andy Gill from the Gang of Four used one when I saw them at Eric's. Mick Finkler, guitarist out of the Teardrops, also had one, so I had some knowledge of that beast. And what a vicious beast it is too. The harsh terrible treble bite is enough to make your gob's teeth splinter and clatter onto the lino. The high-squeal feedback would, given half a chance, decimate your eardrum lugholes to a frayed string vest now used for washing the car. But they look groovy, with a green light that glows behind all the controls. Andy Gill had no fear and was the master of this strange and scary high-pitched feedback squeal. He could almost tame it, charm it out of the speakers, then command it to hover in the air for ages as he held his cobra-like pose. Meanwhile, he would fix the crowd with a glassy stare, as they are waiting transfixed for his next explosive strike to the petrified strings of his long-suffering Stratocaster. I had seen him work this evil at Eric's and loved it. But there was something a bit too modern about these amps. I wondered back then, *Would the Velvets have one?* No, they wouldn't. And I would not be able to subdue and tame the squealing feedback as Andy could.

I searched on YouTube for the Gang of Four using this mythical amp but can only find videos of him using Carlsbro amps. I decide he might have just borrowed it for that gig. I wait with bated breath for some wag to pull me up on this via Twitter.

In 1979, used Fender amps were priced in the low hundreds; today, they are in the low thousands. We want that arcane growl and grunt radiating from the glowing guts of a Fender's smoking-hot valves.

Gold is struck. Mac finds a super reverb. It looks like a Twin Reverb, but it is bigger: four speakers hide behind the woven silver cloth. That's the amp to pair with the newly acquired Telecaster, Pinky. I keep searching while Les finds what he's been looking for: the Bassman amp and a huge cabinet all dressed in the lovely silver cloth of Fender. Then I hear Bill call me over.

'Will, look at this.'

I shout over to Bill across the stacks of amplifiers, 'Yer what, where are ya?'

I spot Bill's head popping above ramshackle heaps of amps, looking like houses tumbling down the hillside, a black plastic-coated Jerusalem. And it is the promised land that I seek.

Bill continues, 'Will, come over here and have a look at this monster.'

I lose sight of him but I am hurrying to where I can hear his voice coming from behind a stack of PA speakers.

I finally find the cramped corridor between the amps. There it is. The biggest Fender amp I have ever seen. You must realise that I am very stupid, and at this point to me big is best. I have yet to learn that to get the best out of an amp you have to drive it, that is turn it up loud; this makes the signal crack up and the valves in the amp create a lovely warm tone. I just see a massive amp, a Fender amp, and my tiny mind is chanting big is best, big is best! It's a Dual Showman and I believe Chuck Berry, Dick Dale, Jimi Hendrix had them at various points in their careers. This is the amp for me. I still have it, and it's an absolute beast of a thing. Two fifteen-inch speakers are housed in a massive cabinet. It has the most amazing reverb; a plastic bag full of witchcraft and springs is screwed to the amplifier's chassis to provide this effect.

Bill pays by cheque. Yes, in those days people were trusting enough to take a cheque. But just to make sure you are not a crook, could you put your name and address on the back of the cheque? Wouldn't work nowadays, would it?

We set about lugging the amps up the narrow stairs and into the van, and set off home. Back in Liverpool, we head over to

Yorkie's and instal our lovely new amps in the basement. They look magnificent. The sound is crisp and biting, and you can get a thin sound for those Talking Heads funky fast rhythmic parts or a thick evil growl for the heavy crunch of the Stooges. For once, we are all happy bunnies.

CHAPTER 7

Plan K and the Mersey
Tunnel to the Mystic Land

'Where's Captain Kirk?' – Spizzenergi

It is January 1980, and the new decade starts with an invite from some young Belgians. It seems the blossoming post-punk scene that is emanating mainly from the grim and grimy north of England is now making waves across the Channel. Quick off the mark, a group of young hipsters have become musically infatuated. They have set up a series of gigs at an old sugar refinery. Starting out in October 1979, Plan K has already had Cabaret Voltaire, Joy Division (twice), Swell Maps and Spizzenergi, who have all come over from England, plus the homegrown Belgian band Digital Dance, who fell into the post-punk format with the profuse use of the flanged bass guitar, which is currently popular. Not with us, by the way. We are anti-flange and phaser. The Bunnymen are the seventh band to play at Plan K.

I had thought very little that being in a band could lead us to travel across the English Channel to Europe. Most of the bands I loved came from the UK or USA. I was only aware of a smattering of European bands. From Germany, I loved the Rattles' minor hit, 'The Witch'. I had some vague knowledge of Krautrock, Kraftwerk, Tangerine Dream, Can, etc., and the big rock hit 'Radar Love' by Golden Earring from Holland. Surprisingly, one of Macul's favourites. I always thought the Bunnymen could have done a half-decent cover of 'Radar Love', but on reflection, it lives on the wrong side of the Dutch cheeseboard. I had been subjected to that annual horror show, the Eurovision Song Contest (haven't we all?) and the odd 'Boom Bang-a-Bang'-type song may have drifted into my fevered subconscious, with the Singing Nun harmonising in the far-distant reaches of my mind. It seemed Europe had very little to offer this post-punk rocker. The only punk band I had heard of from Europe was Métal Urbain from Paris.

Interestingly they, like us, used a drum machine, though their box of beats was set to warp factor ten. Such speed is befitting the punk philosophy. I refuse to count Plastic Bertrand's enthusiastic bouncing around in a zip-laden pink biker jacket anywhere near punk. Rotten would be spinning in his grave if he was dead. God, I hope he doesn't die before this comes out because that will look like awfully poor taste. Having said that, now when I hear Plastic Bertrand's song 'Ça Plane pour Moi', I get some perverted pleasure from it. Young Plastic had missed the punk target by a long chalk in the same way several so-called punk groups released other horrendous records back then. Top of the list must be the Boomtown Rats, which I get no pleasure from, perverted or otherwise.

With only a few Boy Scout camping trips to the Lake District, a junior school camp at Staithes in Yorkshire, and one trip through the beautiful white-tiled and art deco-ornamented Mersey Tunnel to the mystic land of Wales under my belt, I was hardly Phileas Fogg material. The thought of going to a European country was incredible. I had no clue what to expect.

Pete is the only one of us that has a passport. His photo in the old dark blue booklet is of a little boy of about twelve or thirteen, issued from Port of Spain in Trinidad and Tobago. The rest of us head down to the passport office, housed inside the imposing India Buildings. This soot-encrusted solid stone edifice dominates Liverpool's Water Street, which steadily slopes and swoops towards the Liver Buildings, the Pier Head and the River Mersey beyond. The entrance is a magnificent affair with vaulted stained-glass ceilings, where many carved cherubs are glaring down, keeping a beady eye from high above. To get yourself a passport, you need a birth certificate. I have no such thing. There has been a panicked rigmarole of trying to find mine in our house and failing, so I have a form signed by trusted professional people that live in the village: the doctor, the vicar and even my mate Billy Besant's dad are all happy to guarantee I am, in fact, me.

Our passports, or pazzies as they are soon dubbed, now secured, we set about rehearsing and getting our new equipment ready for the trip over to Belgium.

Very soon, the day comes, and we head down to the end of the country to get the ferry from Dover to Calais. We're travelling with The Teardrop Explodes and very few Belgian francs in our pockets. On the ferry, it all feels like a school trip. We pass the time between seasickness bouts by playing cards. Dave Balfe manages to win all Gary Dwyer's meagre spending money. The Teardrop's drummer forlornly heads to the back of the boat to stare at the frothy wake created by the ship as it steams along. He sparks up a ciggie and reflects on his bad luck. In the cinema of his mind, he is Humphrey Bogart, starkly noir-lit as the imagined soundtrack orchestration swells and adds to the poignant image.

Plan K poster, Brussels 1980

Back in the bar, our pleas of 'Don't be such a tight arse, Balfy; give Gary his cash back' are met with a resounding 'No chance.'

(I like to think we had a whip-round for Gary, and we gave him a few quid to get him by. But as we were all skint, we probably didn't.)

Back at the stern, as we are approaching the harbour, Gary is watching seagulls swoop low behind the ferry as his romantic notion of the hero who has taken a chance and lost everything continues to play out in full 35-mm noir glory inside his head.

My head is filled with different films. So far, late-night BBC Two French and Italian films complete with subtitles have been my only way of knowing what Europe is all about.

BBC Two was good for slightly risqué movies. Now, I can pretend that I was a pseudo-intellectual teenager and watched them for the camera work, the arty angles, the acting and the plots. In truth, I watched because there was a fair chance in foreign films that some gorgeous actress would get their tits out. If any teenager from back then tells you otherwise, I suspect they are lying. Hey, a young lad with testosterone-flooded veins and hormones going nuts cannot live by the sensual delights of the lingerie section of Mrs Mazenko's *Freeman's Catalogue* alone. Europe seemed so mysterious, chic, artistic and erotic. Alongside these spicy flicks sat TV documentary clips from the war series *All Our Yesterdays* – lines of German soldiers marching through the Arc de Triomphe or the SS lording it up at cobbled kerbside cafés. These were my only impressions of Europe.

As we approach Calais, I believe that the so-called 'Johnny Foreigner' is not trying to conform and is not in the slightest bit besotted or seduced by the US-of-A, like we are over in Blighty. Back home, all are brainwashed, including me, by the ideal of the white picket-fenced American Dream. *Huckleberry Finn*, *The Beverly Hillbillies*, *Petticoat Junction*, *Green Acres*, *Mister Ed*, *The Munsters*, *The Man from UNCLE*, *The Addams Family* and countless other American shows have distorted our minds.

We reach Brussels early in the morning and are met at the hotel by a gaggle of very well-dressed young trendies: Annik, Michel, Natasha, Marc, Pascal and their friend Bert. They all seem like kids to me but are a couple of years older than us.

We check into the faded glory of Hôtel Central right opposite the Bourse. This turns out to be a great location as it's near the Café Falstaff, where we'll meet up with our new friends for a drink later. After dragging our cases through the revolving door, I am issued a key and I am sharing a room with Les on the first floor. Though they call it the second floor here. The Europeans don't have a ground floor, which is a little confusing for the novice traveller. Les and I dump our bags, quick swill or cow's lick (as my mum used to say) in the bathroom sink, and then we are out. Keen to explore, we note there is a café to the right of the hotel, the Chat Noir; many cheese omelettes and chips will be consumed here over the next few days. We head past the columned Bourse building and on through the little lanes that eventually open into the most impressive Gothic medieval square we have ever seen. Well, in my case, the only Gothic square I've ever seen; I don't think they have one in Liverpool. The Grand Place; it's a place, and yes, it's grand. We soak it all in. It has incredible carved rock finials and squinting gargoyles, ornate spires, Gothic archways and window frames crafted out of stone. Centuries old and still standing. Why have we never heard of this place before? At all corners, the square has little lanes and alleys feeding in tourists to gaze at this magnificent structure. These passageways are home to some interesting shops. There seem to be many shops with *Tintin*-related books, cards, posters and models.

Along with Les, I am a big fan of children's TV from the golden age, the 1960s and 1970s. *The Adventures of Tintin* was one of our favourites. Seeing all this Tintin merchandise, we are in our element; shops in England never had any of this cool stuff.

Back at the hotel, one of our hosts, the very beautiful, soft-spoken and warm Annik Honoré – her accented voice is enough to fill your body with butterflies – is chatting with us.

Annik is very proud of her country and fuels us up with local knowledge. The creator of Tintin, Hergé, lived and worked in Brussels.

'And, of course, Will, you must know Jacques Brel?'

'Er, no, never heard of him,' I answer.

It turns out the singer-songwriter Jacques Brel, who died a year or so earlier, was from Belgium too, and recorded and played some of his most famous concerts in Brussels. Annik provides us with some cassette tapes and a VHS of Brel.

At this point, I may not have heard of Jacques Brel, but I was unwittingly aware of his songs from a few cover versions of his songs I had heard: the Sensational Alex Harvey Band, 'Next' ('Au Suivant'); Scott Walker, 'If You Go Away' ('Ne Me Quitte Pas'); David Bowie, 'My Death' ('La Mort'). Also, one of my favourite Bowie songs was 'Amsterdam', perhaps because it had lyrics about 'sluts', 'whores' and other wild goings on. Fascinating imagery of a grown-up underworld to a teenage kid still wet behind the ears and just discovering sex. I was not used to such words being used in a song. But these Europeans, eh? Always were ahead of us Brits in the saucy department.

Many of you will know Canadian singer Terry Jacks's hit, 'Seasons in the Sun', which Brel originally called 'Le Moribund', usually translated as 'The Dying Man'. All cheerful stuff, right up my morbid boulevard.

I can't remember whether we saw the videos of Brel in Belgium or when we came back to England and watched them there. VHS video players were a very recent invention and cost a small fortune, and I only had a minuscule fortune. No, that's a lie: I had no fortune. So it is unlikely I had a home video at this point. I was still living at my dad's house, and there was no video player, that's for sure. There were scarcely any lightbulbs. I remember in one of the videos, Brel is picked out of the darkness by a single spotlight. I go into book research mode and look it up on YouTube; of course, it's there. He is dressed in a sombre black suit with a dark tie, loosened; top button undone. He is not a classically handsome fellow but then who is? His somewhat gaunt face is home to a goofy mouth. Lug holes just like our brand-new King Charlie's bookend his head. But his voice and the expression he gives to the songs are all that matters. Probably his most famous song is 'Ne Me Quitte Pas'. A lone camera is up close and fixed on his face. A single shot of a singer's mug would be unheard of in today's zero-attention-span world. The song sees Brel begging his lover not to leave him. He is a fine actor; every line is accompanied by a delicate expression that leaves you in no doubt about what is going on in his tortured mind. He is in utter anguish and, as the song progresses, he permits himself to think that maybe his lover will not leave him, and the slightest glimmer of hope flashes across his face. Then reality hits him hard, and he is dragged back into a bottomless lake of misery. You are an easily ruined man when love has you in its vicious grip. The pain he is in is so real, his eyes distant and glazed, the sweat on his face adds to his distress. It is difficult to view but it's impossible to look away. As I watch, emotions are wrenched out of me, feelings I do not wish to feel. Everyone has a song like this, and 'Ne Me Quitte Pas' has become mine.

Manchester's finest exponents of the darkness, Joy Division, have already been over to Brussels and played at the Plan K twice. Coincidentally, and very appropriately, the venue is on Rue de Manchester. I am very happy to follow in their footsteps as I have been a big fan since first seeing them at Eric's. I often wonder how they took the rock 'n' roll format of bass, guitar, drums and vocals and made it sound so fresh and new and timeless. It's all the usual components that have made rock from the very beginning. But the four of them freshened it up somehow. It must be something in that Macclesfield water. I am going to have to stop thinking about this now; it's twisting my brain up.

We are invited to one of the young promoters' houses for a drink before heading off to the Falstaff. It's a fantastic flat with massive hardwood doors and floors. My council-house manners are out of place here. I'm not in the least bit erudite. They all seem to be a lot more sophisticated than us, especially as they can speak perfect English, more than likely better than me. Our gang and the Teardrops are all in attendance. Something is happening in one of the rooms, involving the top of a fancy sideboard. The others are bending down and sniffing something. I'm not used to this, and my curiosity is fired up.

'What's that, Balfy?' I ask.

'It's Cocaine, Will. Have a go.'

Les and Pete have already had a go, so I think, *Why not?* As I'm doing it, Mac appears.

'What the hell are you doing, Will?'

'I dun know, just thought I'd have a go.'

He looks at me, disgusted. I don't seem to feel any effects and think it is just a bit of nonsense. A couple of beers and we are out of the flat, heading to the Falstaff for a couple more. The Falstaff is quite like an English pub, all carved wood, the funk of stale beer and of dead tobacco; the only difference is that waiters in black clothes and white aprons are floating about, ready to take our drink orders. After about a couple of hours in there, it's getting on for midnight; I think, *OK, this must be the end of the night.* The servers are starting to stack up the chairs and wipe down the table spillages. But no, incredibly, our new Belgian friends are just getting ready to go out to a club. Then we go to what I'm assuming is Brussels's number-one nightspot, but this is no Dixieland Showbar in Southport.

We are given a VIP entrance to the Klassik. There are white Venetian blinds all around the room, like we will soon see in 1980s videos to convey a feeling of sophistication. It all seems a bit naff now but at the time, and compared to Eric's, it's all very suave. The reflective surfaces of the blinds are picking up the flashing colours of the disco lighting, the pulse, accompanying music from Kraftwerk, Bowie and James Brown. 'Sex Machine'

Our lost friends Annik Honoré and Bert Bertrand

is a big hit in the Klassik. As James Brown invites us to get on up, I am doing my best: I am getting on up. Cocaine has removed some of my inhibitions, and I think I am the essence of cool. In reality, I've now got my hands held up right in front of my face like I'm going to take a bite out of a massive sandwich while doing a repetitive side-to-side shuffle kind of deal to the beat of Kraftwerk's classic 'The Model'.

'She's a model, and she's looking good.'

I am not a model, and I'm pretty sure I'm not looking good. But the lying nosebag tells me I am, and I keep trudging my way through song after song. I suppose it could loosely be called a dance. I'm sure it is not what Mr Brown had in mind when inviting people to get on up and do their thing. My moronic leaden sidestep dance continues until the sun opens its sleepy eyes and peeks above the horizon. The cars and trucks start their Saturday deliveries. Shop people and cleaners are on their way to work. Six a.m. arrives, and it's kicking-out time.

I'm not impressed with coke. I think it never did much, but Mac loves to remind me that I danced until 6 a.m. It's the first and last time I willingly take it.

After a sleepless couple of hours back at Hôtel Central, suddenly, it's gig day.

Our equipment is successfully lugged through a brick archway into a courtyard, then on into an industrial complex. The substantial brick-built disused sugar refinery is now empty of all the sugary goods, but a sweet molasses bite still hangs in the air, along with the familiar smell of dead rats. A small stage has been set up in one of the larger rooms. The dressing rooms are high above the factory floor. In the rafters, steel grid walkways are suspended on metal rods. I'm not too keen on heights; it's a challenge to get to the stage without freaking out and crapping myself. Les has no such qualms, and it's all a breeze to him. Les is a salty seadog; he is no stranger to the crow's nest and is often to be seen shimmying up a mast. It is all in a day's work for our recently resigned boat builder. He takes great joy in shitting us all up by wobbling the walkway as we nervously creep to the stage high above the heads of the crowd of Belgian post-punks below.

It all seems so modern and exciting, bohemian, continental and free. That some kids could do such a thing. England is so tightly nailed down with rules and regulations. Pubs are still closing at 10.30 p.m. in the week and on Fridays and Saturdays at 11 p.m. For clubs, it's 2 a.m.

We are on stage first. The Teardrops will have to wait till we get through our few songs. The new amps look cool; silver sparkles matching the sparkling Fender sound. I am wearing my finest charity-shop leather jacket and beatnik turtleneck; I've hardly ever had this top off since I found it. Mac is wearing a suit jacket, sandals and jeans. Les is in a blue work shirt. Pete is keeping cool in a simple T-shirt. By the way, I think that by this time, Macul's name has been shortened to just Mac. So, I will be calling him Mac from now on.

Mac alternates between the newly acquired fender Telecaster Thinline (Pinky) and his Yamaha Acoustic. I have my black Telecaster. Les has his recently spraypainted blue Fender Jazz Bass. We are still getting used to having Pete bashing seven kinds of shit out of the drums behind us. But the set and songs are improving every time we play.

Playing at the Plan K, Brussels 1980

CHAPTER 8

The Skilled Loafer Could Make a Pot of Tea Last for Hours

Music for Airports – **Brian Eno**

Without the rather tiresome burden of a job to take up my days, I drift into the life of a musician. This entails mainly hanging around in the centre of Liverpool. Most of the bands stemming from the Eric's punk scene gravitate to the Mathew Street area of the city. The current favourite hangout is the Armadillo Tea Rooms.

It was almost certain you would see someone you knew in the Armadillo. Our good friend and former Teardrop Explodes keyboardist Paul Simpson worked there on occasion, serving the food and drinks. He would craftily top up our teapot when the boss, Martin, wasn't looking. It was a good place to keep warm for a while. The skilled loafer could make a pot of tea last for hours.

As we sat keeping out the cold nursing a cuppa, we would talk shite about the Liverpool bands. The main topics of conversation would be what bands were coming to Eric's? Who was going? Have you heard such and such's latest record? And generally, what a load of shite it was. Much gossiping about who was shagging who. I obviously never featured in this tittle-tattle, being a very late starter to the world of sex, or 'the beast with two backs' as Mac used to call it. I understood the imagery but had no clue the reference was from Shakespeare's *Othello*. Shakespeare wasn't for the likes of me and my schoolmates. I'm pretty sure Pete would have got the reference, though, posh school and all that.

When the teapot was completely empty, and we had our fill of bitching about bands, I would drift into Probe records looking for the latest releases. Probe had a blackboard at the back of the sales counter, a musical menu with all the new singles and albums chalked up. Probe always seemed to be full of punks. I expect not all of them were buying records, but records were flying out of that shop. After being in Probe for a short while I would walk a few hundred yards to the tucked-away basement shop, Penny Lane Records. There on the counter was their bargain rack. Full to the brim with twelve-inch singles, mainly from Joy Division. An *Ideal for Living* EP. The shop couldn't get rid of them, they were there for months. So many times, I was going to buy one but was put off by the simple fact it was in the cheap bin. We knew it was from before they were really Joy Division. When they were still in the transition from the more punk Warsaw to the much darker and moody Joy Division. Very collectable now, as you would expect.

The Bunnymen were starting to get mentions in the weekly music papers: *New Musical Express* and *Sounds*. It seemed like that was the pinnacle of being in a band, getting a mention in a music paper. When we did get namechecked, it would increase my belief in the band. My growing, deluded, youthful arrogance was giving me a sense that everything I said and did was the right thing. I thought all the other Liverpool bands would have spotted these little mentions in the press, and they would be thinking, *Wow, the Bunnymen are getting noticed and are ahead of us.* Knowing the competitive vibe most of the bands had they were surely thinking, *Why are we not in the papers? And I wish the Bunnymen would fuck off.* Our contemporaries' jealousy, around that time, was very obvious.

I was starting to grow into a peculiar mix of arrogant prick and self-doubting knobhead. This was all heavily tinged with punk rock's distrust of big labels and the music business in general. And just for good measure, a handful of shameful feelings of being a sell-out. Back then, selling out, or not selling out, was a very big deal. If I met some mates on the street and they would ask me how it was going, I would always feel slightly awkward that we seemed to be becoming flavour of the month in the music press. I would not allow myself to have pride, it was more a sense of embarrassment, and I would almost apologise for having some small success and always play it down. I felt a weird sense of guilt. While a lot of my mates languished on the dole, we had a chance. It was a slow build, but we were getting to be number one in the 'hip parade'.

My idea of success was creating cool, innovative, timeless music, not chart positions and becoming a household name kind of deal. I wanted success on our terms. I wanted very much to be given those most elusive of accolades: cool, underground or even hip. In my blinkered opinion, our band was not like the rest of the up-and-coming crop of Liverpool post-punk bands, some of which seemed to be doing it for fame or even money. This never entered my head. It's hard to believe now,

Pete wearing my groovy sweater

but I had no concept that the band would lead to a musical life, a career – that word still makes me cringe a bit; careers are for others, not for the likes of me. On the other hand, Mac had known he was going to be a successful singer since he first saw Bowie on *Top of the Pops*. I suppose it can be summed up in our approach to chord sequences. I was always into the darkness of the minor chords and Mac was more of a major-chord kind of fella. So much so that when I had some basic chord structures of the songs, 'Villiers Terrace' for example, I would insist on playing E minor and he would play E major, and this created a slightly discordant element to early Bunnymen tunes, which probably made them sound slightly edgy and unnerving to most lugholes. I saw using major chords as selling out, too sweet, too nice and too obvious. This would clearly cause a tension that still exists today. It's a ridiculous carry-on. In fact, I know now both elements are needed for the song's journey. To have dark you also need light to travel to, or vice versa.

We both have the skills to shoot ourselves in the foot. I won't say who has the best aim, but I did win a cup in archery once. Just saying. I was something of a crazy, mixed-up kid.

The nearest station to my dad's house is Kirkby. It only takes a few minutes, a short hop to the top of Station Road and then a couple of hundred yards through the slightly safer parts of Kirkby. I can see the trains sitting next to the only platform.

Quickly now, I'm skipping down the ramp with my Saveaway ticket clasped in my hand, day and month freshly scratched off with a halfpenny coin. The guard is looking out the window at the back of the train, poised to close the sliding doors and give two rings on his communications bell. This will let the driver know we are good to go. He gives me a hurry-up-mate look, and I jump on. It's only a sixteen-minute ride to Liverpool Central.

It's another day wandering around town. I peek into the Armadillo but unusually no one I know is in there. Off to the record shops, and charity shops looking for booty, but today's haul is poor. I decide to head up to Rodney Street to see if Paul Simpson is in his new flat. Always good for a chat, a brew and listen to a few records.

A right turn up Bold Street and a ten-minute walk on ahead, past the bombed-out church, and a little further up Hardman Street, past the Silver Plaice chippy, it's a left turn into Rodney Street. About halfway along the shabby Georgian terrace is number 14, opposite the neglected Scottish church. I glance through the church railings at the fascinating pyramid-shaped tomb, unkempt and shrouded in long grass and nettles. Then I turn to face the black front door of number 14.

Paul lives on the first floor. Often on the way back from a

night at Eric's, with no lift or cab money, it would be a wise move to swing past Paul's for the possibility of a couch for the night. Ringing the bell would be too loud at that time of night so a stone would be thrown up at his window. I'm not the only one who takes advantage of his hospitality and often find other denizens of the Eric's scene already on the couch or the floor, an overcoat for a blanket.

I ring the bell for flat 4. Nothing. I try again; I'm thinking maybe he's in the bog? The third time of ringing, the sash window slides up and a hand drops the key to the ground. I unlock the heavy, glass-panelled door and let myself in. I clatter up a flight of stairs, I turn right and knock on the grey door to Paul's flat. It's a bedsit, only one room, but it seems to be taking him ages to get to the door. I knock again.

A wispy voice asks, 'Who is it?'

I reply, 'It's me, Simo, who do you think it is?'

'Who's me?' the voice asks.

'Me, Will, you div,' I say with a chuckle, thinking it's some sort of joke.

The door handle turns, and I am in.

'All right, Paul. What's going on?' I ask.

'Er, Yorkie is here. He keeps making creaking sounds like a galleon,' he whispers.

'Eh! What you on about?'

'Shush. Listen.'

I listen. Yorkie changes his position and looks up over the top of the sofa. He is wearing his thick leather Canadian Mounted Police gaiters and, as he moves, they rub together, creating the sound of a creaking galleon straining the ropes of its mooring in some far-away grey lagoon.

'Ha, that's ace. It's a supernatural power.' I have a chuckle and ask, 'Do it again, Yorkie.'

'Do what?' Yorkie says with a slight bemused smile on his face.

Then I realise all is not quite what it seems. They are both acting a little strangely: they are with me but somewhere else at the same time. This can only mean one thing. LSD. Their eyes don't look right.

I had first come across this drug when Les had taken a blotter in the Zoo office. He was sitting by the window, just quietly looking out towards the parallel stripped frontage of Beaver Radio on Whitechapel Street. At the time, no one knew Les had taken acid and he was silently taking in all our chat and clamour. We just thought he was not in the mood for chatting and left him to it. The scant office was now a wondrous place to him, but with one annoyance: us, that is. A few days later he told us what he was thinking at the time.

'Why are they doing all that talking? Do they not know there is no need of words any more?'

He was on one of those trips where everything is clearly coming into focus – the 'I can see our place in the cosmos, we are one with the universe' kind of trip. That's right, the stuff that Timothy Leary would come out with, the higher consciousness stuff. The sort of thing that you hear about when people take weird mushroom concoctions in some South American rainforest ritual. Seemed a little out of place in a rainy, grey Liverpool with hordes of shoppers laden with Woolworths bags trundling about. But I don't make the acid rules.

Back in Rodney Street, Yorkie might be communing with a god for all we know and wants to embrace him/her/it/them. It looks like he is going to try and put his fingers through the protective, very hot wire cage towards the even hotter one-bar electric fire, the only source of heating in the freezing bedsit.

'Oi! Yorkie, don't do that!' I say with a concerned and urgent tone.

The situation starts to unwrap in my head. His eyes are black; the pupils are dilated, massive. Yorkie turns with the now familiar creaking sound and I shepherd him away from the fire. I look around and realise Paul is now drawn to the glow. He is slowly bearing down onto the red-hot element, the orange radiance bathing his pale face. He is like a dying man compelled to go into the light.

'Paul, stop!' I shout with a little panic entering my voice.

He stops for long enough to get distracted by some other wonder in the room, of which there are many. Phew, that was close. All seems OK for now.

I decide there is only one thing for it. I head to the stash of LPs leaning against the wall. Quickly leafing through, I dig out *Music for Airports* by Brian Eno. Fire up the Dansette record player. The static crackle of the needle coming to rest in the grooves is soon replaced by the glorious sound of slow, so slow, so very slow treated piano. It's filling the freezing room with warmth and a feeling of total calm.

With a distinct gaiter rasp, Yorkie flops down on the couch and Paul hits his eiderdown-strewn bed in the corner. For now, the electric fire emergency is over.

I put the kettle on and settle in for the next few hours. I don't want to leave them to get into any more danger. It may be a while until the touchdown brings these two cosmonauts of inner space back to Earth.

I recently called Paul up and remind him of this day. He divulges that Kev, the local supplier of psychotropic tinctures, had told him, 'There is a bit of a drought on the pot front. I do have some microdots, acid, LSD, though, if you would be interested?'

And of course, he was interested. Earlier in the trip, as Yorkie had been lying on the couch with his leg gaiters making the uncannily accurate galleon creaking sounds, Paul had been getting harassed by one of those animatronic clockwork monkeys that crash cymbals together. The cheeky monkey had been jumping all about the architrave and picture rails of the room, annoyingly clattering his cymbals. Paul never owned a monkey toy.

In the soft-drug world, cannabis in the form of hash aka Rocky and the slightly softer version, Black, was pretty much all you could get back then. Skunk and its derivatives were extremely unusual.

These were the days when attics and lofts all over this land were used for storage of junk and not collectively for growing acres of weed. Now, look up and you can always spot them around any estate. The sizzling grow-lamps below the roofs create cosy roosts for pigeons. But back in the post-punk days I was a novice hayburner. I saw pot as a hippy throwback, something to be avoided by punks at all costs. As a fifteen-year-old, I had only managed a few drags on a jazz cigarette. One of our more out-there schoolmates, Trog, had brought a joint into school. And somehow, I had got hold of it. Back at Ian Campbell's house for lunch, more than likely beans on toast, and very near Maghull's number-one hotspot, the Country Club. The Campbells' soft furnishings were about to become impregnated with the heady fumes of Moroccan hashish. After about two puffs, my fifteen-year-old brain was banjaxed, and I felt sick and extremely nauseous. Dinnertime over I then had to go back to school and get on with chicken-killing lessons or something equally as nuts, and still in the woozy state of a trainee pothead. I'm still not a committed exponent of the world of drugs. I occasionally have a bit of weed in the States if the tour bus has become boring and we must hang about for a while. I have had my psychedelic moments, though, and I will be detailing them as my story goes on.

CHAPTER 9

Demo-itis and a Demonic Bunny

Live at the Witch Trials – The Fall
'Typical Girls' – The Slits

We are now getting enough songs under our belt; soon, we will have an album's worth. The next stage of song development is the demo stage. We recorded a couple of tunes at John Peel's radio show in the summer of 1979 that we've been using as demos, but we need proper recordings.

Bill Drummond had been up to Amazon studios in Kirkby. He tells me, 'I found the experience a bit dry, lacking in atmosphere.'

It's all about the atmosphere; places have got to be suitable and vibey for things to work.

Meanwhile, Bill's occasionally talking to Tony Wilson from Factory Records. Tony tells him about a studio they use.

'Bill, you should go to Rochdale.'

'Why?' says Bill.

'There's a great little studio there, Bill, Cargo, run by a bloke called John Brierley; you need to get your Bunnymen over there.'

Within days, Bill is cracking the whip and we are heading to the promised land: Rochdale. Birthplace of the Co-op and home to a creepy legend about a satanic beast, the Baum Rabbit

10 HOUR BOOKING DAY OR NIGHT

8 TRACK RECORDING   £9 per hour
                     £70 per day
16 TRACK RECORDING   £13 per hour
                     £110 per day
CARGO RECORDING STUDIOS
KENION ST (off Drake St) ROCHDALE,
phone (0706) 524420   LANCS

a NEW deal from

(tape and vat extra)

Cargo Studios. Thirteen quid an hour, bargain

or, as they say around those parts, Baum Rappit. A boggart or demonic bunny. A far-out coven of Lancashire witches possibly conjured him up – witches that prefer their demons all cute and cuddly with floppy ears. The unfortunate spectral creature is summoned up and then, I presume, left with no return ticket to Hell. The poor little fellow is destined to hop around the Rochdale area for eternity, mainly St Mary-in-the-Baum grave-yard. Baum? I look up baum; it means tree. Not sure what Mary is doing in a tree, but it takes all sorts. I think of the rather disturbing puppet Hartley Hare from the seventies kids' TV programme *Pipkins*. If ever there was a demonic rabbit, Hartley fits that bill. Give yourselves a nightmare and look up the scruffy little fucker. Before you start, I know a hare isn't a rabbit, but who's counting? Not me. Anyway, the Baum Rabbit has been actively putting the shits up the locals for centuries and is used by parents to get their kids to obey them.

'Get to sleep, or the Baum Rappit will get you.'

The kids are now wide awake with the terrors till dawn.

This is all true. I'm not making this up for Bunny-istic effect, by the way.

I find this fascinating. It's an odd coincidence as our Echo and the Bunnymen logo is a demonic rabbit, which we call the Bunny Devil or the Bunny God or sometimes the Bunny Creature.

Rochdale is perched just to the north-east of Manchester. Rochdale's roots are knitted into the woollen industry, which means, by 1980, it is on its arse. Like many northern towns, Rochdale is now forgotten and neglected. The textile mills stand silent; the static cling and electric zing of nylon, rayon and other cheapo synthetic fibres are now the thing. I still remember the sizzle, cling and pop that happened every time I slid out from my freezing nylon sheet and sleeping-bag combo. I'm sure this static fizz contributed to many of the spontaneous combustion cases we always seemed to be reading about back then. That and a bad diet of overcooked sprouts.

Cargo Studios had become the regular recording studio of many north-western bands in the early eighties, most coming from Liverpool and Manchester. We were impressed that the Fall had recorded *Dragnet*, their second album, there in the summer of 1979, in only two days of August. The Fall's first album, *Live at the Witch Trials*, took even less time. They don't hang about, them Fall guys.

Some incredibly steep steps access the studio. I can't imagine the gangly figure of Mark E. Smith lugging the Fall's amps up those stairs. I assume the band do the humping. Just like in our taut unit, it's every man for himself. So, we begin the assault on the north face of the studio staircase. Bravely we climb without the aid of ropes, crampons or even a lone Sherpa to help us. I struggle to the summit by dragging the amps one clunking step at a time. The recording room is a no-frills kind of place but in the control room, they have a sixteen-track recording machine, which is incredible. We can layer up guitars and add extra sounds. We record about six or seven of the songs that will be on the upcoming album.

Now, there is such a thing as demo-itis. This condition is brought on by listening to your demos too many times. Your mind becomes clouded, and you start to believe the demo is the best version of the song. To the sufferer, no other version will ever come close to the raw, visceral energy your band has been able to commit to magnetic tape. Demo-itis can only be cured by not listening to the demos for several years. The freshly recorded album versions have got to take precedence. When recording, it is customary to play guitar parts repetitively, especially when timing and execution, at this time, are not my most apparent assets. Cargo's engineer John Brierley is constantly playing and rewinding the tape in short sections, dropping the machine into the record mode so I can insert my guitar; it's all part of the normal recording process. By the end of this procedure, you will have listened to the new recording several thousand times.

Listening to the constant playback of the new versions should cure the demo-itis condition but can often worsen it. For example, if you hear the demos unexpectedly because you need to reference part of the old arrangement. You will already be fed up with the constant repetition of the track you are now recording, so you can quickly be dropped back into demo-itis hell, thinking the new version is missing the original's fresh vitality. So, it goes on; eventually, you have to learn just to let it go.

Me and Mac

I need to mention this: beware of giving out copies of demos to mates as, inevitably, it will get back to you that they think the demo is better than the finished record.

As you contentedly trundle up Bold Street with pride in your pants thinking you are the centre of the creative universe just because you have a record in the shops . . . Oh God, look who's coming down, a rival band member, a 'friend' who you foolishly let hear your demos or, worse, made them a cassette copy. They are still yet to get a record out and in the shops so, full to the brim with envy, they invariably chime up with, 'All right,

Will, heard your album. It sounds good, but I like the demos much better.'

Arsehole.

After you have spent weeks perfecting the parts and the sound, and you have plunged yourself into a mammoth debt with the record label, it pisses you off and is highly annoying. This is, of course, the aim of the often-jealous rival band member. He then carries on his merry little way as an evil, satisfied grin creeps across his mush; he has successfully managed to piss on your chips. He has sown a very nice, festering nugget of doubt in your head.

Torment ensues, and you start to question yourself.

Maybe he's right? I did like that guitar sound on the demo; we never did manage to recapture it. Is it all too polished? Have we lost our punk-rock roots? Oh my God, have we sold out?

After being in the studio, I never want to hear the bloody songs again. When I take them home, I never play them. They remain stacked up in my collection. Of course, I hear the songs repeatedly in the live versions. Which somehow always makes them sound fresh. I expect this is because they are never the same twice. The onstage sound and things that happen when playing live can be unpredictable, sometimes pleasantly, as some little thing you chance throwing into the mix works, and a shimmer of joy goes around the band. You know the others have spotted it when they respond with their off-piste expedition. It's all part of the subconscious language of a firmly bound-together band.

I talked to Big Bill about the Cargo demos a few weeks back, and he is still suffering from demo-itis, the poor fellow. He tells me, 'I remember the Cargo demos were much better than the *Crocodiles* record versions of the songs.'

Soundcheck somewhere in the Midlands, 1980

He continues, 'Somehow, they had the raw essence of the band in them. They were a lot more real.'

And then, 'Grittier, and even though there were anomalies in the playing and the band's tightness, they were better.'

For almost fifty years, Big Bill had held the sound of the demos from Cargo in the furthest reaches of his mind. Annoyingly crackling away and now and then brought to the surface, the demo-itis takes hold once again. It's a nasty case, the worst I have ever had the misfortune to witness close hand: unfortunate kid, all those years of suffering. If you are suffering from demo-itis, there is help available. Log on to www.wedont-giveafuckandgetoverit.com. It is time to get real; it's only music; it won't change the world. It hasn't changed the world. It has changed some people's worlds involved in music. It has changed my world and sprung me from a life in the kitchens of Liverpool's low-end establishments. Some music fans' outlook on life may have been revised, or they may have met people they have fallen in love with because of music, gigs or dances. I do not doubt this in the slightest, but that's all. It has not stopped wars or politically altered any state, and the planet is in as much shit now as ever it was.

'Eh, Will, you are so cynical, man; what about the Beatles? They changed everything.'

Oh really?

Even John Lennon, when asked, 'Did the Beatles change the world?' replied: 'Yes, some people grew their hair long for a time.'

Or words to that effect. So, get real people; it's just entertainment.

After we had left Cargo with our final mixes, the multitrack tapes were recycled, rubbed off and used again for the next band who came into the studio. I have been trying to track down the Cargo demos without much luck. I would love to know if I could get the same thing from them that Big Bill mentioned.

I am not immune to this sickness; I have been blighted with a kind of demo-itis. An incurable offshoot live-gig-itis. It has manifested itself several times over the years, firstly with Dr Feelgood, whose live set was so electric that their first record, *Down by the Jetty*, was just too flat and dull. The volume of live gigs could take you to another state of consciousness. I played the record at a high volume, but it didn't cut it; it was just the same only, as you can imagine, er . . . louder.

Something else in the live gig couldn't be recreated by turning a few knobs to eleven. There is a live at Southend video of Dr Feelgood on YouTube, and you will see and hear it for yourself. The fact that the band are going for it, and if they don't play the sections of the song as crisply as they could, it adds something to the menace of the band and the uneasy feeling twinkling through the crowd.

Liverpool loved the Slits, and I saw them a couple of times at Eric's. They were always great nights. The Slits' anarchic stage personas and the rough-around-the-edges renditions of the songs were what I wanted. It intrigued me; they were like a female Fall. When the record came out, everything was too clear, too crisp, just too bloody good. I know this is my problem; most would disagree and say the songs are much better this way. But they hadn't been in the sweaty cellar down Mathew Street when these not-so-typical girls were producing magic.

I'm not sure we always managed to get the essence on the record. In our case, it's best to think of the recorded works and the live shows as two independent entities, which is exactly what they are. Some bands I have seen have managed to be as good on record as they were live. Early Roxy Music did it for me, and Led Zeppelin never disappointed on record or when I saw them on stage. Ramones and the Buzzcocks were always great too.

A few years later, Cargo Studios was rechristened Suite 16. Hooky from Joy Division was involved with it. It continued being the epicentre of northern post-punk recordings. Eventually, it closed as a recording studio in the 1990s when everyone drifted into a gurning ecstatic funk brought on by consuming bucketloads of horse tranquillisers. This initiated an insatiable need for repetitive bass drumbeats and squelchy synthesiser pulses. Many turned to the home computer (including me) as the primary tool for music construction. This was the beginning of the end for thousands of studios in the land.

CHAPTER 10

Stuck Down a Blues-scale Cul-de-sac

'Biff, Bang, Pow!' – The Creation

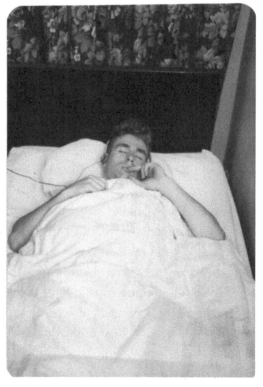

Les having a snooze. More than likely listening to early Bowie

When I'm not wandering the streets of Liverpool city centre, my head is filled with all things Bunnymen. I am playing the guitar in the back room of 15 Station Road. I am constantly getting more and more to grips with my idea of a guitarist and the techniques. Not always what real guitarists would do, but I tread my own idiosyncratic path. I am coming up with chord sequences and little sneaky riffs incessantly; it's hard to stop this stuff from just arriving. No thought is given to how it all happens. It just happens. Like the telly advert for *Yellow Pages* says, I just let my fingers do the walking. I don't try to analyse this too much; my thinking is if I get too much under-standing, my creativity will be channelled down the well-trodden path that many have travelled before, and then, before you know it, I will be stuck down a blues-scale cul-de-sac. Forever to be chugging out the blues. Spending all my crea-tive days learning 'Stairway to Heaven' or, worse, 'Smoke on the Water'.

I have no musical theory in my head, and I don't want any. I know what I like. And not just in my wardrobe. Simply put, it is only combinations of notes that make you feel something inside. A lot of trial and error is involved; I record everything I can, so I can remember what I have come up with. I also write down the sequences of chords in a little book. My terrible handwriting is sometimes hard to decipher. I do it all in my own way and generally take the shortcut or easy route. My fingers are not the leanest or longest, so reaching for fancy augmented chord shapes, well, that's a non-starter. There is nothing too clever in these chord structures.

We now have almost enough tunes for an album, usually about ten.

When a band signs to a label you are assigned an A & R man. It seems it is always a man. Well, it was back then anyway – I never heard of any A & R women. Korova's creator, boss and our A & R man was Rob Dickins. Rob and our manager Bill Drummond knew we needed a producer. They thought we would be floundering around, taking ages to record, and more than likely end up arguing about unimportant and irrelevant things. I think they were right about that but, at the time, I was so full of spunk and spit that I would have likely said we don't need a producer – any producer. Truthfully, I was not happy with bringing in anyone from outside our very close group. Producers seemed to me like they were in the pay of the record company. In truth, they are in the pay of the band; everything is in the pay of the band, and that's what the debt is all about. They kind of keep this from you, but every expense eventually creeps into your debt. A producer's job would be to try and make us sound in a way that I did not want us to sound, basically too cheesy or, to use the buzzword at the time, make us sound 'commercial'. More palatable to the majority. This was not what I wanted at all. It's another example of me shooting myself in the foot, or was I? It sounds ridiculous, but if we had gone down the cheesy route, I'm not sure we would have had the longevity we still enjoy. Music that is easily digested is easily shat out too; it becomes boring and bland. I think the best music is the stuff you as a listener must work at enjoying. It becomes more engrained in your soul.

I never trusted anyone back then. I was extremely precious of the band, the sound, the whole concept. Sire Records boss, Seymour Stein over in New York, had piped up with the suggestion that the great Del Shannon, he of the number-one smash 'Runaway' fame, should be the one to produce us. Bill knew us extremely well by then, and he decided to swerve this madcap idea from Mr Stein; it was not even suggested, and I have only recently found out about it. He would have definitely got a solid 'You can fuck right off with that plan.' From me, at any rate. We did know Seymour was a fan of Del and, somehow, he had managed to glean that some of that Del 'Runaway' vibe was present in the organ sound on our minimalist first single on Zoo Records, 'The Pictures on My Wall'.

Er, I'll have a pint of what Seymour is on. It was three notes I had put down on a random organ, possibly a Philips Philicorda; this was added to break up the twelve-string acoustic strum, which was all the way through the song.

Don't get me wrong, 'Runaway' is a fantastic record and I love it as a piece of sixties rock history. I was all about going forward, weirdly, by looking back to the sixties, maybe not quite as far back as Del Shannon in 1961. I know this is a contradiction; some sixties bands were so ahead of the game they have never been surpassed in the creativity stakes. Modern bands are still trying to catch up creatively with the likes of the Velvet Underground, the Doors, the Beatles, Cream, etc. I could go on. All right, I will. The Rolling Stones, Love, 13th Floor Elevators, the Creation, the Kinks, the Small Faces, and the Who. Sorry, I drifted into a sort of mod vortex there. All are great bands. So, when I hear a guitar-based record on the radio, my mind automatically thinks, *Hmm, do I like this? It is sort of good, but it reminds me of this track from the sixties in its tune or sound.* This sixties song is inevitably much better, and it is swathed within a nostalgic bubble wrap that can never be fully popped by some new kids on the block. No, not them. I mean new bands on the street. Some things are just cool, and some things are just so flipping uncool, for example, New Kids on the Block. Yes, them this time. Del may have been extremely good in the sixties, but he was not cool in the eighties. Bill had elected wisely, in my opinion, to keep shtum about Seymour's wacky idea.

To be fair, we were all naive when it came to studios and what could be achieved. I hardly knew what a producer's role was. We had been in a few small studios and in with the BBC producers on the John Peel sessions. The Radio 1 producers, as far as I can remember, just wanted to get it all done and dusted, with us lot out of the studio as soon as possible. Ideally, before the pubs closed. You can't blame them, being stuck in a tiny control room with a gang of grumpy punks chosen by Peely every day would have driven me nuts, that's for sure. I have tried my hand at producing, but I have never pursued it seriously. I remember how awkward I was and how ungrateful to people who had worked their balls off, only for it all to be dismissed as crap by me. What a cunt I was.

Bill Drummond and Dave Balfe had been with us when we worked on the demos at Cargo. They were more vibe merchants than producers. They did try and keep it organised, but real producers have a plan and usually jot it all down in a little book they can refer to. As the recording progresses, they cross out the things that have been done or make notes if parts of the song need adjusting or redoing. A bit like a foreman on a building site, producers make sure we are working hard and on budget. They can add ideas to the pot, too, but they are not always welcome. There had been a few arguments in the studio between us, Bill and Dave, usually when Dave was trying to add keyboards all over the tracks. He had invested in an ARP Odyssey synth, and he was determined to use it. We were determined he wasn't going to use it. I think Bill was not too keen to be in the role of producer – he could see trouble ahead with us lot.

At this point, we were sent to Rockfield Studios near Monmouth in South Wales for a couple of days. The in-house engineer/producer was a nice fella called Pat Moran, who had worked on a lot of records, mainly rock or progressive rock: Van der Graaf Generator, Budgie, Rush, Dr Feelgood. He was currently working on Iggy Pop's album *Soldier*. Pat had a few days off from Iggy duties and could work with us. We recorded a version of 'Villiers Terrace' to be our first Korova single, but it failed to impress the label and was shelved. All I remember about this recording is Pete de Freitas and possibly Pat Moran doing some lisping backing vocals. I did not like this at all: it was a saccharine sweetening too far. I saw 'Villiers' as a garage rocker; for once, I agreed with the label.

Who the hell could deal with this band? Robert Plant was even suggested as a producer, as apparently he sometimes hung out at Rockfield. I was really the only one in the band who was impressed by this as Led Zeppelin was my favourite band as a kid. Bill spoke to Rob at the label, and between them they dreamed this one up. This idea was a total non-starter. No, that was never going to wash with our punk-rock credentials. It would have been the kiss of death. I loved Zeppelin, but even I knew that this was a nutjob suggestion. I don't think Plant was asked or was even aware of this crazed idea. It was just a thought that, like many others, just appeared and then faded out.

Discipline was not our strong point. We really were going to need someone to make it all happen. Someone who was ultimately in charge, a person that was organised and could push us to greatness. Someone who knew their way around a studio and was versed in all the technical stuff a studio can provide. We had no clue how to get an LP together.

Then, out of nowhere, Bill and Dave come up with Ian Broudie.

Broudie was only a kid at the time but, then again, we all were. We were mates with him from Eric's and from gigs by Big in Japan, Bill's former band which Ian had joined as a guitarist. We all liked Ian a lot. He was funny, had a great take on things, and was a kind of sensible voice in all the punk-rock bollocks that were flying around. We had given him a lift in Les's van and played some demos for him. We hated them, but he liked them and saw that he could rearrange them and add to them. So, it was kind of fate again working in our favour.

A big clock and Mac

After Big in Japan had imploded, he had gone on to record with the singer from Deaf School, the artist formerly known as Enrico Cadillac Jnr, now simply Steve Allen. Together they had formed the aforementioned Original Mirrors. Broudie had been in a studio with the Original Mirrors; they had made a full LP, so he was a lot more experienced in this band recording lark. He knew a hell of a lot more than any of us, anyway. I've never been able to understand this; how did he know so much about studios, the equipment and all the way-out stuff in there? I knew about guitar effects, a few of them, at any rate. Phaser, flanger, wah-wah, echo, chorus and reverb, that sort of thing, the basics. But not all these other gizmos, stacked up in rack upon rack, all plumbed into the mixing desk via a complicated patch bay of spaghetti wires: compressors, de-essers, harmonis- ers, noise gates, graphic equalisers, etc. Broudie even knew which microphones were best for recording different instru- ments or the best ones for the individual drums. He must have had a bloody good crash course on all studio techniques during that Original Mirrors album.

If America had got their hands on the Original Mirrors, they could have done well over there. They were serving up a much more agreeable version of punk the Yanks called New Wave. Lots of pastel suits, skinny ties, chorus guitars, big drums and jumping about, looking like you are having too much of a good time. That kind of thing was the opposite of any of the bands I liked. If there's going to be any jumping about, it can only be Iggy Pop after he's rolled around in a few broken bottles or Jim Morrison getting shot by an imaginary firing squad and hopping about like a Comanche dropout who's just stubbed his toe on his wigwam.

The first time I noticed Broudie was when the two sevens clashed, yes, seventy-seven. Jayne Casey, Big in Japan's singer, was in Eric's. No surprise there – like us she was always in the club. The Queen of Eric's, she had to be there to take care of her realm. But also, this night, Big in Japan was set to play. She was chatting with Les Pattinson, Paul Simpson and me as we were doing our usual hanging around in the club, nursing a tepid bottle of Eric's finest Pilsner for as long as possible.

Jayne says, 'Wait till you see our new guitarist. He looks about fifteen and he is amazing.'

He did, and he was. He was wearing denim dungarees. Not the most punk-rock item of clothing at the time but, somehow, they fitted in with the Big in Japan vaudeville vibe. He had the appearance of an undernourished kid from a Midwest farmstead on the outskirts of a one-horse dustbowl town. In reality, he was from Childwall, an affluent area of Liverpool. Ian had been in a rather short-lived ensemble before Big in Japan, the O'Boogie Brothers, along with a few early-doors Eric's loyalists, Dave Knopov, Ambrose Reynolds, Nathan McGough, plus drummer Bernie Goodheart. This band was named with serious reverence, a nod to John Lennon's alter ego Dr Winston O'Boogie.

Bill pushes the idea of Ian Broudie as a producer, as he was there when Ian had taken the reins on the Big in Japan sessions and seemed to know what to do instinctively.

He phones Broudie up and asks him the question. Broudie promptly says, 'No thanks, Bill, I've got my own band going, and we are just about to go on tour with Roxy Music, so I won't have time to commit to an album.'

Bill hangs up rather dejected; his mind is spinning. How can this be turned around? His gut is telling him Broudie is the man for the job. Bill quickly rings back.

'What if you just do a couple of tracks? Just a few days in the studio?'

Broudie thinks about it. He's not soft; he knows the single is the track that gets all the attention. And he did like the demos he heard in the van.

'OK, Bill, I will do a single and one other track.'

Bill agrees even though we have no obvious single now that 'Villiers Terrace' has been rejected.

CHAPTER 11

The Glowing Brazier of a Cocky Watchman Drifts Smoke into the Salty Air

'Life During Wartime' – Talking Heads

It's early January 1980. I'm back in my village of Melling. My stumpy digits are getting a right royal workout on the guitar in the back parlour when the cheery chirp of my dad's trimphone interrupts the proceedings. It's Bill Drummond, our manager. News just in. Bill has found us a new place to practise that we can call our own and keep all our gear there, permanently set up. Ian Broudie is going to be there in his role as producer.

'What tracks do you have? He said he will be producing two tracks for us. He wants to do some preproduction. Get the songs into shape. before going into the studio in London,' says Bill.

'OK, Bill. We will go through everything we have, and we will see what he thinks,' says I, following on with, 'Where is this rehearsal place, Bill?'

'It's down on the docks. Brunswick Dock in the south end.'

We are essentially a north Liverpool band; the south side of Liverpool, in my head, is a tough and scary place. It is truly uncharted waters. A nervous fear and excitement fills me.

How could a couple of miles upriver seem like a world away?

Easy, when you've had no experience of the adventure of life. In the next couple of years, our world is going to expand beyond all of my expectations.

Back in 1980, the Liverpool docks were a completely different place from what they have become today. No plush apartments, art galleries, fancy shops, car dealerships or restaurants; all that was yet to arrive, starting with the renovation of the Albert Dock, then in 1984, the Liverpool International Garden Festival. Some effort was put into getting Liverpool back on the map. Even the Beatles were not really cashed in on back then. Now, you can't move for memorabilia museums, Magical Mystery Tour buses and the odd taxi driver offering trips around the lads' old homes and haunts.

Roger Eagle, the imposing moustachioed boss of Eric's, had somehow got the keys to a small, abandoned building, teetering close to the banks of the Mersey a few miles south of the cleaned and now gleaming Liver Buildings. Roger was intent on using it as a well-out-of-the-way rehearsal room. After all, this sprouting crop of post-punk bands would need somewhere to practise, and no one down here would be moaning about noise, apart from the odd cormorant or gull.

Bill was no stranger to these forsaken docklands. He had stumbled upon the area in the early seventies while roaming around the waterfront, purely in the pursuit of solitude and skiving from art school. With an 8mm cine camera for company, Bill would wander around being arty. He had remembered this old desolate dock area from these art-school days of mooching about. He loved it down there, and was convinced this would be a creative place for us.

A day or so after Big Bill's call, Les's van is tightly crammed with guitars, amplifiers and Bunnymen. Off we go, drifting down the docks, heading to the riverside destination. The van clatters over a grey metal girder bridge crossing the deep dark water of the Brunswick Dock, and we pull up into a large, cobbled yard.

Strangely, there are no barbed wire fences or a security man sat in a little gatehouse with Radio Merseyside blasting out of his tranny. Nothing here is guarded or manned twenty-four hours a day. There's not even the slightest acrid sniff of the glowing brazier of a cocky watchman drifting in the salty air. It's possible to wander unchallenged in this area of the old docks. Just a few hundred yards off the main road we are now in what feels like a forgotten and forbidden zone, a no man's land.

Giant storage warehouses stand completely empty to our left and right. Cold and quietly haunted by the distant ghosts of dockers. The only sounds filling these voids now is the wind off the river, the scream of quarrelling gulls, the sharp yell of starlings and the frantic flapping of fornicating pigeons, homing in on the vinegar stroke.

The warehouse's enormous sliding doors are kept wide open, I suspect for the same reason parked container lorries leave their doors open; this is to let thieves know there is no need to smash a padlock or damage a door because no booty is housed within.

There is a large redbrick building, the harbourmaster and lock keepers' building. This must be where the practice room is housed.

I'm taken by the area's bleak, mysterious, forgotten beauty. 'This is ace, Bill.'

We all agree.

'Wow, Bill, this is brilliant, where is the practice room then?' we ask excitedly.

Bill points not to the well-kept and slightly imposing Victorian redbrick splendour of the harbourmaster's building, but to a two-storey, rather ugly, slightly dumpy afterthought of a brick building sitting alongside to the left. Looking at it, I'm not too impressed. This little outbuilding must have been used for storage or as an electricity substation.

Not knowing the Roger Eagle connection, I'm wondering aloud, 'How the hell has Big Bill found this place?'

A battered door like a kicked-in mouth sits in the centre. This is flanked by two windows, now blinded and bricked up. Above, two more windows squint down at us past the broken glass. We stand by embedded rusty train tracks, snaking all over like veins set into the cobbles. There must have been trains shunting and grunting in and out of this place years ago. Now they have seen the last of their shunting, grunting days. Exploring around at the side of the building we find a swinging chain, a safety barrier strung between hefty cast-iron bollards, and a warning: you are near a dangerous waterfront. We creep forward and peek over the edge. Peering from a greasy bank, the actual river channel is some way off. The riverbed is a putrid colour somewhere between grey and brown. I'm sure you can find it on one of those hipster paint companies' colour charts, with an esoteric name like 'Elephant's Memory' or 'Vanilla Fudge'. In the sheen of the surface, the smooth glistening mud is peppered with the trident-like prints of seabirds' tracks. Old tyres and bikes languish in the silt.

Les notes, 'The tide is coming in.'

The salty seadog knows about such things.

We watch the River Mersey slowly flood the sludge-covered riverbed below as the tide crawls in from the Irish Sea and heads towards Runcorn. Pete and Mac's fag butts are flicked into the mud, and we head back to the front of the brick cube.

Bill grins nervously as he produces a key from his pocket and opens the battered door.

We poke our heads inside, and are greeted with the sight of piles of rubbish, bits of wood, bricks and other debris.

A thought flashes through my head: *I wonder who's paying the leccy bill for a derelict brick shed down the docks with no other living soul in sight?*

The thing that I find strangest of all is that there is power in this abandoned and broken-down dump. A bare light bulb is swinging in the breeze, glowing like it has been waiting to welcome us in.

The responses to this new practice room are along the lines of 'Think again!' Followed up with, 'What a sodding hovel!' Maybe even, 'Shithole!'

I can't speak for the others, but the disappointment on their faces says it all. However, there is a quiet, desolate beauty about the place that suits the band's post-punk dark and sombre vibe.

We are here now, so we elect to set up anyway. In no time the bunker's trash is lashed out of the battered door and piled in a heap on the cobbles. In goes Pete's kit and we arrange our still-glistening second-hand amps in an arc formation, facing Pete. One of the important similarities about playing live and writing or rehearsing is communication. After a couple of years of being together, the communication becomes magical. It transcends into a mystical level, and it's hard to fathom how it works. Telepathy starts to happen. The music becomes a conduit for thought, even before you think you have thought the thought you are thinking of. Your fizzing mind sends impulses out of your brainbox. They shoot down your neural network straight past your elbows and wrists into your hands, and then the electrical impulses start to flourish and twitch, the tactile touch of the fingers on the metal strings.

This is especially true if the right combination of minds is as one. It speeds up the process. At this stage of the band, we have the right mix of personalities, humour and serious intent, and it all works very well. We are as one.

Broudie wants us to play through the songs we have. I am slightly apprehensive of his scrutiny but go along with Broudie's request. We complete our usual practice routine and run through the songs.

'Do you have any others that you are working on?'

He's obviously not that impressed with our half-dozen or so songs. He is very musical and, as we all know now, a fine writer of pop tunes.

'What about that new one we were doing at Yorkie's the other day?'

'Oh yes, we do have a new one but just a kind of slightly funky Talking Heads-style riff, really.'

'OK, let's have a jam around it.'

Yuck! A jam. I hate the word jam. It kind of stinks of some old smelly rock band getting all bluesy and frugging out while passing around the well-stocked bong. Punk rock and our whole new scene are rejecting the old dinosaurs in brushed denim, beads and cheesecloth.

A slight argument breaks out.

I say, 'No, we are not having a fucking jam. I hate that fucking word!'

'OK, what are we calling it then?'

We need a new word, a cooler word, to describe what is

happening in this grim brick bunker. Some suggestions come forth.

Broudie looks on bemused. I suspect he's thinking, *I'm glad I'm not doing a whole album with these nutters.*

'Tootle about?'

'Nah, that's crap.'

'Scratch around?'

'No, too itchy.'

'Play around?'

'Pervy.'

'Chug?'

'Give over, will ya?'

Try as we might, we can't think of a better word, so sod it. I hate saying it, but yeah, fuck it, jam it is.

My once chubby and soft fingertips are now hard as nails; I am always searching for the next combination of notes that will ignite and delight my pleasure zones. We have been in the brick hut for a few hours. We are getting too cold and too fed up, we are just about to pack up and go home when out of my guitar pops a melodic combination of chiming notes. I follow this up with a rhythmic attempt to sound like the scratchy funk of David Byrne from Talking Heads. Everyone starts to jog in and, yes, jam along. OK, don't rub it in.

Ian Broudie instantly picks up on my little guitar motif and says, 'What was that you just did, Will?'

'Er, dunno.'

This happens on occasion when I am playing the guitar. I will run past a riff or combination of notes without noticing their worth.

I try to retrace my steps and get back to the part of the guitar's neck the notes had magically materialised from. After a few attempts, I have the little motif back in my fingertips.

Ding-dong dinga-dinga dong-ding-dong-dinga-dong-dong.

Or words to that effect.

Broudie says, 'That would work as a great intro.'

It also gets used in the chorus. When Mac adds the vocals, this rough jam becomes 'Rescue'. With Broudie's melodic ears on our team, we soon pull it all together, and we have a new song to add to our growing list. This will be our first single on the brand spanking new Korova label.

It's the first and last time we use the brick bunker. It is back to Yorkie's for our next practice session. We do return to this area of the docks soon after, though, for a photo session. Bill Drummond's Northampton art-school friend Bill Butt has been drafted in as a photographer.

I have an instant, not exactly dislike, but a mistrust of any newcomer to our team. And I, like a proper arsehole, deem it wise to be as uncooperative as possible. And take the piss as much as possible. Everyone seems to want a piece of our action. Plus, Bill Butt is wearing brown leather jeans just like a mullet-sporting German. As we all know, the brown leather jeans target audience is the German mullet man. Oh God, what have we become? What the fuck is going on?

Without lighting and with the dark of the evening closing in, this photo session has not really been thought through correctly. We head into one of the big sheds open to the elements. It's even darker in the shed. Bill Butt tries his best to light us up with the van's headlights, but it's a losing battle. I have set my mind against him. We are not the chirpy friendly northerners you see on *Coronation Street*. I am downright antagonistic, working against him, not with him.

This was a trait we all displayed on occasion, maybe not Pete so much; his southern posh-school manners would not allow him to be this way. It was a kind of power trip; we could be intimidating if we wanted to be. Most journalists and photographers got the sharp end of our collective spite. This was a sort of 'attack is the best defence' kind of thing. Consequently, not a lot comes of this photo session.

What I didn't know was that Bill Butt had travelled all the way from Bristol to do these photos for us on his BMW motorbike and the leather trousers, far from being a fashion affectation, were hard-wearing pants designed to protect the soft spongy flesh of his arse cheeks. If the unthinkable happens and you end up scooting down the road arse first, the soft fleshy backside ends up like grated Red Leicester all over the tarmac. A wise and practical safety aspect for a biker. Goes with the helmet, lights, brakes and . . . er . . . the bird. That one is for the unreconstructed old codgers in the audience.

Trainspotter fact: the bunker can be seen a year later in The Teardrop Explodes video for their song 'Reward'. It's the building where the late Jake Brockman, our then-future roadie, keyboard player and occasional rhythm guitarist, is crouching, looking rather cold, tired and wretched, squatting among all the debris we had cleared out, which had somehow found its way back into the brick bunker.

Soon the day comes to record 'Rescue'. Ian Broudie in tow, we arrive at Eden Studios in the lovely borough of Chiswick, west London. After setting up, we box off the backing tracks fast.

Then it's down to me working on the guitars. I'm sure I played all the guitar parts on both tracks. We are now familiar with Ian Broudie; we like him an awful lot, so he has been honoured with a rechristening. He is now simply Brod.

Ian Broudie outside Brian's Lean and Hungry diner
on Stanley Street, Liverpool

I remember some of the techniques we employed at Brod's suggestion. On 'Pride', Les Pattinson's bass had a slight flange sound. We were not huge fans of these 1980s flavour-of-the-month effects, but somehow it worked and ended up on the song. Brod must have been quite persuasive for us to let that one go. Les is normally a purist; secretly, I think he liked the way the bass sounded. It really popped out of the mix. I know when I listen to a mix, me and my ego are only really listening to my parts and I want to make sure they are getting heard. Basically, am I loud enough? I think we all do this ego-mania thing whether we admit it or not. We may be a team, but I want to be heard all the same.

Brod had been reading up on the Beatles' studio tricks. He had me double-track the guitar intro on 'Rescue', you know the ding-dong one from the brick bunker. Back then, tape machines had a cool little feature called varispeed; the tape could be sped up or slowed down by tiny amounts. And I mean infinitesimal amounts. This faintly changes the pitch of what is recorded on the tape. The nature of the electric motors means that the speed is not constant and can fluctuate but this was exactly what Brod wanted. This is something that is difficult to achieve on digital recordings without a lot of faffing around. If you slow a digital recording down, it is completely constant; the digital realm never wavers. It cannot change unless you program in tempo changes. The fluctuations in the anomalies between tape machines are useful sometimes: the imperfections create the sound. When Brod recorded my second pass at the guitar intro and chorus riffs, he slowed the tape down by a minuscule amount. Afterwards, when the tape was up to normal speed, the two guitar tracks would cause a sort of out-of-phase sound; this had the effect of making the guitar peal out with a crystalline jangle that made the guitar riff really stand out. Hey, we are all suckers for a bit of crystalline jangle; I know I am.

The big upset of the session was my guitar sound in the verses. What I had in my head was a slightly funky rhythm. It turned out to be more George Formby than George Clinton. It was like a night down the Old Bull and Bush. Knees up, knees up, try and get the breeze up. This still troubles me today; why did I let it go? I can only think we must have used up all our time at Eden. I just had to accept it.

We had a saying back then: 'Forget it; tomorrow there will be a new hurt to heal.'

Such was the difficulty of getting the idea that grows in your head to transfer to what ends up on the records.

Now, it all seems so minor and petty; back then, it was a major thing for me. I would have to live with the sound of a fucking banjo forever. Today, my relationship with the song 'Rescue' is only from the live gigs. I have improved the sound of the rhythmic guitar on the verse bits to something more like how I wanted it to sound on the single.

Our next mission is we need a B-side for 'Rescue'. It's back to Rochdale and Cargo Studios to knock out a song. It came quick, this one being quite a simple construction. Dave Balfe and Bill Drummond are with us, and after we have the song down on tape, Balfy is trying to foist his synth on the track. We relent, and Dave creates a very rounded sound, almost a marimba. He tries a few things. We all agree they are shite.

Then he makes a little flurry of notes on his ARP. Engineer John Brierley had set the monophonic synth to an echo effect in the hope of making Balfe's efforts sound a bit more interesting. The flurry repeats steadily in time with the track, and the echo's gradually decaying repetition has it fading off into the distance. We all prick our ears up.

'That sounded cool, Dave, do that again.'

Chuffed he has done something that meets our approval for once, Dave is beaming.

It sounds good. God, we have a synth on one of our records. We will be dressing like robots next.

Weirdly this little sound of Balfe's gets us the reputation that we are all heavily into the 13th Floor Elevators. The part sounds a bit like the electric jug that Tommy Hall of the Elevators played. In fact, we had never heard of the 13th Floor Elevators at the time, but when the single gets reviewed, it is pointed out that the B-side, 'Simple Stuff', has an Elevator flavour about it. My brother Steve read this review. He was one for trawling the charity shops, and he found a copy of the Elevators album *Easter Everywhere* in an Oxfam shop in Rickmansworth. He sent me this record, and I still have it today. It had only just been re-released in 1979 on Radar Records. I must say you would be extremely unlikely to find such a record in a charity shop today. In some way, this album and band do become a heavy influence on me. I love the record and have started to collect all the other 13th Floor Elevators records. This weird happenstance of fate reverse-engineered my brain and opened up a whole new area of American garage rock from the sixties to me. The Seeds, Chocolate Watchband, Electric Prunes and many others all become essentials on the cassette tapes we played in the van.

We are gathered in the Zoo office in Chicago Buildings. Bill says, 'We need a cover for the seven-inch record; any ideas?'

Having pretensions of being some sort of artist, I push myself forward for the cover art. Incredibly, I am given the job. I make a stencil out of the first single cover by cutting out the Bunny Devil creature, then smearing soft pastel crayons red-orange on a background and then black across the stencil to form the outline of the Bunny Devil/Creature/God. I am pleased with the results, and everyone seems OK with it.

Next on the agenda is recording the rest of the tracks for the album.

CHAPTER 12

Ultimate Cock Rock Stance

'The Faith Healer' – The Sensational
Alex Harvey Band

We have been playing gigs up and down the country, sharpening the songs. They always come together better in the live arena. The effervescent buzz that washes over you from the crowd spurs you on. It is weird how being on a stage brings forth the dormant bravado of the introverted. In my mind, I'm going for it like a rock-crazed freak but, in reality, I'm just looking at my feet for most of the gig.

I have never been one for the rock 'n' roll cliché, and the ultimate is the foot-on-the-monitor pose. This is peculiar because, as a fourteen-year-old, I loved it when Zal, Alex and Chris Glen from the Sensational Alex Harvey Band ambled to the front of the stage. In unison, the three parked their stacks, creepers and platforms on top of the on-stage monitor speaker. Then they fixed the crowd with a deliberate glare just like Rotten would do a few years later. Was I too shy or too cool for the foot-on-monitor pose? I would say both. I would have loved to have had the balls to do it. For a laugh when we are doing sound checks, I have had a crafty go at this ultimate cock rock stance. I was and still am, to a lesser degree now, self-conscious. It's crazy that I have ended up on stage at all.

Playing shows inevitably results in us becoming much tighter. The pressure of the crowd's scrutiny gives you a good kick up the arse. With that lot gawping at you, you'd better be good.

We are gelling now in the way that only playing gigs can. From the beginning, both me and Mac had been trying to be percussive on the guitar. We are playing in that Velvets way, like on the track 'What Goes On' on *1969: The Velvet Underground Live.* Their interplay is magical; some strokes are deadened by releasing the grip of the left hand on the guitar neck, creating a percussive chug we both love. If it wasn't so white, it could almost be called funky. All those years listening to the Velvets have paid off. Mac is much better at this than me. He can add strokes between strokes at the speed of light and remain in time with the band. This way of playing is excellent for the chugging interplay of two guitars going at it like rattlesnakes' tails. It is a great way to improve timing.

We are all four of us becoming more competent. OK, Pete was brilliant from the start, and Les was solid; his timing had the accuracy of an atomic clock. It is a dream to sloppily ramble about and get creative while the reliable safety net of Pete and Les is there. The drum machine never cared about us in this way. Echo would tick away, aloof and nonchalant with an air of superiority. We are always going to get better with a human foundation.

In March 1980, we were at the Lyceum Ballroom, London. It was a new venue on post-punk radar, though not precisely a new venue. It has been there since 1765 in one form or another. Straight Music had started putting on shows with the up-and-coming post-punk bands; it all felt cool. Surprisingly, the somewhat classy Lyceum had let the likes of us in. Still damp with a punk attitude, many new bands had skipped up the stone steps and on through the Doric-columned portico. The Cure, the Clash, the Slits, the Damned and Gang of Four. This was a seal of approval for us to know these bands, our contemporaries, had played the Lyceum. Some of whom we even liked. Many others had played there in the sixties and seventies. Among these were the Groundhogs, Taste and Hawkwind, all great bands.

EATB play the Lyceum in London with U2

We were playing with The Teardrop Explodes. Bill Drummond's idea was to get both bands playing live as much as possible. There were the beginnings of a rivalry between us. I suppose he thought this would help – the competition between us. We were trying to outdo each other. We always thought we . . . now, this was the phrase we used back then, so don't be getting any ideas . . . blew them off. I mean blew them off stage, as you well know. Get your mind out of the gutter. We were better. I'm sure Scott Walker lookalike Julian Cope at the Teardrops' helm would be thinking the same thing, that they had blown us off . . . but I was there, and we blew them off big time. We would not allow ourselves to admit any defeat, ever, even if we had doubts. In some gigs, we came off satisfied that some magic had happened; in other gigs, I would come off stage thinking: *Oh my God, that was awful.* Usually, this would be because I had fluffed a guitar part or played a wrong note somewhere, which I often did.

In the crowd back then, there were hordes of long overcoat-wearing nerdy oiks. (If you were one of these nerdy oiks, read that as 'dedicated fans'.) They would shuffle to a prime spot in the centre of the vast PA stacks. Cassette recorders were smuggled in pockets, badge-strewn Army and Navy gasmask bags and duffle bags. At the first sign of the lights going down and the intro music beginning to creep up in volume, illicit buttons would be flicked to the record setting, and VU meters would twitch into life. The small condenser microphones hidden up the sleeves of bootleggers were a completely different ball game to the quality you can achieve today on the cheapest phones. The old condenser mics latched on to the nearest sound, so if the said bootlegger was standing next to some div that wouldn't shut up about all the birds he'd shagged, you'd end up with the band as merely the background muzak to matey boy's erotic adventures. Most were there just for the private collecting of gigs, like a trainspotter or stamp collector. We never had a problem with this taping of gigs. And there was a nice tape-swapping scene among Bunnymen fans. The way I looked at it, the people who are taping the shows had everything we released anyway. I don't believe that anyone ever said, 'I don't need to buy the new Bunnymen record, cos I have a really shit recording from a gig, though the chatter around me is more audible than the band.' Highly unlikely.

As for taping records at home, the record companies got the right hump over it and even tried to make it sound all frighteningly illegal and shit. 'Home taping is killing music', accompanied by a terrifying cassette and crossbones logo. Yeah, right, I'm quivering . . . I was never bothered if fans recorded the LPs for their mates; it gave us another audience that maybe had limited cash. Some would come to our gigs and go out and buy the records eventually.

There was an evil side to all this live-gig bootlegging, though. Hmm, yes, an extremely amusing cassette going around in the early days, crammed full of all my guitar fluffs and fuck-ups. Yeah, very funny whoever put that together. I was learning on the job, OK! God, now that I have mentioned it, it won't be long until some wag finds it and bungs it up online. Doh! Why don't I learn to keep my big gob shut?

With a couple more months' worth of gigs, the country is warming up and getting deeper into spring. We now find ourselves blistering at the breakneck speed of at least thirty miles per hour towards Rockfield Studios, this time for more than a fleeting visit. The Trannie van is on a rollercoaster ride up and down the hills of the Welsh borders. Only 166 travel-sickness-inducing miles from Liverpool. I get sick at the slightest motion; it's a pity I would like to be on the water, away from everything. It would have been nice to sail with Les Pattinson, our resident seafaring bassist. Back to the van, I claim the front seat, always;

Me blurred

this is a perk I get as co-founder of the band. I am Les's wing-man. I always ride shotgun. I look straight ahead and focus on the horizon.

Rockfield is a residential studio – the first residential studio, the one all others are modelled on – and it is tucked away in the countryside. Not many distractions; this is where we can get our teeth into recording without interruptions.

We leave the motorways behind, and now the road is becoming narrow; it's flanked by freshly leaved tall hedges dotted with trees. The trees are peppered with large dollops of parasitic mistletoe. This is something unusual for me to see – we don't seem to get so much mistletoe in the north; it must be the slightly harsher climate or the varieties of trees. The sun peeks through the verdant canopy overhead. The afternoon light is making the mistletoe berries glow like pearls, while speckled points of light bounce off the Transit van's heavily rust-pocked nose.

We are heading to the outskirts of the old Welsh market town of Monmouth, where the River Monnow trundles through the town, flowing across weirs, under bridges and towards the valley to join the River Wye. The Monnow, in part, denotes the border between England and Wales. The surrounding country-side is a patchwork of beautiful rolling hills and farmland for as far as you can see. Everything is bursting up out of the ground in eye-popping shades of green.

If we could sneak into the Doctor's TARDIS, hotwire the craft, then set the controls to slide back through the space–time continuum all the way to 1963, Rockfield is just being born.

It's the brainchild of two music-mad farmers, the Ward brothers Kingsley and Charles, acolytes of the inventive and, well, a bit mad Joe Meek – he did shoot his landlady and himself, after

Rockfield Studios' plate reverb units

all. Even by our standards, not the sanest way to act in a studio. The Ward brothers' first recordings were for their own fun – a love of music and the process. They recorded themselves in various group incarnations. They started recording with other bands in 1965. In 1970, they have their first real chart success, with the Dave Edmond classic 'I Hear You Knocking'. Dave's rootsy vocals sound like they are sent through a guitar amplifier to give them that hot-valve grit; this effect was actually achieved by the simple use of a cardboard tube on the vocal mic. It is an old trick used by the Beatles and very likely Joe Meek. I remember this song being played at the Melling Tithebarn youth club; it stood out. Dave Edmonds isn't why we have come to Wales, however. We are not on some Rockfield pilgrimage. I have no clue that track, or the Queen epic 'Bohemian Rapsody', had been recorded here. With my mindset at the time, the information that Queen had been there might well have put me off the place.

Big Bill Drummond and Dave Balfe have come in Dave's yellow Citroën. They have now assumed the role of producers and given themselves a snappy production team name: the Chameleons. Not to be confused with the Manchester post-punk band with the same name. (If I had a penny for every time someone has asked me if the Chameleons band produced our first album, I would be about thirty-seven pence better off now.)

Eventually, after the van has gobbled up the 166 queasy miles, we turn into the studio gates and head up the track to the farmhouse and studio office. It's a relief to jump out of the van and feel the solid earth beneath my feet.

My first impression on this proper visit is that it is in a beautiful location, still a working farm, as the odd tractor is clattering in and out as we get to grips with the whole scenario.

We are shown our accommodation in the old stables, now neatly converted into individual units, each with a first-floor level housing a double bed. We all pick a room; I go for one on the right-hand side. I unpack my few clothes and sit on the bed, looking through the big window and onto the daffodil-bordered fields that softly swoop towards Monmouth.

Rockfield Studios viewed from the house on the hill

Soon, Les gives me a knock. He is impatiently waiting for us to go exploring the place. We check out the kitchen, which is close to the rooms. A large fridge is stocked with loads of food, including quality cheese, not a Kraft slice in sight. Crusty bread, eggs, bacon, sausages, all things my dad's fridge seldom had – the complete works. We head around the back of the stables. A field rises to a small clump of trees. We can see a clear track; many feet have trodden a trail through the wet grass. More than likely, bands that had previously stayed at Rockfield had made the same trek. We climb up to the small copse of trees and look down onto the farm complex. This is as far from the MVCU four-track studio back in Liverpool as it is possible to get.

Back at the studio with mugs of tea in hand, we are introduced to Hugh Jones, our engineer. He is a slender fellow who can make you feel instantly relaxed in his company. Soft-spoken and gentle. To my bleak industrial northern eyes, a bit of a hippie. He is decked out in a flamboyant wardrobe: faded jeans, suede chucker boots, a silken scarf around his neck, a cheese-cloth shirt, beaded bracelets, etc. The control room is the beating heart of any studio. The mixing desk sits in the centre of the room. It looks complicated, and it really is. Massive JBL speakers are set into the wall left and right. In the centre of the speakers is a large soundproof window with layers of thick glass. This looks into the recording room.

Hugh is busy setting up the microphones he wants to get going, and is positioning all the instruments that we will be recording. Guitar amps and drums are isolated behind large soundproof screens to prevent spill. Spill? The sound of one instrument getting recorded or contaminating another instrument's tracks is called spill in the recording game. Pete's drums are the most complex part of our equipment to mic up. The snare drum has two mics, one pointing at the top skin and one at the bottom skin, near the wire snare that gives the snare drum its distinctive crack sound. Pete's toms are closely micced, too, as are the bass drum, cymbals and hi-hat. Then there is a set of ambient mics high above the kit. This will add a live feel to the drums and the overall room sound. Hugh expertly places all the microphones with confidence, experience and an understanding of the equipment.

Every recording room has its own distinctive sound. Think of the sound of 1960s Tamla Motown records; you know instantly it is a Motown record because they were recorded in the same small room at Berry Gordy's studio 'Hitsville USA' in Detroit, usually by the same musicians.

Many studios can change the room's sound by changing the studio walls' surface. The walls at Rockfield are covered in hessian and some carpeting to deaden the sound. In some areas, there are harder surfaces where the sound isn't overly deadened. Stone, for example, is used as the backdrop to the isolated drum booth. All possibilities are available to the engineer. At Rockfield, they also have a reverb chamber: a large stone room complete with toughened glass panels that can slide on rails suspended from the ceiling. These can swivel to change the dynamics of the reverb. A hefty speaker is set at one end of the chamber and microphones at the other; any recorded sounds can be routed to this speaker and then sent back to the control room and back onto tape.

We raid the fridge in the quadrangle kitchen and, after scoffing chunky, cheesy, crusty sandwiches, washed down with tea, we are set to record the backing tracks. We have been rehearsing in Yorkie's basement for a couple of weeks before we got to Rockfield, plus the live shows have helped to get the songs in a neat arrangement. We are all ready to go. There is a nervous excitement in the room; this is it. We are concentrating on getting the bass and drums down first. Mine and Mac's guitar parts are not the priority. If we fluff up, it's OK; we keep going.

Bill, Dave and Hugh are after the feel of the drums and bass. We do several passes at each of our songs, and then they are meticulously listened to for something you can't quite put your finger on, but the word 'vibe' gets used often. Getting the backing track process completed takes a few days, and I am impatient to get cracking on my parts.

Coach House Studio, Rockfield. *Crocodiles* was recorded in here

Mac is next to work on his guitar and will get the rhythm down over the next few days. He has two main guitars: Pinkie, the lovely Telecaster Thinline, and Blondie, a beautiful Gibson ES-335. He uses his Gibson for the thicker, meatier sounds and Pinkie for the crisp, ringing sounds. We've also hired some acoustic guitars. Ovation guitars are currently in favour; apparently, they sound good for recording. They have a rounded plastic back that I think is very ugly. I am not a big fan of these guitars, mainly because I feel they looked horrible, and that's enough for me not to have anything to do with them. Mac uses them here and there. Acoustic guitars have always left me cold, probably because I'm intimidated by people who can play them very well. My style needs the power of amplification and guitar effects to compensate for my lack of skill.

After about a week, it's my turn; I have a real problem recording a little arpeggiated guitar part on 'Villiers Terrace'. Hugh painstakingly helps me build up the part by switching the tape machine in and out of record mode as I attempt to play the section as best as possible. He can drop in single notes, a process called punching in and out. This takes split-second timing, and the result is that I sound like a much better guitarist than I actually am. (Today this would be easy with a computer and a recording program such as Pro Tools; you could copy the note and plonk it in position seamlessly. In the two-inch twenty-four-track tape days, it was complicated and a real skill for a recording engineer to master.)

We are resentful of Balfy, who's always trying to steer the band in a poppy direction that we are not into. At one point, something is said by Balfy that is too near the knuckle, and it flares up into violence. Mac grabs Balfy by the throat.

Balfy chokes out the words, 'I'm not going to fight with you. Get off. I'm not fighting with you, Mac.'

After a bit of a scuffle, Mac releases his grip and the tension subsides; Balfy flops onto the couch.

It's an ugly scene in the control room. It has become a battleground. I get my usual kick out of this fight, just like back in my dad's house in Melling in the good old days when my parents would be going at each other like cat and dog.

Over the next few days into the recording, stress begins to increase. It's not all plain sailing in the studio. There is an immense feeling of frustration and anxiety coming to the surface. It's the idea that you must let go of control and let others put their oar in. It gets on your wick.

After I have recorded a guitar part, it is played in the control room in a prominent position in the mix. This is done so Hugh can check that the sound works and the tuning is spot on. It doesn't take long for me to start wanting the part I've just done to be louder, as loud as I heard it when Hugh was reviewing it. When it is turned down, I get a cob on. Now, of course, I realise that everything can't be louder than everything else. It's impossible. Back then, I was very new to the process and had a lot to learn.

The strains of the situation lead me to ask Hugh, 'Can I do a screaming solo?'

Hugh turns away from the desk and says, 'A what?'

'A screaming solo. I want to scream on the record to get the tension out.'

'OK, let's do a screaming solo then; which track?'

'"Happy Death Men".'

'That seems appropriate.'

Hugh is a little bemused but agrees to my request and places a microphone at the far end of the corridor that adjoins the control room. He instructs me to go to the other end of the hallway and get ready. The track is lined up, approaching the area where he wants me to scream. It's about one minute and thirty-six seconds into the song. Hugh has headphones on and stands at the other end of the long corridor.

'When I give the signal, you scream.'

I give him a thumbs up and wait.

I can hear the tinny sound emanating from his headphones, and then he waves his hand, and I scream as if I've just fallen down a well.

'ARRRRRRRRRRRRRRRRRHHHHH!'

All the pent-up emotions and angst flood out. The pressure of recording is spewed out in one almighty howl. In the control room, Hugh soaks it in reverb, and it's done. My voice is in tatters. It takes a couple of days for my croaky speech to return. It hasn't really helped. I am still full of anxiety that my band is getting diluted by others, by outsiders' ideas.

I want a heavy sound on the track 'All that Jazz'.

Big Bill pipes up, 'The only guitar that is fit for this job is the Gibson Les Paul.'

I'm not so sure; the Les Paul has the stink of old-school rock about it.

Hugh assures me, 'It will be OK, Will; we'll keep it under our hats.'

Hugh gets on the blower to the musical instrument hire company. The Gibson is loaded up in London and, within a few hours, a man in a van drops it off.

This thing is heavy but not as heavy as my Fender Telecaster, the heaviest guitar in Christendom. I'm talking weight here by the way, not tone. In the world of heavy guitar sounds, Les Paul is the top dog, mainly due to the humbucker pickups that add a nice thick crunch to the sound. The Telecaster is great but can't compete with the grunt of a Les Paul. This axe – yes, it should be called an axe – it's the ruler of the world of rock. Mick Ronson used Les Pauls, Jimmy Page, Marc Bolan and even Steve

Jones of the Pistols, all did. Plus numerous seventies rockers. The Gibson was here to bring heft to my straightforward riff. Listening back now, it is not as heavy as I remember it. I was worried I had overstepped the mark and drifted into territories where post-punk should not go. Now, I can see how wound up I was getting. I'm still worrying about a bloody guitar sound I made over forty years ago; I need to get a grip.

Another memorable track for me on *Crocodiles* is the title track. I was trying to channel the late great Wilko Johnson, my teenage hero guitarist from Dr Feelgood.

I decide to record the guitar while standing on top of a Fender Twin Reverb amp; God knows why. I ask Hugh to turn the headphones up loud, and I imagine I'm on stage at the Liverpool Stadium. I am Wilko, and I'm just about to kick off big time.

I hear the steady click of Pete's drumstick count in. Click! Click! Click! Click! And we're off! This track is fast and furious, and I'm flaying at the strings like a crazed nutjob. I'm trying to keep up with the incredibly fast drums and bass. I catch my finger on the metal strings. Now blood is splattered Jackson Pollock style all over the guitar, but I'm a brave little soldier, so I carry on through the immense pain. You must suffer for your art. I get to the end, and then I'm rushed to hospital and given a blood transfusion and the kiss of life. No, not really. I have a Band-Aid wrapped around my poorly index finger, wipe the blood off the Telecaster's pickups and scratch plate, and put the kettle on for a brew. Wilko Johnson did this every night. I'm surprised he had any fingers left. Now, he really was a brave little soldier.

Mac begins getting the vocals down. He works best at night, I work best in the daytime, so, after I had done my guitars up till around 7 or 8 p.m., Mac would take over and work with Hugh, Dave and Bill till all hours. Me, Pete and Les would leave him to it. It would have been a bit off-putting to have us lot in the control room fucking about while he's trying to get his soul down on tape. Likewise, the band left me to my own devices when I was recording guitars.

In between, Dave Balfe did some bits of keyboards, piano mainly. He also instigated the trumpets on 'Happy Death Men' and put the Hammond organ on 'Do It Clean'. All of which I hated at the time but was outvoted. Now those tracks would sound odd without them. It's all water under the bridge now, and hardly worth fighting over. I like the trumpets now; hey, I've mellowed, OK! Want to make something of it, do you?

We are up early. The spring sunshine is warming up the quadrangle nicely. The morning dew is starting to steam. Rockfield has a cook who comes and makes us grub every day. It's always great. It is so lovely to be pampered in this way. We are here to record and all other concerns are secondary to that, so food is provided. We are scoffing at our breakfast, more than likely a full English with tea and toast, when we notice a long-haired geezer walk past the window. It's only fucking Robert Plant. (Eh, Will, I think you dropped something.) As I've said, Led Zeppelin does not mean much to the rest of the band, but I am a massive fan. In the post-punk fallout, all things from the past must be denied, destroyed and forgotten. Robert is friends with the Ward brothers, the owners of the studio, and has been living at Rockfield for a few weeks. Now that my guitars are done and it's Mac's turn to do vocals, I am OK to go home for a day. Dave Balfe must return to Liverpool for some reason, so he gives me a lift home. I pick up my Led Zeppelin albums and bring them back to Rockfield. Planty, as we are now calling him in that Liverpool way of being overly familiar with people you do not know, is still mooching about the place, so I collar him by the office and ask him to sign my records, which he does.

As time goes on, all recording is done. We have some time off as Hugh has begun the mixing process, and decide to go to Monmouth for a pint. Planty gets wind of this and offers us a lift in his Mercedes. What the hell is going on? Five years back, I watched Zeppelin at Earls Court, and now I'm in Robert Plant's car getting a lift.

Cock-a-hoop with the excitement of this, I claim the front seat and chat with him.

'You looking for a house?'

'Yes,' he says.

Along the leafy road to Monmouth, we pass several large houses. I spot one particularly nice one with a for sale sign.

'What about that one? Looks a bit spooky.'

'I won't worry about that. I would get Pagey to go and scare any ghosts off.'

We all laugh at this; it is common knowledge that Page is a fan of the occult and had lived in the Great Beast Aleister Crowley's house on the shores of Loch Ness.

Now that I'm familiar with Planty, I can offer some condolence to him in my increasingly arrogant way.

'Don't worry; Zeppelin will be back,' I say.

I know they have been called dinosaurs by the punk-drunk hacks in the music press. He surely would have known about this and would have been freaking out.

What am I doing? What am I saying? Who the hell do I think I am? A few music journalists say we are good, we've had a single of the week and John Peel seems to like us. I am so full of shit I can tell Robert Plant not to worry? Worried? He's probably a billionaire. This is one of the most cringe-worthy things I have done so far.

Planty laughs it off. He knows a knobhead when he hears one.

CHAPTER 13

The Rickmansworth
Psychedelic Wood Caper

'Paint It Black' – The Rolling Stones

Now that we have finished all the recordings, the mixing has started. We are not exactly banned from the studio during this process, but you can tell Hugh Jones doesn't want us around, at least at the beginning. This is when he gets a rough balance. He doesn't need us poking our noses in every two minutes, slowing the process down. Most of the time, Hugh is working on the drums. This seems to take ages. He is tweaking the sounds and balancing everything.

We have been hanging about for a long time with little to do. We go to Monmouth a few more times and have a visit from our new press agent Mick Houghton. We all love Mick and his hypnotic, soft voice. He knows so much about music we could do with him in our pub quiz team. He is the one who is getting us in the music press just about every week now. Even if it is a small article, we are steadily seeping into the consciousness of the record-buying public. Well, the ones who buy the music papers, whom I like to think of as the cool ones. It's the way it works; the record labels have a tried and trusted method of building a band, ways to make them seem interesting. This is how it all builds up, and the next thing you know, the band has the seeds of a solid following. Anything could go in the paper; it brings a cocky 'aren't I important?' kind of thing to my character. Not the most attractive trait. I start to believe the hype. This is a dangerous thing to do. The slightest knockdown from the press cuts deep into you.

We are hanging around the studio now. We are getting bored. One of the Ward brothers (I suspect it's Kingsley) notices we are just sitting around, usually near the kettle in the kitchen or watching the telly. He brings us a shotgun and a box of cartridges to play with. Rockfield has a clay-pigeon launching device at the back of the farm buildings. We fire off a few clay discs and miss. The rusty old launching mechanism is more frightening than the gun; it terrifies me. It looks like the powerful rusty old spring could easily snap back at you and rip off a finger. Only the brave few come forward to load the gadget.

We wander off in search of better targets. We spot a piece of old plywood and prop it up. The shot quickly makes a hole through the half-inch ply. A couple more hits from the twelve-bore's twin barrels, and it's blasted to bits; I think the word is smithereens. Now, it seems a bit nuts to hand over guns to people in bands, who are usually not the most well-balanced of folk.

'Here you go, run along and play with these weapons of mass destruction.'

These are the glorious carefree days before the nanny state and pesky health-and-safety nonsense.

After Hugh, Bill and Balfy have worked on the mix to a listenable point, we can come and have a listen. We all gather around the mixing desk and man the faders. Everyone is piping up, including me, saying the same thing: 'I'm not loud enough.'

Lots of arguing generally ensues and, eventually, things come to a compromise, and we are allowed to get near the desk again.

With no fader animation back then, some parts might need a little tweak; we are instructed to push up some of the faders to increase the volume of the guitar, voice, bass, drums or even pan parts from side to side at key points in the songs. Hugh uses a special grease pencil called a chinagraph to scribble marks on the desk to indicate the start and finish points. Well, you expect me to stick to the rules? I sneak the guitar a touch past the line and get a couple of decibels more guitar in the mix. And I'm sure Mac does it with the vocals and Les with the bass. It's all part of the fun and games of recording.

Overall, I think it's a pretty good mix. It could be a little rounder in the overall sound, a bit fuller and, if anything, the bass more prominent with a deeper sound. Les likes the bass's treble kick, which makes it pop out and be noticed.

We are approaching the end of our time at Rockfield. Three short weeks. It's enough to make Rockfield a special place for me. I have loved every minute we spent at the studio, even with the arguing.

Big Bill and Balfy have booked the studio again for the next three weeks. It's The Teardrop Explodes' turn. Before we got to Rockfield, Iggy Pop and Simple Minds had been in. The studio is busy all the time, it seems.

Things are starting to move fast; summer is just around the corner and a UK tour looms. First, we have to get the LP cover image in place. We are having a conversation, discussing what we should have on the cover. Someone suggests having a circle of 10-foot-high wooden stakes hammered into the ground, soaked in paraffin, and then set on fire. The blazing light from the stakes would somehow illuminate us in the darkness.

'Hold on a minute, won't that look like a Ku Klux Klan cross burning?' someone chimes up.

'Oh, shit yeah, we best bin that idea.'

The flames are swiftly doused.

We move on. However, we like the idea that the photo is taken in the dark.

Rob Dickins at Korova is drawn to the work of a brilliant photographer, Brian Griffin. Brian is more well known in the glossy world of colour supplements and magazines. High-powered businesspeople and workers alike are viewed through his Dada-influenced lens. Brian's pictures place the subject in exciting poses or unusual situations.

Rob has one of Brian's photographs on his Korova office wall. It's called *Rocket Man*. The setting is a pebble beach in Dungeness, Kent. A man in a suit stands facing the sea, and he holds the childlike stance of a rocket about to take off. His arms are on a slight angle, pushing downwards like the fins on a missile. The man is cast in shadow, silhouetted by the bright white trail of a large firework burning in the sky. The photo was taken with a one-second exposure to capture the wake of the rocket. It is a stunning image executed with precision timing.

Rob sets up a meeting with Brian and tells him, 'This band are psychedelic. Can you make them look trippy in a wood someplace?'

Brian knows what to do. He lives pretty near Rickmansworth in Berkshire. There is a farm that was used by the now-defunct

Denham Film Studios for rural exterior shoots. Brian heads over, has a look-see and finds the perfect spot.

Brian had only in the last few years been getting work taking photographs for LP cover art. He had taken the cover shot of Joe Jackson's 1979 album *Look Sharp*, in which Joe's white winklepickers are picked out in a shaft of light. I wouldn't have been seen dead trotting up and down the South Bank wearing those shoes. Not my cup of tea musically either, as you might imagine, but looking back over my shoulder of time, it's a great cover shot. Brian had applied his Dada sensibilities, and the record label fell for it. It was lucky I was unaware of Brian working with Joe. If I had known, it would have been a hard no-chance and fuck off with the horse you rode in on from me. Things could be easily tainted for me. Brian had also taken the photo of Iggy Pop for his 1980 record *Soldier*, which, incidentally, had been recorded at Rockfield in the weeks before we had arrived. Iggy is bathed in a square of light. He looks like some unseen sniper has just shot him; there is no blood; the only shooting was Brian behind the sights of the large-format Hasselblad.

We are sitting in the van and heading to Rickmansworth. I am in charge of map reading but the massive roadmap on my lap is unnecessary: Les doesn't need a map. He is navigating by the stars. Even in the daytime? Yes. Les has an inbuilt navigational gene spliced into his DNA. I stick with the map anyway. The van's heater is not exactly effective and it's keeping my thighs warm.

There is no stylist for us, no white leather jackets, nothing to say 'hey look at us, we are buckled, strapped and stack-heel-booted, leather-panted cool punk dudes!' and no King's Road garb. We wear what we happen to have on that day. It's all Mark E. Smith chic, charity-shop suits and long overcoats.

Eventually, we leave the main road and turn onto the farm track leading to a small patch of trees. It's now late afternoon. The cold sun is on its descent; the sky is beginning to enter the time of twilight. The farm is now used for location shooting for such TV shows as *Dick Turpin*, currently a must for the British Sunday-evening viewing millions. We spot a shadowy dandy highwayman riding his horse along a ridge a few hundred yards away. We convince ourselves it's Richard O'Sullivan, the actor playing Dick Turpin in the show.

Bill Butt and Brian Griffin up to something, God knows what

Brian had arranged for the film lighting company Lee Lighting to bring a generator lorry. It sits high on the track with cables snaking into the trees. The lorry's low hum provides power and a pleasing ambient soundtrack to the scene. The geezers from Lee have wired up 50,000 watts of spotlights. Brian, with the help of his trusty assistant Ricardo, has meticulously placed the lights. The multicoloured beams are shining up into the trees so any roosting birds must be well freaked out. As the light fades and dusk creeps up on us minute by minute, the coloured washes begin to take over and the cluster of trees is slowly changing. The English countryside ebbs away and a new psychedelic landscape appears.

We are told by Brian to find a spot to sit or stand. He tries several variations until he is happy with the composition, and then he takes some test Polaroid pictures, warming these snaps under his arm to aid the development process. When ready to view, we impatiently grab the pics. The small images look great, but we are just checking what we look like personally, looking for bad angles emphasising double chins or open gobs and noses looking like half-eaten turnips. I have all of the above, so for the proper pics I look down at the ground and get all enigmatic. We've done a few pics earlier, standing by some trees before the darkness descended. These are good shots but nothing like the cosmic glory of the evening shots. After about an hour of position variations, the cold creeps into our bones, and the gripes start.

'Come on, Brian, how much longer?' grumbles Mac.

I add, 'We're fucking freezing.'

Brian surrenders: he has what he needs. He wants to take some last-minute pictures of the suddenly not-too-cold Mac, now willing to lie in the thicket again. Brian has had strict instructions from Rob Dickins to get the singer's image alone. I can see where this is heading, and I'm not happy about it. We are a band. There are four of us on this adventure. We want to be represented as a band. But there is little I can do about it except look pissed off, which I am quite good at, to be fair.

Brian looks like he didn't really want to take the solo photos, but he does it anyway and applies the same meticulous care as he does to all his photographs. It's all over fairly quickly. Brian is confident he has got the photo for the cover.

We leave Brian, Ricardo and the lighting people to pack up all the equipment, and we return to Liverpool in the van. As we weave down the cart track, the illuminated coppice becomes visible. The night is becoming quite misty, and the clump of trees is glowing, vibrant like a UFO had just crash landed. Through the trees, shafts of light are picked out in the night's haze. It is a sight to behold. I will never forget it.

A week or so later, we are heading south to London to pick the cover photo. There is much arguing, more than likely something like this:

'I looked better on that one; I look shit there.'

'No, you look great.'

'Get stuffed, you look great on that one, but I look crap.'

'Fuck off; I look like a spud.'

'Think again, you turd; I'm not having that one.'

With four people to please, it's almost impossible for everyone to be happy with their pose. It goes on and on till, at last, we agree on the one to be used. Then we wait for the record to be pressed, so it is back on tour for us.

We head off around the UK. During these dates, the Bunnymen urban-guerrilla-army-surplus-clothing image is born. This is precisely how it happens. Les and I come out of the hotel room to go to the gig, and we haven't noticed, but we both have some item of military clothing on.

'Ha Les, we look like we are in the army.'

'Yes, the Bunnymen army.'

The spark of an idea is born.

'Let's start dressing in army surplus clothes.'

Recently the press has written that we are the band with no image. What? Have they not seen our smorgasbord of spectacular haircuts? Mac with his gravity-defying Bowie bouffant, Les with the ultimate quiff, Pete with the schoolboy floppy-foppish mop top, and me with my self-sculptured bowl haircut, fashioned after my favourite Stone, Brian Jones. How many bloody images do they need? We'll give you a fucking image. Over the course of this British tour, in every town we visit, the first stop is the local army surplus store: We increase our urban guerrilla wardrobe. Pants, jackets, vests, shirts and boots. Les even buys a bulletproof vest. I'm unsure if it's lead-lined, but it weighs a ton. However, the ludicrous weight does not hinder the signature Les Pattinson shoulder shimmy. I give Mac a spare combat jacket I have hanging about.

Mac wearing camo (the square insignia was from my dad's WWII uniform)

Two major Vietnam War films were released in the late seventies, *The Deer Hunter* and *Apocalypse Now.* We watch these films constantly on the newly invented VHS video players. We are fascinated by the inexplicable juxtaposition of peace-loving hippies being forced to go to war. We all start to dress in camouflage even when we are not on Bunnymen duties. The camouflage look is abbreviated to camo, as you would expect. It's a great move, we are creating a look, and it's a growing image that says straight away Bunnymen. Many of our fans have a bit of army surplus kicking around. They throw it on and become part of the gang. If they need to buy anything from the army surplus store, it's hardwearing and, above all, cheap, so it's easy to be one of us. Our crew are joining up, too; they are all dressed in combat jackets, khaki keks and boots.

Big Bill's college friend Bill Butt has been drafted in and is now our lighting designer. He creates the light show, and his background in theatre brings a fresh feel to rock 'n' roll lighting. Gone are the multicoloured flash fests of the past. Now stark white light is the thing. He places spots at the front of the stage that flicker and cast our giant shadows onto the backdrop. It's a stunning and simple effect. We introduce massive smoke machines to pick up the lights; Sometimes, the smoke is so strong I can barely see my guitar neck. If a white light hits me while I'm shrouded in this smoke, the blinding effect is otherworldly. I feel like I'm floating in a cloud. I love hiding in the fog. While I'm on about it, punters always call the smoke effect dry ice.

'All right, Will, we couldn't see you in all that dry ice.'

I would usually reply, 'Good.'

It's not dry ice; it's fog or smoke. Dry ice is the sort of mist that hangs around your ankles, and is favoured by Hammer horror films, seventies light entertainment shows and prog-rock acts.

A couple of oil wheel projectors are dusted off and set up. This old-time effect had been assigned to the far-out scrapheap; the swirling oils had not seen the light of day since they illuminated the almost naked dancer Stacia's more than ample bosoms at Hawkwind's last freak-out. The projected churning globs of colour complement the plain, bright white lights and add to our smoky, psychedelic, sonic mayhem.

Butty, as we now call him, has the brilliant idea of draping the whole stage in camo nets. This hides the ugly lighting rigs and makes every stage we come across our own. The next step is for the crew to go out foraging for foliage to tuck into the netting. Before every gig now, a crack team armed with secateurs are sent out looking to decimate the local area of any suitable shrubbery. Don't panic. The branches are sprayed with a fire retardant. Safety first, kids.

A few weeks after the album shoot, we were sent the record. It is a magnificent cover. We had given little thought to the back cover but, as we should have expected, Mac is featured alone, looking out from some undergrowth. We were never given a chance to object: it was a fait accompli. Even Big Bill was unaware of Rob's plans. I got a serious cob on, but as we were getting used to saying: 'Forget it; tomorrow there will be a new hurt to heal.'

The album was released on 18 July 1980 and hit the British charts at number seventeen, not bad for a first record. 'Rescue' got pretty good reviews but never made an impression big enough to be noticed by the BBC's *Top of the Pops*. I can't say I was bothered at the time. *TOTP* was all a bit too cheesy. It had a kind of foul smell about it. I saw it as selling out.

CHAPTER 14

Rumble on Leuven Square North

'I Must be Mad' – The Craig

At a gig in London, Rob from Korova has an issue. In the new song 'Do It Clean', he doesn't like Mac singing the words, 'I have a handful of piss.'

Rob has only seen the song live, and without the clarity of the recording, Rob mishears some of the lyrics Mac is singing: 'I have a handful of this.' How he can get that mixed up is beyond me. And why would he have a lyric like 'I have a handful of piss'?

It's ridiculous.

I'm not sure if this was the reason why Rob removes the song 'Do It Clean' from the United Kingdom version of the *Crocodiles* album. I also feel that 'Do It Clean' isn't good enough for the album. Indeed, the live performance always has a lot more vitality. 'Do It Clean' is relegated to the status of the eternal flip side. It gets used many times as a B-side, and it also becomes a live favourite. I love to play the crashing chords; I'm waiting to kick off into the psychedelic wig-out sections and the drop-down that gives Mac free scope to conduct us and extemporise to his heart's content with stream-of-consciousness words and the melodies that pop into his head. He also fits in lyrics from other people's songs, and we try to follow where he is taking us, building up and then detonating into a display of incendiary violence. Madness takes over at some gigs, and I literary try and destroy the guitar, not in the traditional way employed by Hendrix or Townshend, setting it on fire or bashing the thing on the floor or twatting it on an amp. By the sheer force of the power of my right-arm strum. No real damage has ever been done to my Telecaster besides a few strings getting reamed off the petrified neck; it's a tough cookie, that guitar, built like a brick shithouse. Some of these improvisations are so good that they stick and become part of the live song.

Korova wants to put 'Villiers Terrace' out as the next single off the album. It doesn't feel good to us. Records with lots of the songs released as singles seem cheesy. It's very uncool. We lie and tell Rob we have a great song and not to put out 'Villiers Terrace'. He falls for it. We quickly get the song together. Rockfield Studios is booked, and we go in to record 'The Puppet' with Big Bill and Balfy (the Chameleons) producing. It's fast and furious and turns out pretty good. We play it live a few times after it is released, but it gets nowhere. Over time, Mac starts to hate it. I'm not sure why; it may be his lyrics.

September 1980. We are offered yet another gig at the Lyceum; this will be our third visit. There is an American film crew that wants to film one track, and because 'The Puppet' is our current single, naturally that's the one they decide to film. We are steadily creeping up the bill, and only a few months have passed. Our standing in the post-punk hierarchy has increased, and we are now headlining. U2 are also on the bill, along with the Au Pairs and Delta 5. U2 had constructed a giant letter 'U' and number

'2' out of grey drainage pipes at the back of the stage. We think this is hilarious, with the Irish builder stereotype in our minds.

Bono collars me during the sound check and is talking to me about Jesus. I'm not the type to be preached at. It is all a bit odd. We have heard about U2's religious zealotry, and now here it is in action: young Bono is trying to turn a snotty heathen to the light. Even when I was in the choir, the vicar never bothered with that idea.

It's fair to say I'm not a fan of any organised religions. They seem to cause more trouble than they solve. The fact that men make up these religions should be a massive warning. Where I live, Jehovah's Witnesses come knocking around quite a lot. They are annoying, but I will talk to them for a laugh. How can you take people seriously that believe the earth was made five thousand years ago? The last time they came, they showed me a picture of paradise: a group of smiling people sitting on a sunny hillside in flowery dresses and colourful shirts. One has a guitar and is happily strumming away with the usual moronic grin on his gob. I doubt it's a version of the Pop Group's classic 'She Is Beyond Good and Evil' he's playing. Now that's What I Call Music for Paradise Volume 25. Kiddies and young people smile and play on the hillside. They always smile in paradise. I'm a lot happier when I'm not smiling. Sometimes I think I am smiling, say when someone takes my photo, but when I see the image, I have a face like a wet weekend. Must be some disconnect between my brain and the chuckle muscles in my mush. Anyway, back to the Jehovah's Witness bloke. I looked at the image and said, 'That is my idea of Hell.'

He went quiet. He has always got a passage from the good book ready to go in any circumstance, but this time the Bible doesn't appear.

So, I asked him, 'Do you remember what it was like before you were born?'

JW looked perplexed. 'No.'

I replied, 'Well, that is what I think it is like when you are dead.'

It worked; he never came back.

I don't know what to believe any more; maybe I'm just getting scared as I head towards the grave. Well, more likely the top of the fridge, as that's where my dad's ashes are still. I must put them somewhere more permanent. I would like to think there is something else going on. I have seen strange things, things I believe to be ghosts. Odd things have happened, but I'm just not sure it has anything to do with an old dude with a white beard living in the sky watching everything we do. This nosey god who is dead interested in every little thing we are doing? Hmm, it feels a bit pervy to me.

Christ almighty! One mention of Bono and it all got heavy. I got lost down a right righteous rabbit hole; time to dig my way out.

Since those post-punk days, I have chatted with Bono, and religion was not mentioned. He's a charming fellow. This is surprising, given the amount of shtick U2 got from us over the years. It looks like he practises what he preaches. He has forgiven his enemies, turned the other cheek, etc.

I have been trying to remember when Jake Drake-Brockman (usually known as just Jake Brockman) arrived on our scene. Jake was an actor and one of Butty's mates from the Bristol Old Vic theatre. Bill had brought him along as a roadie to help out. Jake was very handy and could fix just about anything. He would always be on the ball with any problems that needed to be solved.

Jake had grown up in a house in Sarawak, Borneo, the son of the local big white chief. Their home was built on stilts with tins of paraffin wrapped around the legs. This was to prevent army ants from marching through the living room and devouring the family as they snoozed, half listening to the BBC World Service on the wireless. To gain entry, the army ants would have to swim through a small lake of paraffin. They don't like a paraffin swimming pool, so they would go around the Drake-Brockmans' colonial hut. Jake had grown up in a jungle with deadly things around every corner, ready to kill him, and he came back to Blighty with a mild form of malaria. I saw him in this state occasionally; it looked pretty grim. He always played it down as just a fever. It generally lasted a few days, and he was back on form. He had a stiff upper lip, like the more adventurous posh people used to have.

Jake Brockman plays Mac's beautiful Gibson 335 known as 'Blondie'

Thinking about Jake, who died in 2009, prompts a dream in which he is standing before me.

'Jake, Jake! God, this is ace. I need to ask you a question.'

Jake looks on. He is as clear as day in my dream, and there is no hint of fear or weirdness engulfing this odd happening. He wears 501s, a checked shirt and a nut-brown corduroy jean jacket. It was his usual garb from when he lived in the flat with Les, Pete, Tim Whitaker and me in 1983.

I ask him, 'Jake, when did you start to work with us?'

He replies, 'Towards the end of 1980, the tour that started at the Bains Douches Paris.'

There was no more chat; it was all very matter-of-fact. No, *Oh my God, Jake is dead, and I'm talking to him.*

It was very ordinary. I wake up buzzing. I can't believe what has just occurred. I need to double-check this out.

Butty states that Dream Jake is correct: it was on that tour.

I also get in touch with our mate, Bernie Connor. Over the years, he and Jake had become very close friends, and he confirmed this timeframe. He tells me he and the Teardrops' drummer Gary had been in the Grapes on Mathew Street, just a punk spit from Eric's. Back in those days the pubs shut at 3 p.m. (I know I've already mentioned British pub hours, but they were very, very important.) Just enough time to empty the ashtrays, a quick cat lick around the tables and bogs, then open up again at 5 p.m. for the evening's horde of seasoned boozers. Bernie and Gary had been whiling the afternoon away in the pub.

Along with the odd pint, they have dropped an LSD chaser. At 3 p.m. closing, the acid starts taking hold; they need a safe haven. They wander around to Chicago Buildings, up a flight of stairs and into the Zoo Records office, where they find a stranger sitting on top of a desk; our latest recruit, Jake, has just arrived. Jake is merely trying to keep warm; in the freezing office, his knees are up and he has wrapped himself in his RAF-issue great coat, but this is highly disconcerting to the vulnerable space cadets flying high on acid. Acid trips and strangers don't mix. You need to feel comfortable and safe. Jake looks up from behind his long, straggly strawberry-blond hair. He is no stranger to the thrills and spills of tripping and instantly realises the situation. He knows precisely what Bernie and Gary have been up to.

These two Herberts are out of their tiny minds.

Sensing the stress they are feeling at his presence, Jake immediately and instinctively defuses the situation. He picks up my Fender twelve-string guitar and serenades them with a song by the Incredible String Band fittingly called 'Way Back in the 1960s'. It works its magic, and Bernie and Gary have found a new friend for life.

Along with Jake, we have got ourselves a soundman, Harry DeMac. Harry comes with a homemade PA system. In those days, it was typical for bands to bring a massive PA and lighting system with them to the gigs. Along with a truck to transport all this crap, Harry has a couple of mates to help set the gigs up. Both are called Dave. Little Dave, who won't eat anything with butter involved, and tall, spectacled Dave, not sure what his butter requirements are; I don't recall it ever being an issue. Both have adopted the camo look and are solid team members. Our Bunny family is growing. The band and the crew are travelling in two white Ford Escorts. Everyone is wearing camo gear. When we all pile out of the cars at service stations to fill up, it looks like a ragtag army has just invaded, here to liberate the garage of pasties and crisps.

Jake Brockman became an invaluable part of the Bunnymen

We are heading to Europe via the ferry to Calais, then on to Paris, Amsterdam and a few other places in Holland: Apeldoorn, Utrecht, Groningen. These last two are best said with the rasping sound of coughing up phlegm from the back of your throat. The tour is set to end at the Rainbow Theatre in London.

Doping up on quells, I float across the English Channel without much vomit. The first gig we are playing at is at Les Bains Douches, translated as 'bathhouse'. It is now converted into a swanky nightclub. Apparently, this was the place to be, a kind of Euro Studio 54. More like Le Studio Soixante-Neuf if we know anything about the saucy Frenchies.

Many of the features of the building's former life are still intact. The walls are dressed in rock-hard white porcelain tiles. This has the undesirable effect of making the band sound particularly horrible. The reverb whooshing around is mammoth, like playing in a bloody swimming pool. Er, it was a swimming pool. Yes, there is a small pool still in place. We battle through the gig, and as it progresses, we get used to the music coming at us like a swarm of mosquitoes from all angles. After the gig, with the sound of 'Do It Clean' still bouncing around the room, the club is cleared of the punters that had come to see us play. We are allowed to stay. Parisian Bunny fans are replaced by a shedload of Parisian millionaires, Les poshos, Les toffs and Les toffettes. We soon find out this is a very exclusive place. We have a few beers in our dressing room, but they soon go. A bottle of beer is sixty francs, translated to about six quid. We only have about one hundred francs cowering in our pockets, so not much beer is drunk that night.

We are suddenly mingling in a sea of the rich and famous. Wall-to-wall fur coats and well-turned-out Parisians reeking of expensive perfume. They are steadily filing in, well, only the good-looking ones; the bouncers on the door with faces like a bulldog chewing a wasp are not letting in anyone with a face like a slapped arse. I feel like a right fish out of water; in my mind, my face is undoubtedly on the wrong side of the slapped-arse tracks. Pete, our French-speaking drummer with his perfect face, is not intimidated in the slightest. Private school had taught him how to converse with the aristocracy. A nouveau riche somebody presented him with little problem. Pete is getting on swimmingly; he is definitely a fish in water. If Pete had been able to fund a few more beers, I'm sure he would have been in the pool with the plethora of decadent show-offs now giggling and splashing about like, well, you know, decadent show-offs. Pete is never afraid of baring his body; he has a six-pack before they have been invented.

As a practical chap, I am thinking, *How will these dripping wet bell-ends get home?* They'll be trotting down the Parisian boulevards, warming themselves with nowt but a *rue*-side Nutella crêpe, not even the chance of fishcake, chips and gravy to warm their innards as they shiver and skid along the *merde*-strewn *rues*, gifts of the plethora of that most art nouveau of dogs, the sausage dog. These foolish things will have to wait in a taxi rank for hours on a freezing Parisian November night. But hold on: I forget this is not England, where everything shuts at 2 a.m.; this is Paris, and this discothèque will be open till baguettes by the truckload are lobbed out of ovens all over the city. By then, they will have danced themselves dry, and the Métro will get these fools home with no bother. Hold on, what am I thinking? Most will more than likely have a chauffeur lurking down a nearby alley. Patiently waiting with a stubby Gitanes clamped between yellowing fingers, I reckon.

After a few gigs in Belgium, we have a stopover at Leuven, the home of Stella Artois beer, known in Britain as 'Wife Beater'. We are sitting at a table in the shadow of the gigantic Saint Peter's Church in the Grote Markt with our friend Annik Honoré from the Plan K venue. We take in the quiet ambience of the ornate square and appreciate the medieval architecture surrounding us. Suddenly our quiet chat is interrupted by the buzz of about six bikers turning up on, it has to be said, pretty shit Japanese bikes. They park them and head to the tables next to us. There is nothing remarkable about these bikers – hardly Steve McQueen or Marlon Brando material.

Now, Belgium isn't as fiery as Northern Ireland – guns and bombs and shit like that are very rare – but there is still a certain amount of sectarian religious bullshit going on between, yes, you guessed it, Catholics and Protestants. My magic man in the sky is better than yours. The Flemish north is predominately Dutch Protestant, and the south, called Wallonia, is predominately French-speaking and Roman Catholic. Weirdly, Richard Jobson from the Skids is having a drink with us. He has formed a new band called the Armoury Show, and there is some connection with Annik and her Belgian hipster chums from the Plan K gigs. They discuss doing a record with Jobson on the newly formed Crépuscule label.

He is soon referred to as Jobbo, in our way of giving out nicknames like Parma Violets in the playground. Basically, not everyone wanted one.

Annik is chatting away with Mac, me and Jobbo. Her unmistakable Belgian-French accent lets the bikers know we are not from the north. Add to the mix Mac's very scouse accent and his high spikey hairdo, and these dickheads know something exotic dares to be in their square.

The bikers decide to intimidate Annik. We have no clue what is said, but the jeering laughter says it all. Mac's fiery temper starts to boil up, and it's not long till he's verbally going at these idiots. It is pretty quick to turn to scuffles and then a full-on fight is happening. I don't know what possesses me, but I have a fair idea it must have been the several glasses of Wife Beater that are now sloshing around in my belly. First, I stand on a chair, and next I am on the table with the chair in my hands and jumping into the biker throng, just like John Wayne in the films. I now realise John Wayne is usually standing at the bar keeping his cool, sipping whisky, as the mayhem ensues all about him. He stays calm and clocks a few cowpokes in the mush as he heads out to saddle up his steed. Wayne lets the disposable numpties do all the table jumping.

As I fly through the air, the bikers are not impressed and merely step aside, and I crash onto the solid, cobbled square chin first. A biker steps on my head, and I'm done. This is the only fight I have ever had. I quickly figure out that I'm no street brawler.

Jobbo is using his superpower, a high-kick dance move perfected on many stages. He could have been a Scottish kick-boxer champion, but no one had heard of kickboxing in 1980. I suspect he knew that can-can would be useful for getting the boot in one day. Outnumbered, Jobbo wisely retreats and shouts from the periphery, Monty Python-style, 'Run away! Run away!'

A few more of our crew turn up, the bikers are outnumbered, and the rumpus dies. There is much staring across the square in a *West Side Story* way.

Jake looks at me and says I'd better go to the hospital and get stitches. I hadn't noticed that a rather chunky flap of skin is now hanging off my chin. I trot off to the nearest hospital and get stitched up. Note to self: John Wayne never does the jumping off tables. Leave that to the stuntmen and real-life dickheads.

We play the Paradiso in Amsterdam. It's a great gig at a converted church. They sell pot and even have a menu just like they do in many states in America now. The items mainly consist of that weird hard black or brown stuff, not much in the way of the weed, which is oh-so-popular now. Our Pete and Jake are the team's champion potheads, and spliffs are sparked up in no time. Inane grins are the order of the day. They are on cloud nine and doing fine. I don't indulge . . . well, that's not exactly true. Les and I have had a go, and it made us laugh our tits off, but from then on it never had the same effect; it only creates a comatose state, with no laughing or fun. I'm not saying it wasn't pleasant, but I've given up the world of pot as being pretty much counterproductive. You might have good ideas, flights of fancy carried by plumes of smoke, but you are too stoned to be arsed to carry them through and they're soon forgotten.

The Dutch fans are among the best we have played for so far. Not sure if it's the stupor they are in, but they love the gig. It is cool meeting with foreign fans. Most of them can speak English better than we do.

The next gig is in Rotterdam. It reminds me of Liverpool, not so much the architecture but the rugged ambience of a port. It's a hard city with a tough reputation. We get talking to a couple of fans outside the gig. They are English and have been mooching around Holland. One of them asks me, 'Do you want some microdots?'

'Eh? What are you on about, microdots?' I ask.

'You know, acid trips?'

I have heard of LSD, of course, and some of my friends have already taken it, but I'm still unsure what it is all about. I know the Beatles experimented with trips, and Syd Barrett from Floyd had gone too far to return. Some of the sixties groovier music was made either under the influence or with the memories of dropping acid.

'Sure, yes, thanks,' I reply, not really knowing what to expect. One of them hands me a small plastic bag with a few poppy-seed-size granules in the bottom.

'So, these are microdots?'

To my way of thinking, these tiny granules are so small that they look perfectly harmless. How can this be a powerful mind-bending drug? They look like they would do nothing. Wrong!

I am scared to take one then and there, but I take the gift and pocket them for later.

We have a few more gigs in Holland, and are introduced to our promotor Willem, who becomes a firm friend of the band; over the years, we have teamed up with him many times for our Dutch gigs. He is tall, wears a long black coat, sports a huge Asterix the Gaul-style moustache and has long hair; he exudes a dash of underworld menace. This is added to by the fact that he carries the biggest switchblade I've ever seen. The blade must be nine inches long and flicks out almost like a sword. Funnily enough, we have never come up with a nickname for him.

Back home, we are on the front page of the *New Musical Express*. This is a massive deal for us. The whole band is featured on the cover. The photos were taken in the dunes at Formby Point, a few miles up the coast from Liverpool, and not far from my drowned bike incident (documented in my first book, *Bunnyman*, available at all good booksellers).

We are dressed in camo gear and sit among the clumps of marram grass spiking out of the dunes. The pictures inside the *NME* feature us outside a sizeable Victorian house as it is slowly getting eaten away by the inevitable creep of shifting sand. Dunes never stay motionless; the wind off the Irish Sea sees to that. They are built and rebuilt one grain at a time. The house is abandoned and lonely; it is an unsettling place. Why build a house on such unstable ground? I can only assume there were many more trees or grass with roots to anchor the sand from wandering about and devouring the house sooner. Cracked and crumbling, it is fascinating and warns us of our impermanence. I returned to find it a few years ago; it's completely gone now, engulfed by dunes. The same fate fell to an entire caravan site in the sixties; occasionally, as the dunes dance along the coast, the crushed bones of a caravan are revealed. This will be an archaeological dig in someone's future.

CHAPTER 15

I'm Not an Expert
on Gnomes, But . . .

'Autobahn' – Kraftwerk

East Berlin

After our short spell of shows in the lowlands of the Benelux countries, we have a long drive ahead, approximately 430 miles to West Berlin. We have to leave Rotterdam and journey east into West Germany. The two Ford Escorts head off together. The small truck with our equipment left a couple of hours earlier. Our destination is the town of Helmstedt. Bordering the GDR, this little town is the location of Checkpoint Alpha. We set off in convoy, Les puts his foot down on the autobahn, and we soon separate from the car with the crew aboard.

The beautiful German countryside flows past us. I gaze at sweeping fields bordered by leafless linden trees and dark green forests of pines surrounding quiet hamlets. Red-roofed cottages are, in turn, gathered around spired churches. I am very excited that we will drive across East Germany to Berlin. It feels so strange that the West has this little outpost right in the middle of East Germany, a tiny island of capitalism in the heart of Soviet-style communism. I am a big fan of spy films and books. Len Deighton's classic *Funeral in Berlin* and John le Carré's *The Spy Who Came in from the Cold* are among my favourites. No, not for me the, er, inconspicuous white dinner-jacket, bow-tie-wearing James Bond, bombing around in a very discreet gold Aston Martin. I prefer at least an attempt at the grubby reality of espionage.

The hundred miles or so go by fast. Les is no slowcoach on the autobahn; there is no speed limit. After a couple of hours, we pull up at Checkpoint Alpha. The car creeps under the covered inspection bay. A couple of miserable-looking guards approach; we are ordered out of the car and into the checkpoint building flanked by the border guards. A couple more guards head to the car and look casually around it. They are not that arsed; they are not looking for people trying to get into East Germany. They open the boot and have a root about. Luckily, I have forgotten about the acid I have tucked away in my pocket. The level of paranoia that would have been triggered in this very totalitarian place would have had me in bits. I more than likely would have dumped the microdots and tried to grind them into the car's carpet. After about fifteen minutes or so, our documents are discerned to be in order, and with nervous grins on our faces, we accept the stamped passports that are handed over. We can go.

Berlin transit road, checkpoint alpha

Les slowly pulls the Ford Escort onto the only permitted road to Berlin, the transit corridor. As we head east, the weather starts to get nasty. The tame swirling snow flurries turn into full-on snowstorms, and now snow covers the road. Hardly any traffic has left tracks along the corridor (Berlin is not exactly the tourist destination it is now). There is no sign of snow ploughs. This doesn't worry Les, who is still putting his foot down. After all, he is on an empty autobahn. Mac and Pete are snoozing in the back seat. Those two can sleep anywhere.

For much of the remaining 103-mile journey, the road sits on a manmade bank. I suspect this is for the purpose of surveillance. We pass many grey concrete watchtowers with searchlights mounted on the roof. Windows at every aspect command 360-degree views of the road and the surrounding countryside. It's a strange sight with a lo-fi sci-fi element to it, like an old black-and-white episode of *Doctor Who*, the early ones with William Hartnell playing the Doctor. I imagine we have just stepped out of the TARDIS on a strange authoritarian planet. But this is Europe. We have driven here, not that far from Liverpool, and it's only around the corner globally.

Shadowy uniformed figures are visible in the watchtowers, constantly observing through glinting binocular lenses catching the drab winter sunlight. We are being watched all the way; everyone is. No turning off the autobahn. We pass a few unappealing rest areas on the way – no services or cafés, not even a sniff of bratwurst sausage. We don't stop. Cameras swivel on their rusting metal mounts, lenses twisting and focusing their optics on our every move.

From our high viewpoint on the autobahn, we can see above the fence into remote and ramshackle farms. Communist farmers ride on ancient tractors; they trundle around the barns and outbuildings, trailers loaded high with *kartoffeln* (spuds to you and me). It's such a strange land, mainly for the actual fact that it is very normal-looking, but we are peering at another world where not much has changed since the war. We spot the odd person on the other side of the fence going about their business on foot, in little cars or on bicycles as they have done for decades. I wonder what they are thinking, seeing these Western-style cars whizzing along the road,

Along the route, the Volkspolizei – the People's Police – sit in huts with little green and white Lada cars parked outside. It feels like this is the epicentre of the Cold War. This ridge really is an iron curtain and we are driving along it. Now, I finally remember that I still have the few acid microdots the Rotterdam blokes had given me. To be caught with LSD in the GDR would not go down too well, to put it lightly. I'd probably end up in a Soviet-style Gulag eating one of my cellmate's boots while he was asleep. If you are going to get paranoid, this is the country to do it in; the whole place is built on foundations of paranoia. I prize open the collar stitching on my Israeli army jacket I have recently picked up at a surplus store. After a bit of pulling and twisting, the stitches give way, and I create an opening big enough and slip the small plastic bag and its psychedelic contents inside; close shave: if the Polizei had turned out my pockets at the checkpoint, we would all have been in deep shit.

The snow is now coming down in a swirling flurry of white; visibility has dwindled. Out of the washed-out landscape, faint lights are glowing pink up ahead. As we approach, the pink light turns deeper red, and two huge Russian-made trucks become clearer. I have looked up trucks of this period; they are called Urals, after the mountain range in USSR. We are soon close enough to see they are laden with enormous freshly felled pine trees. Heading towards a proletariat sawmill, no doubt. Les soon catches up with the battered slow-moving vehicles and sits behind them. The swirling vortex of snow caused by the trucks' draught is worsening our visibility. Our speed is reduced to around twenty mph. This is no good; at this rate, we will be bloody hours before we get to Berlin.

Les decides he has to overtake the trucks. Pete and Mac are still snoozing in the back seat, but they won't be for long as Les turns the wheel and sees his chance, putting his foot down hard. The Ford Escort's engine responds and accelerates. The car suddenly slides into a spin. The engine is racing as the wheels lose grip. We twist into an ugly pirouette in the snow; traction is impossible. We are now doing what young petrolheads call a doughnut. In this case, an iced doughnut. Grabbing the dashboard to steady myself, I abruptly lose a hopeless battle with inertia plus several tons of g-force. I am flung hard against the car door. Mac and Pete are in a heap in the back and have awakened with an angry start. Les is still battling with the wheel and trying to control the skid, as we do a complete three-sixty on the ice- and snow-covered road. The trucks are still moving. Somehow, we have managed to miss colliding with them and come to a halt. The good news is that we are facing in the correct direction.

Mac, now wide awake, is not too pleased.

He screams at Les, 'What the fuck are you doing?' And follows that with: 'We are not in a fucking video game.'

Everyone is OK. We have survived without hitting either of the trucks or sliding off the road edge, down the embankment and into the fence, which will more than likely be electrified, judging by the way these East Germans carry on. The truck's lights fade out into the distance. It takes a while for the rest of us to get over the shock, but Pete takes it all in his stride, sparks up a fag, sucks the life out of it. He is soon back to sleep. Pete really can kip in any circumstance; even life-threatening ones don't faze him.

I can only assume that the visibility had become so bad that the surveillance cameras trained on the sparse traffic could not pick us up as we did our icy twirl. No little green and white Volkspolizei car showed up. We can't stay stopped here long; who knows what will come out of the snowstorm and plough up our backside? We get back in motion quickly with a few more fucking hells, Jesus Christs, 'That was close' and a 'What the fuck were you playing at?'

With terrible grins of relief on our pallid faces, we compose ourselves and are soon back to thirty mph. A little further on, the flurries subside, the road widens and the snow is much less thick; maybe the ploughs have been along, or the wind has cleared the dusting away. But we are back again, right behind the huge logging trucks. We have no option; we have to try the overtaking manoeuvre again. Les moves out carefully and smoothly. This time the tyres grip, and we sail past the trucks with no bother. On we go. Berlin, here we come.

At last, we reach the end of the tarmac transit corridor or *Transitstrecke* in German. We are at Checkpoint Bravo near Drewitz. A tatty Red Army tank sits on guard atop a concrete plinth. A Soviet red star is emblazoned on the turret's khaki paintwork – a rusting relic from the Second World War. Our documents are checked once again, our passports are stamped, and we can move on to West Berlin.

We are playing at the premier punk club in Berlin. It's located in Kreuzberg, still a largely battered area. The Second World

War's Allied Bomber Command virtually wiped it off the map, and it's now populated by squatters and Turks. As the cars roll up, we spot our truck with the equipment; we jump out and say hello to the already hard-at-it crew. Time to kill, we wander around the streets like an invading army. Several Turks poke their heads out of windows; their flats are looking down on the SO36 club opposite. Bewildered by this sudden invasion, they shout to each other in Turkish.

Inside the club, the high roof is not entirely watertight; the melting snow is finding its way to a hole or two, and a steady and persistent drip is hitting us on the stage. The gig is a rowdy affair; pushing and shoving seem to be the thing to do here. Attendees at Berlin's top punk club want to live up to the punk-rock reputation they have read about in the papers. Spit is raining down. One carefully aimed gob hits me right between the pickups. My Telecaster's strings are coated with thick green jelly, and this goop deadens my playing. It's a horrendous thing to try and play with this shit on my strings. I get a towel off Jake and try to rub down the guitar.

There are a lot of British Army squaddies in the crowd, and the tensions with the Germans are pretty obvious. The vibe in the gig is edgy. There's more pushing and the odd skirmish in the crowd. Nothing gets out of control, in any case. It's all seems to be part of a good night out to these punks. Berlin is bang in the middle of East Germany and it has a strange frontier-town vibe; the feeling is that anything goes.

The West German government has a policy that if you live in West Berlin, you don't have to sign on to do compulsory national service. Rents are cheap; squatters are tolerated; hence the city has a lot of young people avoiding the draft.

Not many people would want to live on the Cold War front

line, with the real possibility of the Russians deciding to roll in and take over the western half of the city, so it's occupied mainly by young people; punks, artists and outsiders have headed here. There's a fear in Britain that the Russians will kick off some nuclear war crap at any moment. While in Berlin, we put that to the back of our minds. It just adds to the strangeness of the place, where they say fuck it, let's live for today.

Me in west Berlin

After the gig, it's back to the hotel. Everyone is a bit out of it; the crew are drunk or stoned, even Harry, the sound man. He is ill with a cold; a few whiskies and some codeine tablets, and he's zonked out in bed.

Les and I decide that now is the time to take the acid. Please accept my word for it: now was not the time to take the acid.

Half-drunk in a strange land at 1 a.m., your body is tired after a very sweaty gig. All you want is to go to sleep, not get your mind bunged in a blender and have your neural pathways tangled into spaghetti, but we do it anyway. This may be my first time, but back home, LSD has been gaining in popularity in the city.

There was a big acid factory setup in Wales, which was closed during a massive police raid called Operation Julie in 1978. The far-out boffins, now in the nick or on the run, had made millions of blotters and microdots before the fuzz caught them. I suspect quite a lot of their stock was still floating about the underworld for a few more years to come. And Liverpool's new psychedelic scene was a great market. LSD was definitely on the rise at this time. Most bands we knew were into the odd acid trip. It was common to bump into a couple of mates tripping away contentedly in the clubs or wandering around town.

Roughly forty minutes after taking a tiny speck of acid, I am slumped on my bed and have my arm over my face. The chrome bezel off my Timex watch has caught a faint glint of reflected light. This has become my focus of devotion, and I am zooming in on it. My watch is close to my eye, resting against my cheek. I can see through the little shimmer into another land inside my watch. An alternative world is opened up to me. Inside the light, there are buildings, sky, vegetation and animals.

I can see small people. Some variety of gnome is wandering about. I'm not an expert on gnomes, but I don't think they are trolls or goblins – that would not be good, judging by the unseemly way they acted in *The Lord of the Rings*. All this is dwelling in a tiny glimmer of brightness reflecting off my watch. Blimey! Who would have thought it? This is what acid does. It takes reality and slides a new reality into it, at the same time, filling you up with feelings of extreme joy or love or anxiety. I want to get inside the watch and escape this room. My senses are heightened; I feel a malign presence. The light fitting above the bed is one of those seventies styles with lots of crystal lampshades on brass tubes; this gives the appearance of a huge spider hanging down from a thread, the cable that the light is held up by. The light is casting ominous shadows in the room.

Les and I are sharing a room, which adjoins the one shared by Pete and Jake. Mac stands in the connecting doorway. He enters the room. In my tripping state, I sense a malevolent spirit entering the room. He's already been to Harry's room, who is out of his mind on booze and prescription drugs. He's shocked at the condition of us all. Mac's perfectly spiked hairdo and stick-thin look cast a shadow on the wall; he gives the Thin White Duke a good run for his money. He's all limbs and cheekbones. He is becoming a spider looking down at me.

'Will, what are you doing?' Followed by: 'What the hell is going on? Everyone is out of their sodding tiny minds. Even Harry DeMac is bongoed on whisky and codeine.'

I try and seek refuge in my watch, but the light has changed. The land I could see has now vanished. This disturbance has returned me to the room.

All I can do is look up and say, 'You were nice; now you're nasty.'

After a while, Les suggests we venture out of the hotel. This is a scary prospect but I want to get away from the room of spiders. Pete and Jake are coming too. This makes it seem like a safe idea, so with the strength of numbers, the adventure continues. We leave the room and head towards the lift. This is not as straightforward as you might think. The hotel wall is coated in granite with sparkling specks in the stone. Every little sparkle could be another world, just like the inside of my watch. It takes us what seems like ages to get to the lift and descend to the exit.

The street is incredible. Berlin is a propaganda tool for the West. The streets are bathed in multicoloured neon. The centre of West Berlin is almost like a small Times Square in New York. There is a huge spinning Mercedes emblem picked out in white light. A glowing wonderland would be visible to the East Germans who live in drab areas in small apartments. This is all done to wind up the communists on the other side of the Wall. As the old saying goes: the neon is always brighter on the other side of the Wall.

An east Berlin street

As we leave the hotel, the street feels very steep (it's not). My mind is well mashed up now that I have the illusion that I am on a mountain, not a normal flat street with trams, cars and people darting about. To make sure I don't fall, I walk sideways, not unlike a crab, after we traverse what I perceive as the north face of the Kurfürstendamm.

In the middle of all this psychedelia, Les is hungry and wants to find some food. My memory of this part of the trip is a bit patchy. (After all, it was forty-odd years ago, and we are off our cakes tripping.) Pete and Jake, who are merely a bit potted up, are there to shepherd us out of any danger. Somehow, we all get on a tram, go for a little ride, and when we see a lot more action on the street after a couple of stops, we get off the tram. We find a street burger seller. Les has problems locating his mouth and tries to eat the burger through his cheek. Eventually, Jake and Pete lead us back to the hotel, and as the dawn starts to fade in, the dark sky fades into the pastel blue of the day. As shafts of light hit the glittering cold surface of the River Spree, we flop into our beds.

An acid trip can last a long time, twelve hours till it all wears off and you can start to feel 'normal' again. I think you never really feel 'normal' after LSD; you have been given the keys, and life and everything will always seem different somehow. The aftermath of the trip is a proper comedown. You feel like a husk; all has been exhausted. It really takes it out of you. To make that journey, you need recovery time. Luckily, the next day was a day off, and we were heading to Bonn, which was the capital of West Germany from 1949 to 1990.

My main recollection of the former capital was the hotel bathroom. This stuck in my mind. It was a beautiful example of the comradery of being in a band. When we were all in it together, they were great days; we all had a common purpose.

I had forgotten my electric shaver. My dad used one, and I naturally followed suit and got one myself. Pre-gig at

Rheinterrassen, I was waiting to get a wash, and Pete was shaving away with a Wilkinson Sword blade loaded in his safety razor. I asked him how you shaved with one of those things. Pete, although a couple of years younger than me, seemed to have a worldly wisdom that I had not been exposed to in my little village life or even while working in Liverpool. It is very odd that Pete was also from a village, but more opportunities to experience life were presented to him.

Me shaving

Pete gave me instructions on how to shave: 'You do this and this.' He pulled his face against the direction of the blade, and squeezed and tugged his nose out of the way to access areas of the top lip. He swept the razor across his skin, often rinsing the blade clean of bristles. The scraping made the familiar rasping sound of safety razors. The next day, I bought a razor, and with a little more coaching, several pints of blood loss and a styptic pencil in my kit, I was away.

I liked Germany, but I'm not sure Germany liked us. I can only put it down to not having enough keyboards on our records. They do love a synthesiser, those Germans.

CHAPTER 16

The Bunnymen's Barmy Army in Retreat, School Bus Riots and Black Pudding on Cocktail Sticks

'Riders on the Storm' – The Doors

Mac *Shining So Hard* at Buxton

We concluded 1980 with a shock. Well, it's not exactly a shock – that makes it sound more severe than it was. A band changing clothing is hardly a shock. Well, anyway, on 14 December, at our gig at London's Rainbow Theatre, we had decided that this would be our last show wearing our ragtag squad of spaced-out *Apocalypse Now* supporting artists' camo clobber or, in short, army surplus clothes.

The Rainbow had the stink of heavy rock about it, and I wasn't keen to do a show there. I was either outvoted or left it too late to moan about this gig. I had no reason other than a few of what I deemed to be naff bands had played the Rainbow, so I considered it uncool, and that would have been enough to put me off back then. Plus, the name reminded me of the band Rainbow, which was not a good link in my mind. Ritchie Blackmore is undoubtedly a brilliant guitarist and he was a key component of heavy rockers Deep Purple. This was where the problem lay. You were either a Deep Purple or Led Zeppelin fan in the seventies. I was the latter, a Zeppelin kid through and through.

It was like in the ketamine-crazy days at the arse end of the last century, when you were either an Oasis fan or a Blur fan. I was neither, by the way. The press instigated this rivalry between the bands; it seemed to me, at the time, a sort of north versus south thing. You would be correct to call the press shit stirrers. All bullshit. They tried the same thing with us and the Teardrops, U2, Simple Minds, etc., and it worked; we concentrated on hating those bands, constantly slagging them off as they happily kept quiet and continued their inevitable quest to conquer the planet. I think this was a combination of Liverpool's natural bitchiness and an unfortunate side effect of being Fall fans and not wanting to upset Mr Mark E. Smith.

We were ready to move on, and the change of clothes was part of that. We were always looking for something different to do that other bands didn't do. Bill Drummond believed we should document the camouflage clothing period of the band's history on film. We agreed to do one last show with the army gear and the stage dressed in camouflage netting.

Around this time, we move into a new practice place called the Ministry of Sound (not to be confused with the London rave club, which came much later). This is a large warehouse down by the old Mersey Tunnel entrance in Liverpool. We are given a ground-floor room, and we become a permanent fixture in the place. Two fellas called Billy and Mike run the place; we know them as the men from the ministry, Billy Ministry and Mike Ministry (I have yet to find out either of their second names). It's a very cool setup.

The only problem is that it's a little bit leaky security-wise. The original drum machine soon goes AWOL from the area where we keep our equipment. Then my Fender twelve-string acoustic vanishes into thin air, only to turn up in a plastic bin bag in Billy Ministry's office a few weeks after disappearing. I spot the silver machine-head-adorned headstock poking from the bin bag. I think, *I recognise that.*

On close examination, I know it's my guitar. I had scratched the headstock while trying to replace a broken string. At the time, I was mightily pissed off that I had made this scratch; now, it is an identification mark. A squiggle gouged into the varnish, and no two could be the same. I take the guitar from the office and bring it into the practice room. And put it in the empty Fender case that I still had. The others recognise it straight away.

Knowing it had been robbed, they ask, 'Where the fuck did that come from?'

'It was in a bin bag in Billy's office.'

'Eh? What was it doing in there?'

'I dun know.'

We get back to rehearsing and writing songs for the next album.

After an hour or some kid from the band Come in Tokio knocks on the door.

'Billy says you've got my guitar?'

'It's my guitar, mate,' I reply.

He looks down at the twelve-string case. 'Is it in that case?'

'Yes, it is, but it's my guitar; I recognise it.'

'I've just bought it,' says the lad.

'OK, where did you get it from?'

He tells a tale that he bought it for fifty quid from some lads. They say that they robbed it out of a van in Birmingham.

'Fuck off,' I say.

Les and Mac look on; they know it is my guitar, too. Mac has played it often enough and knows about the scratch I was so pissed off about. He comes to my aid, points at me, and says something to the effect of 'It's his guitar. You've been had, lad. It's never been to fucking Birmingham, mate.'

I don't know if the Come in Tokio kid nicked it himself or if he really did buy it off a third party, but I'm 100 per cent certain it is my twelve-string. I stick to my guns, and with Les and Mac as backup, this isn't going to turn into a scrap. He can fuck right off, which he does, and we never hear anything about it again.

This sort of thing never happens if you get something stolen; you hardly ever get it back. I still have the guitar, but the scratch on the headstock doesn't upset me any more.

★   ★   ★

Big Bill is hunting for an out-of-the-way place to stage our final paramilitary action. He drafts in his former theatre schoolmate and now our permanent lighting man Butty to put together a film team headed by director John Smith and cameraman Patrick Duval. Butty has recently recruited a chap called Kit, a mate from Bristol, to help out with roadie duties. Kit's day job is that of a fine artist. And he is a very fine artist. I look up to Kit as an inspiration and dream of being an artist. What I don't know is that I already am one. Kit is tall and a keen cyclist, strong as an ox. Along with Jake and Butty, the Bristol gang become an integral part of our team.

The last camo gig film is to be done cheaply, with only one camera. We are paying some of the costs, and the record company is stumping up some cash to front it. This will, of course, go into our steadily growing record-deal debt, but we don't worry about stuff like that. It will be a magical mystery tour. You can only apply for a ticket to the gig via an advert in the music papers and our fan club. The ticket gets you a seat on one of several coaches dotted about the country that will bring you to an undisclosed location.

Big Bill has found the ultimate out-of-the-way place. The hall is the Buxton Pavilion Gardens, a highly unusual home for a rock show. The last time any rock 'n' roll music was heard here was probably Cliff Richard. The circular building has windows wrapped in heavy red curtains to contain the sound. It looks like a high-domed palm house rather than a gig venue. There is a small stage; it seems like the type you would get in a school assembly hall. It sends me back to when the Melling bus kids receive a harsh bollocking from our secondary modern beak: Mr not so Jolly. We deserved it, though.

Big Bill Drummond pre-gig at Buxton

High on that Friday feeling and Cresta soft drinks ('It's frothy, man!'), we're having a mini-riot on the school bus. The driver is freaked out; he doesn't stop to let us off in our village of Melling; we sail right past the bus stop by the scout hut; past the stop opposite the Sergeants' woodyard on Waddicar Lane; past the stop at the Horse and Jockey, and on we go. Obnoxious kids are now anxious kids. The shouting has died down, as has the swinging from the handrails and bag throwing. The hullabaloo is replaced by fearful snotty kids' noses pressed hard against the grimy windows as they despondently watch their village disappear out of sight. My bravado, stirred up by the hysteria of mob rule, is replaced by the hideous thought that I am going to miss *Jonny Quest* on the telly. We are driven to the Ribble bus depot in

Aintree, and are given a dressing-down by the inspector, who lives up to his threat of calling the school headmaster to tell of our insurrection. We are kept on the bus for what seems like ages, probably about fifteen minutes in reality. We are then released to walk a couple of miles home. No *Crackerjack* for us that Friday.

Back to Buxton, we set off a day early. The route to the Derbyshire town is via the slow climb and descent of the Cat and Fiddle Road. It's a beautiful and bleak drive. Dry-stone walls divide high moorland scrub into manageable portions. Dotted with shit-caked sheep, the distant peaks are lace-curtained in a freezing misty vapour, the visibility fading to nothing over the furthest peaks. High tight bends are navigated with care. The often-pranged crash barriers along the road's more dangerous sections had hopefully saved a few from the drop.

We check into the next-door hotel and dump bags; we are wasting no time; we are needed.

Les having his tea, Buxton 1981. His Auntie knitted him that jumper, complete with fluffy tailed bunny

Butty and his team film us in various settings to portray our particular characteristics. Pete has a freshly shaved head. (That went down like a ton of bricks, by the way.) Pete is bookish, so he's captured reading *The Catcher in the Rye*. The camera focuses on a part of the text that says 'never read'. He clumsily spills his drink; I call him 'Spill-o' because, as you can guess, he spills just about everything he's not meant to spill, except for perhaps the beans that he would turn up to the filming with a bald head. Les is seen with a one-star captain's hat, radio-controlling a model launch, reflecting his love of boats and the sea. Mac is filmed in his hotel room, hand washing, being untidy and humming. Lazing around like a pampered pussy cat who loves his naps and solitude.

I'm an awkward and badly acting nature boy lurking in the jungle's undergrowth, not too far from 'Betty' the tea lady. I am floating through the palms with headphones on; music is my constant companion. The Sony Walkman had just been invented. Butty has one of the first of these expensive personal stereos to hit our shores, and I have commandeered it. During the trip, I go for a morning promenade around Buxton, my bonce tightly clamped in the headphone's sprung steel band. At either end, my earholes are all cushioned up cosy to the grey, sponge-covered, tiny speakers. In the tape player, Television's *Marquee Moon*, what else? The unbelievable otherworldly feeling of having what at the time seemed like hi-fi sound directly plumbed into my brain blew my mind as I drifted through the Victorian spa town, skirting around the town's railed formal gardens, with all the soot-darkened stone buildings looking down on the frosted rose beds.

Me feeling out of place, the stiffest acting ever seen

It was unquestionably a lovely and surreal experience, all normal now, as almost every youth is forever focused on the fizzing little plastic inserts glued in their ears. Then, not many had seen such an exotic item as a Sony Walkman. As I trundled the sloping streets, I invited funny looks from passers-by who had no concept of what they had just seen. A spotty alien?

Filming continues until dark as it is 16 January 1981, midwinter, and the darkness arrives in the early afternoon. The Pavilion's large windows are filmed with curtains drawn and then open, in the light and then in the dark. Butty and the crew cut this into a flickering animated montage with our song 'Stars Are Stars' providing the rhythm.

Shine So Hard set, Buxton

The Gig Day. The tension is mounting because this will be recorded, and what we do tonight will be what goes on the *Shine So Hard* extended play record for posterity. So, we have the added pressure of no fuck-ups, but we are still trying to retain the spontaneity and the dynamics of a gig.

We have been steadily writing new songs and want to get some of them into the set. The film will feature 'All My Colours (Zimbo)' and 'Over the Wall'.

'All My Colours' started life as a thing I had been recording for Butty, who had created the concept for a film called *Grind*; Grind, the character, was an out-of-place alien or time-slipped conquistador who had fallen through time and space into Bristol docks. He was outside everyday life like a dark Mr Bean before Bean sprouted onto our telly. Grind was much bleaker; he spent his working days sharpening razor blades. He would come home to the ramshackle dry-dock boat he lived in and eat Pot Noodles for dinner. A small generator would power his telly but the unsuppressed motor interfered with the picture and the noise from the genny cloaked the sound. It seemed he was trying to fit in, but he was all mixed up. He would stack his wage packets up in the corner of the room, unopened. It sounded like my kind of film, with a touch of David Lynch's *Eraserhead* about it. I was keen to help, and it would be my foot in the film-score door. I would be called on to make soundtracks by all the up-and-coming filmmakers. I'm still waiting.

Infuriatingly, before the film was finished Butty had his car stolen with all his cameras, film stock and exposed film still inside, never to be seen again. The wind was taken out of his sails. Then another disaster: his actor-friend Nicholas Farrell, who was playing the part of Grind, became a hot property after playing Aubrey Montague in the four-time Oscar-winning film *Chariots of Fire*. He was in demand now, and Butty's film understandably had to be dropped.

Bill Drummond had fronted me fifteen hundred pounds to buy a TEAC four-track machine so that I could record Butty's soundtrack. Bill needed to claw his fifteen hundred quid back, so I started an indie record label, 92 Happy Customers, and signed a pressing distribution deal with Rough Trade. They would put out the now filmless soundtrack anyway. Rob at Korova realised this record was too weird to impact Bunnymen sales but insisted my name was removed from the front cover. I was happy to comply. Some of my favourite LP covers are not ruined by the band names.

I had been getting to the Ministry early and using our equipment stashed in the leaky band lock-up. I was recording what would become 'All My Colours (Zimbo)' when the rest of the band turned up.

'What's that you're doing, Will?' asked Mac.

'Er, just something for Butty, that film he's making. You know, *Grind*.'

'Sounds good that,' Pete added.

They all seemed to like it, and I was chuffed, so I said, 'It can go in the Bunnymen pot if you like.'

Me and Pete. His hair has grown back so this must have been before *Shine So Hard* was filmed

We spent the rest of the day working it out. Pete started with a simple tom beat, and Les took on the bass part – he improved it straight away – while I concentrated on spikey guitar notes shrouded in reverb. And Mac started mournfully singing, 'Jimbo, Jimbo.'

We had recently been compared to the Doors and Mac's low, distinctive voice to Jim Morrison's. I loved the comparison but I don't think Mac did. He was probably being a touch sarcastic singing 'Jimbo, Jimbo' as he was feeling his way through the song, because I was the only one who really loved the Doors. In those days, Mac occasionally tried words just for the shape and fit when formulating the vocals. It worked, and as he got a grip on the thing 'Jimbo' morphed into 'Zimbo', a made-up word that fits effectively into the song's mood. By the late afternoon, Pete had drummed up a tribal beat that is the song's heart. I have a soft spot for this song. I was happy to give the idea up, and the comradeship created by working together meant, in those days, anything was musically possible.

Back on set, as they say in showbiz, our cameraman Patrick only has one 16mm camera to use. If we need to change the camera angles, we have to stop the gig while Butty and the team relocate to other areas of the Pavilion. Meanwhile, on stage, we just stand around awkwardly while things are moved, and after a few times the crowd is understandably a little restless during these breaks in the proceedings.

On the stage, behind Pete's drum setup, Kit is hunched; his duty is to feed a huge industrial fan with smoke from one of our three smoke machines. At the given signal, Kit is to plug in the mammoth fan, which will hurl a massive plume of smoke forward, with the white lights making the explosive thrust of the fog even more dramatic. It works a treat, and this effect can be seen in the film twice, once right after the drop-down over the wall and then again in a similar section of 'All That Jazz'.

After we finish, the crowd and a few journalists get on the coaches but they don't get home till all hours, and a few disgruntled messages are received about returning to London before the trains started. We feel terrible that the planning wasn't brilliant. But I reckon those people who did put up with all the shit to get to this one-off gig remember that they were there and not so much the horrible journey on the coaches.

A few weeks later, the film is ready. Thirty-three minutes long, it's a strange and slightly nervous, disjointed art film. While all around are making videos with shit pastel-coloured angular graphics all over the place, we are making art. We love it. The record label hates it, understandably; it can only be seen at a few art-house cinemas.

We are getting our songs together for the second album. Every day we head to the Ministry for a few hours. After practice, we spend much time in our new favourite café, Brian's Lean and Hungry. Brian is an ex-boxer; he and Gloria, his missus, run the place. They are a fantastic couple, and lots of the bands are now gravitating towards Brian's rather than the usual haunt, the Armadillo Tea Rooms. Brian is famous not only for boxing but his inability to add up the cost of your food. Behind his eyes, his mind is ticking away and his brow wrinkles; he is trying hard to come to a figure, but he always comes up with the same answer.

'Er, that's just a pound, lad.'

Gloria is a lot better at maths than Brian. She has a heart of gold, and if you are skint, as many are, she would let people off when they didn't have enough cash.

A few odd characters in town are in Brian's regularly. One, in particular, stands out. A thick dirty overcoat encloses his hefty girth, and his dark stubbled face looks grubby. It could just be his complexion; we are unsure if he is homeless, but he looks like a street sleeper and has newspapers under his coat, another layer against the cold. There is a mystery to him; he could have been anything in a past life – soldier, sailor, docker or hitman, who knows? His name is Jack, and Jack likes to display all the tablets he is on. All come out of deep overcoat pockets and sit

Brian behind his counter ('That's just a quid, lad')

on the table. He goes through them, lifting the brown plastic containers one by one, then giving them a little shake to prove there are pills inside. He then goes on to tell you what each bottle is for.

'These are for me legs. This one is for me lungs, and those are for me feet.'

It goes on and on. Jack sometimes has a woman in tow. She sits and says nowt. Her face is covered with copious amounts of makeup, resulting in an incredibly pink face. Her eyes are deeply shadowed in that bright blue eyeshadow not seen since the sixties. She sits and stares, never saying a word. As people used to say at the time, 'I don't think she is all there, that one.'

Jack is all there; maybe he's too much there. He is so much

there that he has gone past the 'there' where the rest of us are, wherever there that is.

Brian and Gloria treat them no different to anyone else who comes to the café, and there is no harm in them. Jack goes off on the odd anti-royalist rant now and then, but then again, who doesn't?

Popular on the menu is chicken and chips, real chips, none of this French-fry crap. It's a big leg of chicken; not sure where they are getting chickens with legs this big from. It gets christened donkey's leg and chips by Gary Dwyer from The Teardrop Explodes. I am partial to toasted black pudding and egg with tinned tomatoes.

Next door to the Ministry is a Yates's Wine Lodge. We often call in to find Mac there with a pint and a fag. It has sawdust on the floor, and the dark bar makes a brisk trade selling Australian white wine. This is a very thick, sweet wine with a potent and teeth-rotting syrupiness. On the bar are little black pudding squares, each speared by a wooden cocktail stick; Like a northern parody of *Abigail's Party*, they also sell sardines by the tin, with punters dropping them into open gobs like seals. I am unsure if crisps and nuts have ever hit Yates's.

CHAPTER 17

Cymbals Are Shit

'Wild Thing' – The Troggs

Billy Ministry (working out how much we owe him)

Now that our combat gear has been retired, even Les's pride and joy, the ridiculously heavy bulletproof vest, gets stored away. His spine must have been relieved that it was tucked up safely in the Pattinson Wardrobe. It will only be called on in the unlikely event of an armed insurrection or, maybe, the Kirkby Militia launching a special operation to facilitate the annexation of Les's home village, Aughton; unfortunately, the last time I visited my village of Melling, it looked like it had already fallen to the advance of Kirkby's sprawling estates.

So, for now, it's back to the long coats; we call them our Bleak Northern Overcoats. We need the warmth they provide us. It is blinking freezing up north in the winter. Not as cold as Scotland, mind you; that is proper brass-monkey weather up there. I am still regularly heading to the charity shops searching for bargain jackets, checked shirts, ties, scarfs or anything else I find interesting. Harris tweed jackets are popular with the er . . . let us call them post-punk kids. I have managed to nab a perfect dark brown one from the Oxfam on Bold Street. (They were dead cheap back then. I think it was only two quid. Two quid? Blimey, two quid wouldn't buy you a sodding button now.)

Tweed is thick and warm but has the drawback of when it gets wet, it stinks a bit. This might be because of the lanolin in the sheep's wool. In my jacket's case, I fear it's likely that the geezer that last owned it was a champion soap dodger. It never occurs to me to take it to the dry cleaner. I have never even been in a dry cleaner. In my mind, that is just for posh people. The tweedy lapel is where I pin my latest Lenin badge. I have always liked a badge since I was a kid, don't know why. It might be a throwback from being in the Boy Scouts, where we got badges as a reward. An encouragement that you have achieved something good. I was pinning on this picture of the cap-wearing baldly Vlad Lenin for what I would consider a hip affectation; I knew nothing of the *Communist Manifesto* or the shit that had gone off in Russia in 1917. It was all a bit naive and stupid. I knew I was left-wing and consistently voted Labour but a communist? Hardly.

Gone are the punk-rock razor cuts, chains, rips and zips. Shirts, ties, tweeds, long overcoats, checked shirts and the occasional cardigan or jumper are in. This garb is paired with stout walking boots like we are going on an expedition up K2 or somewhere. A quick saunter up Bold Street to Café Berlin or ascending high up the stairs into the ciggie-clouded top deck of the number 82 bus is about as taxing as it gets in Liverpool.

The only clothes that are out of bounds are sportswear. Worn by the football gangs, it's a new casual look. Filo, Adidas, Puma, that one with the little crocodile as a logo. The only item you could call sportswear that I sanction is the Bundeswehr black-eagle-badge vest. All we need now is for the sun to make an unscheduled appearance, and hordes of post-punkers will be drawn out of the dark to show off their puny biceps dangling out of these vests' armholes.

Sweatshirts were starting to appear in more cool shops. Some kid made them down School Lane by the Bluecoat Chambers, so I started to see them in real life, and not being worn by a sweaty Steve McQueen fresh out of the hole for some insubordination, as was his usual filmic want. Unbelievably this garment wasn't as ubiquitous as it is now. The material was thick cotton fleece, not the manmade stuff you get now. They had a 1930s boxers' training vibe about them, with no logos or brand names emblazoned on the front.

I still had my studded leather biker jacket with Velvets painted on the back; Lou Reed's face, picked out in white emulsion paint, was now flaking off and adding to the well-worn patina of this jacket.

Meanwhile, the press had been thinking of pigeonholes to bung us in. Post-Modernist, Neo-Psychedelia, Bleak, Dour,

Grim, Dark, etc., all were getting bandied about. The press scrambled to box us up, all nice and neat. What we were wasn't apparent to these specky oiks that wrote for the papers. Mac always said we were a rock band, and I was happy with that. I only ever wanted the Bunnymen to be remembered as a good band like the Kinks or Love. Timeless music was what it was all about for me.

We are in Liverpool at the Ministry rehearsal rooms. It's just a stone's throw from the beautiful gaping maw of the Birkenhead tunnel, otherwise known as the Queensway tunnel. Ornate 1930s-style streetlights illuminate the entrance, still guarded by green and gold art deco toll booths. In those days, no checks were kept on the number of cars going through the tunnel, so the booth workers had a good cash fiddle on the go. As coins were handed over, it was a case of one for you, one for me. They got caught after it was noticed that yachts, new cars and holidays abroad were suddenly within reach of some of their staff.

We have been trying to get to our praccy room at the Ministry as much as possible, up to five days a week. Intensely practising, writing and sorting out the songs for the record. Playing them repeatedly, working out the little niggles and honing the arrangements. We are coming up with many ideas and, along the way, we have got ourselves a new Roland drum machine, which we had premiered on the last couple of John Peel sessions. We intend to incorporate it in a couple of the song ideas. It's a quirky nod to our past as a drum-box trio. But this time, Pete's mighty thump will augment the Roland's metronomic ticktock. A lot has happened in the eighteen months since our first gig at Eric's on 15 November 1978.

Mac said a good few years ago, 'It was a turgid performance.'

It might have been, but it did open all the doors we have now been able to go through. Admittedly we are a much tighter band now. Playing gigs has seen to that.

In the room, Mac and I flirt with the fast and furious, funky guitar rhythms we hear on James Brown or Talking Heads records. Scything, brittle slices of sound. They are getting stacked up into the format of a song. We are going at it like a couple of lumberjacks. Riffs are hacked out of our Fender and Gibson guitars and are becoming a significant part of this record. Rhythmic guitars set the whole tone.

In the future, Mac often comes out with this gem: '*Heaven Up Here* was Will's album.'

In reality, they are all our albums, and all four of us are creatively accountable for what was put on those records as individuals.

Mac Ministry

We recorded a couple of Peel sessions in May and November 1980. This was used, as usual, as an opportunity to demo new songs: 'Over the Wall', 'All My Colours', 'That Golden Smile' (later to be rechristened 'Show of Strength'), along with 'Heaven Up Here' and 'Turquoise Days'. All had been recorded at BBC's Maida Vale Studios for Peel's show.

We've also done some other demos at Cargo Studios in Rochdale and a couple more in Kirkby at Amazon, so we've got around nine songs in pretty good shape, almost enough for an album. We are not fazed, and all agree it won't be a problem; we can think of something in the studio when push comes to shove. It won't be a big deal. So, from March 1981 onwards, it can only mean one thing: we are heading back to Rockfield to record our second album and greet the coming of springtime in the hills and valleys of Monmouthshire.

I was rooting for Brian Eno to produce the second LP. Rob Dickens at Korova said, 'Eno – he's too weird.'

'Yes,' I replied. 'That's exactly why I want him.'

Mac piped up with his choice. 'Well, I want David Bowie then.'

Both these suggestions were not taken seriously. My suggestion of Eno was deadly serious, and I would have loved to have heard what Eno would have come up with for *Heaven Up Here*. U2 got to work with him, plus Talking Heads, Devo, James etc. All very successfully. It seems he wasn't too weird for those bands.

Hugh Jones has been promoted from engineer and now has the producer job. His role as a studio engineer on *Crocodiles* was pretty much that of producer, along with Balfy and Big Bill aka the Chameleons. His contribution is invaluable.

This time we are in the Coach House studio. It is attached to the Ward family's farmhouse. It is a little tucked away behind an unremarkable door. But remarkable records have been made here, that's for sure.

We did some of the *Crocodiles* album in this studio. Most of the mixing was done here, and my 'Happy Death Men' screaming solo was in the corridor outside the control room. I have recently visited Rockfield, and the studios still look the same, at least structurally, since I was last there in the eighties. As you would expect, the equipment has been upgraded and updated. The twenty-four-track two-inch tape machines are still there and are fully operational if needed.

We are accommodated at the top of a small hill directly across a road and opposite the studio driveway. A steep track leads to a tree-shrouded whitewashed house with a scrubby lawn in the front. A couple of lean-to extensions have been secured onto the old stone building, providing a kitchen and dining room. As we had in the stable accommodation when recording the first LP, we have a set dinner time, and a woman from the village cooks and feeds us fresh and tasty food. She stocks the fridge with anything we want.

At the back of the lonely hilltop house is a farm gate that opens to a view across the freshly ploughed fields and onto a pine-wooded hillside. Look to the right and you can see muddy cow-inhabited fields that swoop down to the gentle flow of the River Monnow as it heads to the fortified medieval bridge that guards the entrance to Monmouth. The other side of the hill gives a direct view of the studio buildings.

We all scramble for a room. I get one up one flight of stairs. Les goes for the attic room; this will become our post-recording briefing hangout room. We will head up there to listen to a few records, discuss how the day's work has gone and the plan for the next day. Clutching bedtime cocoa, we have a half-hour or so to come down after the intensity of the studio. It's always very late, 2 or 3 a.m. Somehow Hugh is always up and in the studio before any of us have woken up.

After one late night in the studio, we return to the house. We are playing 'Space Oddity' up in Les's little attic room. Hugh points out an open hi-hat that is way too loud in the mix. He is miming the bashing out of the hi-hat beat as the song plays. We are all suddenly shocked at the volume of the hi-hat. This is the sort of thing that people who almost live in the studio spot. They constantly analyse records and think about what they would have done differently. It must drive them mad. I've owned that record for getting on for ten years and had never spotted it. And now, when I play 'Space Oddity', it does not bother me. I think it accentuates something, and basically was done on purpose; you accept what is down in the grooves and don't question.

Then I have this idea that Pete should not use cymbals.

'*What*, no cymbals at all?' he says.

'Yeah, just do something else,' I say, and carry on twisting the knife. 'Cymbals are shit; they are such a clichéd rock-drummer thing. I hate them; they are crap.'

I was a lot more forthright with my opinions back then and never considered that I could be hurting anyone's feelings.

As I remember, this wasn't a genius idea I had devised in a postmodernist radical stance. This was a totally selfish act. When listening back to the songs, there was a battle between my high guitar parts and Pete's crashing cymbals. A recording is a battleground, and we are all after space. 'This sonic landscape ain't big enough for the both of us' kind of thing.

Pete, far from getting the hump, sees it as a challenge and replaces the high fizz of the cymbal crash with the rumbling boom of tom drums. This greedy act, on my part, has given the record a different flavour, and might even have improved the production or at least guided it down a slightly less obvious path.

As the recording goes on, we are looking for new and interesting sounds to put on the record. We are working on 'All My Colours'. I have been playing the guitar with the rough-edged blade of a pair of scissors, using them like a bow to add an out-of-this-worldly feel to the track, which, to be fair, is pretty out-there from the get-go. Hugh has a brain wave.

'I know what we need on this track.'

My mind is racing; what can it be? Oh, I know that old chestnut, the Welsh miners' choir. We are in Wales, after all; you probably can't move for them around here. Or an Indian sitar might be a good shout, kind of far-out Beatles style. We had met the band Monsoon a couple of days back; they were in Rockfield's Courtyard studio doing a remix of their song 'Ever So Lonely'. Hugh Jones had produced this record. It must be sitar; that's what Hugh is on about. Monsoon were really friendly people, and I got on well with them. One of Monsoon's team showed me the correct way to hold a sitar and let me have a go. Another very kindly sent me cassettes of the BBC production of *The Lord of the Rings* for weeks and weeks while it was getting broadcast on the wireless; that was so nice of him. I really looked forward to getting them in the post.

Then a horrible thought came into my head: a coal miners' brass band? God, no, not a brass band. I soon dismissed that ugly thought. I've got it, mellotron; yes, it's got to be lovely warbling psychedelic string tones of the mellotron.

Hugh puts us out of our misery.

'A recorder.'

'Ya what? A bloody recorder?' we echo in disbelief, trying to suppress laughs.

'Trust me; I know just the chap.'

The next day a fellow turns up with a shitload of small flight cases.

Nestled all cosy inside velvet-lined recorder-shaped spongy cut-outs, several of these woodwind instruments rest in gleaming hardwood livery. They vary in size and all are of a quality you do not see providing the discordant squeak of the back row of the school orchestra. These are no cheapo plastic fifty-pence jobs from Woolworths. This dude has the Stradivarius of recorders in his little collection of road-ready handbags.

He is called Leslie Penny, and he is hitting the wine we provided to loosen him up. Firstly, we run the track in the control room, and Leslie Penny finds the key and starts to tweet along. He tries a few different sizes of recorder and then settles on the middle size of the bunch. It's a rich sound. Hugh sets him up in the recording room. Penny is supplied with headphones and more wine. Hugh points him and the recorder at an incredibly expensive Neumann microphone freshly plumbed into the desk. We are all crowded into the control room; this we have to see, er . . . and hear, obviously.

Hugh lines up the track, and we are off. After a few runs through, he is getting the hang of it; the whole song is pretty much one-chord (D is one of my favourites, by the way). It's not exactly Shostakovich. Mr Penny even manages to bend the notes into heart-wrenching, mournful cries. Hugh was right; he did know just the chap for the job. Not since the Troggs had an ocarina solo slapped onto the middle of 'Wild Thing' has such an innocuous instrument been added to a rock track. Penny hangs around till he finishes the bottle of wine. He is now pretty well-lubed up. We help him pack up the array of various-sized recorders into their velvet-lined sarcophagi, and he is gone, all done and dusted in a couple of hours.

Hugh then gets to work and soaks the recorder sound in reverb via a posh gizmo called a Lexicon. It sounds amazing. This is a valuable lesson learned about recording. Namely, anything can be cool given the proper context, part, sound and treatment. The Beatles and the Beach Boys had known this for years. I really must try and pay more attention.

Sometimes if Hugh was busy doing something complex in the studio, we would head back to the house and watch telly or play records. On one cloudless and moonless night – the pitch-black night was worthy of a Dylan Thomas description, but I ain't no Dylan Thomas, so take my word for it, it was bloody dark, as black as that new black they have just invented – the phone goes. Hugh wants us to come down to the studio to listen to something.

We grab our Bleak Northern Overcoats and head down the hill. Les has been eating his carrots and darts ahead courtesy of his night-vision eyeballs; I cannot see my hand in front of my face. We are creeping down the hill slowly to avoid twisted ankles, our main concern, when Les jumps out of the hedge, growling like a wild dog. The rabid bastard puts the shits right up us, then scampers off into the darkness. All the rest of the way down the track, we are waiting for him to do it again.

Les, Stanley Street by Brian's cafe

After that, whenever we needed to go to the studio in the dark, Les zoomed off ahead of us, and we would be crapping ourselves, tentatively clinging to each other like a load of school-girls, waiting for him to jump out on us again. He never did, though. He only had to do it once; that was enough. We would get to the control room like nervous wrecks to find Les on the couch with a cup of tea and a bourbon cream. Unbeknownst to us, Les was an expert in psychological warfare.

CHAPTER 18

Hawkwind's Coco Pops

'Strange Brew' – Cream

Bill Butt and Mac enjoying the coach

After a week or so, we have a visitor to Rockfield Studios. Butty, our lighting man, has driven the thirty-three miles from Bristol's Redland area. His house down there is called the Palace, which he rents to actors, mainly those at the Bristol Old Vic theatre school. In theatrical jargon, digs. It is also a good source of Bunnymen staff as most actors living in the Palace are 'resting'.

Kit and Jake, our latest recruits drafted in for roadie duties, came direct from the Palace. We've been to visit a couple of times. It's a cool setup. Everyone chipped in when it came to cooking, and a colossal Sunday roast stuck in my head. There was a real north–south divide, or maybe it was the Sergeants' lack of culinary adventure. I had never eaten roasted parsnips, or even heard of them. The next morning's breakfast was the first time I had encountered the glory that is bubble and squeak, fried up from the Sunday roast leftovers. And for that, I am eternally grateful.

Butty arrives in his new car, an Austin Champ; under the dark green bonnet, a meaty Rolls-Royce engine powers what is essentially a military vehicle. If you don't know what an Austin Champ looks like, and you can't be arsed googling an image, it's like an open-top Land Rover or a Second World War Jeep, like the type you'd see in *M.A.S.H.* or *Garrison's Gorillas*. The only difference is that this thing is on steroids and is much bigger than a Jeep or a Land Rover.

Bill has come armed with a Super 8 film camera, a video camera and a BBC-borrowed high-end reel-to-reel tape recorder, used mainly in the film industry, called a Nagra. We have sent for Butty because we have a mission, a field trip. Butty and I are off on an expedition. Our assignment is to record some found sounds. We head for the M48 and then over the Severn Bridge, back towards Bristol. It will be nice to get away from the intensity of the studio for a couple of hours.

Butty reckons we will get some exciting sounds down at the docks. So, we head to Avonmouth. He knows this area well and guides the Austin Champ close to the quay's edge. Heavy wet ropes anchor a few small vessels to large rusting iron hoops. A little way out, away from the granite wall of a dock basin, in the

Pete getting a lift

shit-brown water floats a lumpen and ungainly dredger. This is no sleek ship, no super yacht. It's the bin lorry of the sea. A floating skip with a heavy crane with grabs bolted on. The small boats moored up to the quayside groan and lurch; when the dredger causes a swell, they rise against the wall and crush fenders made from old tyres. The ripples expand until subdued by the seaweed-coated wall, only for the heaving dredger to send a fresh rippling wash to the bank. The dredger drops the wide-open grab, rusty and scratched. It crashes into the water with a mighty splash. After taking a bite out of the silty riverbed, it is hoisted up, jaws firmly shut. The dirty, serrated teeth hold in sopping wet mud. The heavy gantry crane brings the grab up high over the craft; it opens wide, and the soggy mess is released into the dredger's belly with a satisfying splosh. Swinging clear, the grab is soon back over the river and is sent down again into the murky water. And so it goes on.

'That's great, Butty; let's record that.'

He sets up the Nagra, connects the microphone, switches to record, and the quarter-inch tape starts spinning. The needles on the VU meters confirm that we are recording. We have a good few minutes of the dredger's desolate growl.

At the studio, Hugh transfers our dredger recording to the twenty-four-track machine. It slips nicely into the intro of our song 'With a Hip'. As we listen back to what today would be called a sample, what sounds like two words can be picked out among the grinding and screeching industrial sounds of the dredger. 'Good' and, a second or two later, 'crap'. It's an anomaly of the cacophony of noises the recording has picked up. The extraordinary thing is that it sounds like Mac speaking the words. There was no way he could have added the words to the recording, and why would he? It's another slightly weird thing that happens in the world of the Bunnymen.

After a couple of weeks, we have all our written tracks down on tape; the drums are still micced up, so we are at the stage where we need to write a couple of new songs. We go into the studio and Les starts playing harmonics on the twelfth fret of his Fender bass. This technique can be used on all guitars. Lightly rest your fingers on the strings when plucked; a hollow chiming tone is created, called a harmonic. If you listen to the track 'All I Want' off *Heaven up Here*, you will immediately hear this sound Les is making. Pete builds up the drums behind this spacey two-note arpeggio, and then at the height of the crescendo, the bass kicks in along with the guitar, all juxtaposed with the gentle harmonics of the start. There's an ebb and flow as the song rises and falls several times. We jam (yes, I have given up moaning about this word) around this idea for a while. Mac is providing the sharp stabbing rhythms that he is an expert at. And I am weaving in and around the arrangement. It sounds good for something that was just made up in the studio.

Hugh is a font of knowledge regarding unusual instruments and has suggested that Pete plays a slit drum, also known as a tongue drum. No, I'd never heard of it either. It's a nicely finished wooden box with slits cut in the top of the box in the shape of tongues. They weave in and around, and you can make different notes depending on where you strike the drum with little rubber-ended beaters. It's not a million miles away from the sound of a marimba, only with a softer attack. After the vocal is added, the song is a dynamic exercise and a perfect bed for Mac to stretch himself out on vocally.

Bill Butt, black-haired Annie, Pete and Jake's feet. Relaxing in the Rockfield Lounge

Another part of the Rockfield complex is a couple of miles from the studio. It is used for writing and rehearsing. Big Bill and Balfy have booked it for our friends, The Teardrop Explodes, and they are using the place for a week or so. We still need another song, so we head down to the Old Mill on the Teardrops' downtime. We use their equipment and intend to write a new piece for the record. Hugh Jones comes along, too, to oversee the proceedings, and we start to play. Our old friend D is the principal chord, and we begin to follow Les, who is playing a riff on the bass alongside an open D string that creates a flowing drone. This is something that Hooky from Joy Division was very good at on songs like 'She's Lost Control', though I had first heard this technique used by Dennis Dunaway from Alice Cooper's band on the *School's Out* album track, 'Gutter Cat vs the Jets'. And I'm sure it would have been done before that.

The way Les plays it is very repetitive; it has to be. It has a fantastic hypnotic quality that I like. I start to do something similar to Les's idea with the open D ringing as I do a simple two-note riff with a bend in the playing; this at least adds some variation. When the chorus comes, I head up the dusty end, and the intensity is increased tenfold by Mac's weeping cry of 'A promise'.

When we come to record it in the studio, I use a lovely sunburst Rickenbacker 360 twelve-string guitar we have hired. It's a killer on the fingers, but it sounds great. And it cements my deep fascination with twelve-string guitars. We are hanging out with the Teardrops, who are often around the studio for a cup of tea and a listen to what we are up to. They are going home soon, but it's time for one last brew in the Quadrangle kitchen. We brew up and then notice the breakfast tea drinker's nightmare shit: we have run out of milk.

Back at the Old Mill, acid rockers Hawkwind are now ensconced and rehearsing hard for the upcoming *Levitation* tour so we get in Les's van and head over to see if they have milk. When we pull up at the house, we find the door unlocked. Gary Dwyer opens it, but no one is around. We sneak in, head to the fridge and pinch a milk bottle; we flee sharpish just in case.

The next night Les and I decide to return a fresh bottle of milk to Hawkwind, but really it is an excuse; we fancy having a nose to see what's going on up there in Hawkwind world. They have a wild reputation, and we hope to see some spaced-out goings-on. As it happens, our knock on the door is answered by a Hawkwind. Please don't ask me which one, as they all have the same long hair and hippy garb. He sees us through the door's glass pane but does not attempt to open it. He's in a stupor, looking at us but not at us at the same time.

'Mate, we have your milk.'

Nothing.

We are being rewarded, for this is precisely what you want from Hawkwind at midnight after they have put in a hard day's space rocking.

'Er, all right, mate, we borrowed milk from you yesterday; we are just returning it.'

Still nothing.

'We're from the studio down the road; got some milk for you.'

This time he opens the door. We see odd Hawkwind members

pottering about in the house, but they are all in their own little world and have no concerns about late-night visitors.

They are all possibly tripping; difficult to tell without tests. But I suspect they are. We try to hand over the milk. The one who opened the door looks blankly at us, eyes like flying saucers. I think he has lost the use of his hands. To be safe, we decide to put the milk bottle in the fridge. Then we leave. Not one word has been spoken by any of them.

We are good Samaritans and don't want Hawkwind to be milk-less in the morning when it is time for their comedown Coco Pops, do we?

A day or so later, Hugh is deep into mixing; we give him some space and go to Monmouth for a pint. Les pulls up the van, and we are all piling in.

A tall bloke in a leather coat is mooching around outside the studio. He has a small dog with him and is calmly rolling up ciggies. It's the old Cream drummer, Ginger Baker, who is now drumming with Hawkwind. He is a proper lanky geezer of the cocker-nese breed of south Londoner, and says, 'Oi, where are you lot off to then?'

We answer, 'The Robin Hood pub in Monmouth.'

'I'll come with ya.'

It has got to be said that he is a bit scary. But who is going to say no to Mr Baker? Not me.

He follows this with a call to his little dog, 'Toe Rag, get here.'

Toe Rag is a brown and white Jack Russell terrier with a red bandana around his neck. The dog jumps up at Ginger, who lifts him and climbs aboard the van. It all feels a bit awkward. We drive a couple of miles down the road to the pub. At the pub, little is said to our guest, and he says nothing much to us. He sits on his own and buys himself a pint. He quietly sups it with the occasional, 'Oi, Toe Rag, get here.' Toe Rag obediently jumps up on the seat next to Ginger.

After a couple of pints, anxiety starts to creep in; we are wondering if we will be needed back at the studio. So, we decide to head back up the road.

'Er . . . we are getting off now, Ginger. You want a lift back?'

'No thanks, mate, I'll stay here for a bit; see you around.'

Ginger is happy staying in the pub, so we leave him there.

Not the most thrilling of anecdotes, I know. Ginger never hit anyone with a stick, swore or punched anyone's lights out. Just a quiet bevvy in a quiet pub in a quiet town. Well, it is not every day you go to the pub with a living legend. I only include it to demonstrate the surrealist nature of being in a band. You don't know what will happen next – tea and crumpets with Elton John or maybe a game of shove ha'penny with Maurice Chevalier.

We are sweetly oblivious to what is going on back at the studio. All hell is breaking loose. The magnetic emulsion on the two-inch tape reels has started to come off and it's coating the tape heads with dusty brown gunk. Every time it's played, more is coming off. It is disintegrating fast.

When we return from the pub, we are greeted with frantic activity. All the tapes are getting gathered together, and Hugh has arranged to go to Sarm Studios in Aldgate, London, one of the few places where they have two twenty-four-track machines linked up so they can transfer everything from one of the machines to another machine.

Rockfield's mighty Studer twenty-four-track 2-inch tape machine

It turns out there is a fault with the particular batch of tape we have been supplied with, and now after quite a lot of use, it is starting to break down. It's a desperate situation. Everything we have done over the last couple of weeks could be lost. Hugh loads all the tapes in his car and sets off to London. It's already way past midnight, and he will work through the night to fix this situation. The man's stamina is incredible; he is already getting hardly any sleep; he lives on coffee and roll-ups, but it must be done.

The next day he returns with the new tapes. Every track has meticulously been transferred. It is a close shave. Luckily the tape had not degraded enough to ruin the sound of the recordings. And Hugh carries on with no sleep that day.

As things are getting mixed, we are also working hard. Some old pig sheds have been cleaned up, and we have set up the equipment to practise for our up-and-coming US tour. We are called down to listen and help with the mixing. And as soon as we are happy, we return to the pig shed to practise while Hugh gets the next track in good shape to listen to. This goes on day and night. We have nothing like Hugh's stamina, and it is not long till it starts taking its toll on us. A giddiness is taking us over.

We are at breakfast in the house on the hill. We had been up late and are now up early-ish. We have to carry on the mixing with Hugh at the controls. Sleep deprivation is starting to kick in. Pete has a particular way of eating his food; he always saves a choice piece for the last bite, the final tasty flourish to end a top-notch nosh-up. I have finished mine a while ago. Being the epitome of the phrase 'your eyes are bigger than your belly', I eat so fast that I fool my stomach into thinking it's still empty as I stuff more and more food in it. Back then, all this gigging kept the weight off, so it wasn't such a problem.

Anyway, Pete lifts his fork to spear the tasty morsel he had so carefully segregated for his last bite; the rest of his full English breakfast has been demolished, all but the bitesize piece of Cumberland sausage languishing in a small amount of tinned tomato juice and brown sauce. He dreams of that last piece. He will fork it, roll it around in the sauce and tomato juice until it's fully coated, and then chomp it down. He aims his fork; he's going in. Just as he is about an inch away, Les, quick as a cobra strike, forks the sausage and scoffs it down.

Pete's fork hits the plate and makes that horrible scraping noise that goes through me; he can't believe what has just happened. He is used to well-mannered people. Never in all his time eating has anyone had the audacity to swipe his last inch of sausage. Pete is pissed off, I mean, proper pissed off. Pete never gets pissed off by anything; he's the most mellow fellow I know. I've never seen him so pissed off that he is shouting at Les, and it almost comes to blows. Les is laughing. We are all laughing, but Pete does not see the funny side of it at all.

Les comes back with 'Dry your eyes. It was only a bit of sausage.'

We carry on as usual, but this sneaky sausage swipe leaves a bad taste in Pete's mouth or, worse still, no taste at all. The next time we eat in the house, Pete is guarding his sausage like an Alsatian on a council-estate pub roof.

We have been hammering the practice and the mixing, and now the lack of sleep is definitely showing. Everyone is getting irritable, and jokes and sarcastic comments are being taken seriously.

Suddenly Pete blurts out, 'What the fuck! Did you see that? That salt cellar just moved, I swear it did; it moved, I'm telling you, it moved a few inches.'

I'm hallucinating differently to Pete. I feel a bit of an out-of-body vibe and experience a floaty sensation. I am light-headed. And I can remember grinning at Pete's outburst. I felt emotional. I did think the house had an unsettling vibe; the stairs always seemed odd. I do not doubt that Pete saw the salt cellar move. I'm not sure if it was a hallucination or if it could have been that the salt cruet was a gateway to the spirit world possessed and moved by unseen hands. But then again, sleep deprivation is a powerful form of torture, and it is possible to believe any old shite.

CHAPTER 19

Fish Guts and Seagulls

Mr Fantasy – Traffic

Me looking well shifty and wearing an Australian cap

The record is heading fast towards completion. Our late nights and Hugh's hard work are bearing fruit. Our attention is now firmly fixed on the image for the record's cover. We want to continue the naturalistic theme we began on our first LP, *Crocodiles*. Word has come from Rob Dickins at the label. He wants a picture of us on a beach with seagulls. This news had filtered down to us via Big Bill. I seldom agreed with Rob's visions for the band, but I don't remember having any objections on this occasion.

Now the word seagulls doesn't sit comfortably with me as a chap with ornithological interests; I know there is no such thing as a seagull apart from *Jonathan Livingstone Seagull*. But types of gulls, yes, there are many. Common, black-headed, herring, lesser black-backed and quite a few more, around ten species. Rob has no idea and doesn't care which type of gull we will coax to feature on the next Bunnymen album cover. He wants seagulls, and that's that.

Brian Griffin has been commissioned to take the cover photograph. We are all pleased that Brian has been given the job again. We all love Brian; his strange, understated wit is a joy to be about. Plus, the Birmingham accent is funny; you don't need much else. Everything he says seems hilarious to me.

Brian has been summoned to Rob's office. He sets off and heads north from his south London studio perched on the side of the Thames at Rotherhithe. His destination is Soho. Not for anything sleazy, you understand. Soho is a debauched den of iniquity; it is the natural home for record labels and film production companies. Anything with the slightest artistic content and, more importantly, the suits and their commercial interests are located in and around Soho's Wardour Street. Korova Records is in a modern office block on Berners Street, home of the publishing company Warner Chappell. And, for now, Rob's office.

I like that we tie the new cover in with the first LP. By plonking us in nature, it is timeless, not tethered to any structures or people. Rob wants us on a beach with gulls all around. Brian's mind is ticking over.

'How do we get seagulls?'

We need a beach close to the studio. The good news is that you are always fairly close to the sea in Wales. Brian needs more time to do a reconnaissance mission, so he looks at the map of South Wales; he spots that, roughly one hour from the studio, is Porthcawl and its beaches.

The next day we are ready; Brian picks us up in a black Peugeot 505 estate. It has seven seats plus room in the back for all his cameras and other equipment, tripods and crap photographers have to lug about. We leave Hugh to carry on with the mixing.

In the car are the four in the band, one crew, that's Jake Brockman, Brian and his assistant, Ricardo. An hour later, we pull up in a car park near a flat expanse of beach. It reminds me of our beaches near Liverpool at Ainsdale, Southport and Crosby. Southport beach stretches out to the Irish Sea. You would usually have to walk several miles before you encountered any waves, although the tide does come in now and then. But the Southport shoreline is changing. What was sand a few years ago is marsh grass now. The sandy beach is becoming a salt marsh scribbled with little creeks and gullies. It feels like Great Britain is stretching out on the west coast and eroding on the east coast. Eventually, Britain might creep its way over to America and join New England.

At Porthcawl, the tide has gone out. I'm sure salty seadog Les is wondering if Brian has checked the tide times. The receding water has left the shore with a glistening, reflective surface that looks incredible. A lucky accident of timing works to our advantage. Tripods are set up, and Brian asks Ricardo for a cartridge, simply called a back, loaded with Polaroid film for the medium-format Hasselblad camera. He clamps the back on, checks the light meter, adjusts the camera's aperture and speed, and takes a few test shots. The Hasselblad's click and the satisfying shluuuck sound can be heard over the noise of wind and distant gull cries. The Polaroids are squirrelled away under Brian's arm to feed warmth into them and speed up the development process. After a few minutes, Brian tears back the protective sleeve and we all crowd in, keen to see the results. It is not until we see the test shots that we realise how incredible Brian is. On a rather grey day, illuminated by a low sunlight strip on the horizon, Brian knew; he knew it was going to look magnificent. The cover of *Heaven Up Here* will feature a splendid blue of both sky and beach.

Under Brian's instruction, Ricardo ushers us in to form an uneven line. Brian has made an artistic decision that he already knows won't go down well with Rob Dickins. We are to face away from the camera, looking out to sea to the strip of light peeking back at us from the horizon. Rob, I have no doubt, would want to see our faces on the cover, not silhouettes of four blokes on a beach; the only distinguishing features are that Pete and Les are wearing hats. It could be anyone.

Record company executives need to catch on to what their artists are trying to achieve. Brian's photos are of hope and mystery. We will be heading to the USA very soon and are on the brink of a new horizon in the band's saga. It says it all; it fits well with the music we have imprisoned in the record's grooves.

Pete and Les in the Rockfield garden

But what about the bloody gulls Rob wanted? Gulls are flying around the beach as they always are, but far away, scavenging on other parts of the shore.

Brian has a secret weapon up his sleeve. Well, in a sealed plastic bucket. You wouldn't want this stuff up your sleeve. Brian plans to attract the gulls (mainly common and black-headed, in case you are interested) with a proper good nosh-up. He produces, out of nowhere, this large plastic bucket of tiny fish, whitebait, plus a good amount of fish guts. God knows where he got this stuff from, er . . . at a guess, maybe the fishmonger. Oh yes, he got it from a friendly fishmonger. There must be about ten pounds of this bloody, sloshing, stinky stuff.

Jake is given the job of fish-scattering roadie. He is wearing a shemagh desert scarf to keep the biting wind and occasional drizzle at bay. He wraps it around his face in a vain attempt to avoid being overcome with the stench of foul-smelling fish guts. He takes the bucket and tentatively scatterers the mess in a line before us.

It's only a short time till the far-off gulls get a whiff of this goop and realise it's feeding time. Like a scene from Alfred Hitchcock's *The Birds*, they come flapping and swooping. Webbed feet landing gear has been lowered. But we are too close to the frenzied gulls, and they are scared to come so near us; they think it's a trap. These are the days when gulls still had some manners, and you would never hear of one swooping down and pinching your last bit of sausage.

Jake heads a little nearer to the pale blue crack of the horizon and throws more of the silver-scaled whitebait and bloody guts mix on the sand. This time the squadron of gulls reaches a fever pitch of clamouring, excited calling accompanying the flurry of wings, swooping and grabbing, mid-air squabbles and aerobatic fighting as they grapple for as much as they can get into their gullets. Jake legs it out of shot, and Brian goes to work. The Hasselblad only has enough film for twelve images in each cartridge. These are quickly fired off as the birds make short work of the little shining treats on the sand. Brian gestures, holding the used-up cartridge. Ricardo is well versed in this routine and quickly takes it and hands Brian another camera back fully loaded with film.

Clicking it into position, Brian shouts in his soft Brummie accent, 'More fish guts, more fish.'

Jake runs in and replenishes the fish with a sickly sloshing sound.

Brian continues clicking, checking the light, and clicking again. This goes on for a couple more cartridges' worth of film. Then he takes a few last photos with us out of the shot; the gulls' noise and the chaos are deafening as more and more gulls turn up. The word has spread, and the sky is awash with wings and beaks and the noise of screaming birds. Time to pack up and move on.

Brian wants to take some more photos along the beach. He has spotted another area he thinks looks interesting, where the landscape changes, with some rocky outcrops and cliffs. He has brought some distress flares. Carefully picking a spot, he sets up the camera. He positions us gathered around the rocks; a flare is ignited, and red smoke billows in the wind. I am in the centre of the shot, and it looks like we have just landed from another world or popped out of a volcano. Brian shoots a few more at this location. Les aims and fires off one of the flares towards the cliffs; Brian tracks the flare with his camera set at a slow shutter speed. This picture is used for the cover of the twelve-inch single of 'A Promise'. The yellowish line – that's the flare. The seven-inch cover features the gulls with no band in the shot. The picture of the band on the inner sleeve of the album is also by Brian. We had already been down to his studio in Rotherhithe to do this photo a few months earlier.

At the beach, it's getting dark quickly. We cannot do much more; we must get back to Rockfield and see how Hugh is getting on. Now, with the faint whiff of fireworks and fish clinging to our hair and clothes, we smell like workers on our way home from a smokehouse. We all pile back into the black Peugeot, and Brian drops us off back at Rockfield; it's now pretty late, and we have all had a long day. Too late to drive back to London, so Brian and Ricardo are allocated rooms; they are staying the night.

We hang around the studio, listening to the mixes that Hugh has been working on. We only have a few days left now, and most of it is spent practising in the pig shed by the house on the hill. The last full day comes, and we have a final listen through. We pack up the equipment as we will be setting off back home tomorrow; then, a day or two later, we will go to America for our first US adventure.

There was one thing that we didn't like; I'm fairly sure it was on the track 'With a Hip'. It was maybe an edit or a sound that was not to our liking. It must have been something pretty minor, but when you are so close to a project, the smallest niggle can really get under your skin and drive you nuts; we wanted it changed. A second mix was made. Just before the album was released at the end of May 1981, we were on the UK tour, so we had the record delivered; we went into a shop in some provincial town that sold record players and asked them if we could quickly listen to the track.

Somehow, they had put on the wrong mix. We were all fuming and got on to Big Bill, demanding that the album be scrapped and redone with the correct mix. It was too late, but Rob said they would send the already-pressed records to France and alter the record for the UK pressing. By the time the album is released, the whole fuss is forgotten about, and we wheel out our saying, 'Tomorrow, there will be a new hurt to heal.' It is all history now, and I will never know if there are some copies with a slightly different mix still floating about in France. And I have to say it's not giving me sleepless nights, so fuck it.

CHAPTER 20

Futuristic Interiors
Straight Out of *The Jetsons*

'Too Many Creeps' – The Bush Tetras

Les in the Rockfield control room

The USA tour is just around the corner. We all have our brand-spanking-new full passports necessary for this trip, collected from the passport office in the formidable India Buildings in Liverpool's handsome business area. We have a visa agent in London sorting out our American P1 work permits in those days; this would last us for three years. Big Bill has in his possession a couple of thousand pounds in cash. The record company has been kind enough to lend us an advance to get us to the

States. This will go on our overall debt, increasing with every artistic turn we make. We had to ask for tour support as it's so expensive to tour, and tours hardly ever make a profit. Crew wages, lights and PA equipment – all had to be paid for.

We go with Big Bill and his big wad of cash to the Castle Street branch of the National Westminster Bank. Mac, Les and me (Pete wasn't with us). It was a safety-in-numbers thing. We wouldn't want some scally bashing Big Bill and making off with our latest loan, would we now?

The bank tellers are up the granite stairway, and we enter a cavernous circular chamber through tall mahogany doors. Marble pillars hold up an ornate domed and gold-enhanced elaborately decorated ceiling. Everything about this place shouts money. The foreign currency counter has been expecting us. Big Bill has called ahead for this appointment. (Ah, remember when you could speak to an actual person from the bank? When it was as simple as picking up the phone?) It is highly unusual for someone to exchange such a large amount of money. The bank has had to order extra dollars. This cash is for our tour float. All tours need a float to get the ball rolling. Cash for transport and the initial hotel bills; we also have to dole out the PDs or *per diems* – Latin for 'per day'. This is an allowance that everyone on the team gets to cover daily food and living expenses while on tour. It all comes out of this cash at the start. Once we do a gig, the tour manager will get the settlement and the money from the venue. We will be OK when the dollars are rolling in. Most of the fees get stashed for paying the crew's wages, expenses, etc. The band will see little of this cash once everything is paid for. The purpose of the whole operation is to build our grassroots following and ultimately sell records.

Back at the bank, Big Bill has the American money, and

we head out of the opulent domed room and down the stairs. We reach the large foyer with a high ceiling. Big Bill grabs the crisp green dollars from the carefully stacked plastic bag the teller had kindly filled, all neat and tidy like. He launches the crisp notes high up in the air, floating like falling leaves and then spinning and tumbling onto the thick foyer carpet. If money did grow on trees, this is what a blustery autumn day would look like. We are totally shocked, but we also love this act of rebelliousness. It feels like something from a film, like when gangsters have successfully pulled off a bank heist and are celebrating. We are all laughing; we can't believe what Big Bill has just done. On the carpet lie scattered heaps of cash, the most I have ever clapped my eyes on; it's everywhere. We laugh almost hysterically as we scramble to pick up the notes before another customer enters the large stone-clad doorway and wonders what the fuck is happening. This is just another indication of Big Bill's disdain towards cash. Punk's not dead!

Mac waiting at the Rockfield farmhouse

At last, the day comes; socks and undies are washed and packed in my bright red suitcase, recently bought from a Chinese supermarket on Berry Street. It's made of painted cardboard but it seems sturdy enough. It all feels like we are going on holiday. Then we are off to Heathrow for the British Airways flight to New York.

I'm not happy about flying at all. This is the first time I have ever been on a plane, and I'm terrified. I'm sitting next to Les, who is not keen either, though he's not shitting himself as much as I am. Les is a font of mechanical knowledge. (A few years hence, when he played bass for the late great Terry Hall, Terry christened Les 'Messes with Engines' in the style of the Native American names in the then-current hit movie *Dances with Wolves*.) Les has some understanding of how a bleeding massive metal tube weighing over 41 tons can take to the air, and this gives him some comfort. To me, it's all witchcraft, and as the old joke goes, if God had meant us to fly, he would have given us air miles.

The plane starts its rattling take-off, hurtling down the runway. I can see the wings flex through the little window with every clang and bump. Then I feel the plane tilt; the noise from the wheels on the tarmac stops, and suddenly we are airborne. Now we are creaking and jerking in the most unsettling manner. I'm scared the plane will fall to bits at any moment. After a few minutes of this terrifying climb, it levels off; I can almost feel the plane let out a sigh of relief as it achieves cruising altitude. The captain points the nose to the west and puts his foot down.

Three thousand terrifying miles later, we descend to the Earth with a heart-stopping clunk as the wheel's suspension units are tested in the most brutal manner. No, I'm not at all keen on this mode of transport.

New York's JFK airport.

The passport control is staffed by unsmiling and grumpy uniformed border guards, just like the ones we met in East Germany. Having a gob on you at all times must be the requisite attribute of a border guard worldwide. After a mild grilling, we can collect our bags, guitars and other bits of equipment. My red cardboard case has survived with just the odd scuff. We exit the airport buildings, and the first thing that hits us is the air; it's different here, hot, humid, and feels thicker. We are picked up by a van and taken to Manhattan.

Our first view of the city is as it pokes up in the distance as the van navigates concrete flyovers that stride on stilts above swampy areas of marshes and rivulets.

It is truly a mind-blowing site for a kid from a little village on the outskirts of Liverpool. We get closer and cross steel-girder bridges. The streets are busy; cars, trucks, taxis and bikes are everywhere. The sidewalks (it didn't take me long to go all American, did it?) . . . the pavements are packed with people, everyone urgently going somewhere. We get to the hotel. The Taft on 50th Street will be our base for the next few days.

One thing that struck me as odd was that the hotel-room doors had a sort of bowed design. They had a space in the centre of the door itself so that you could open this door within a door, put your dirty towels in, close it up, and then the maids could get the used towels by opening this space from the hotel corridor, without waking you up or disturbing the guests. Gurgling cast-iron radiators coated in a hundred years' worth of paint jobs kept us awake with the ancient plumbing clanking and juddering. Even the dust looked old. These days I realise that hotel was on the cheaper end of things and had seen better days, but I didn't notice it then; I was too wrapped up in the excitement of America.

Post card I sent to my dad from, you guessed it, NYC

We had the rest of the day off to enable us to acclimatise; there was a five-hour time difference to tackle. This only bothers me a little nowadays. When I was a lot younger, I was severely affected by jet lag. I would wake up at all hours and be wide awake until it got light. The best way to combat jet lag is to try and immediately fit in with the local time zone you are in.

After a quick swill, Les and I explored the numbered streets and avenues aimlessly. There was no way of getting lost here. The numbered grid layout of the city made it easy to navigate. We were warned not to stray into specific areas. I remember we were told Alphabet City was out of bounds to a naive couple of guitarists. At one time, it was a bohemian district; by the eighties, by all accounts, it was a very dodgy area. Gentrified now, as you would expect; in fact, most of New York has been.

We were wandering along, looking up at glass-walled canyons. You can't comprehend how they built this cliff-face architecture, but they did.

We had heard of Bleecker Bob's Records – it was the equivalent of Liverpool's Probe record shop – so we headed downtown to the Village, as is referred to around Eighth Street. Bleecker Bob's was great, all the out-there records, rarities, new and old you could ever want. Greenwich Village was great. Punk clothes and vintage clothes. Many weirdos were hanging around. The streets were filthy, with paper and plastic bags caught by the wind flying past. Dirt, litter and all manner of shite, including real shite, are everywhere.

In the morning, up very early, jet lag struck again. We hit a diner for breakfast. After navigating all that 'How do you want your eggs?' malarky, we settled on over easy. A menu with more things for breakfast than I knew there were things for breakfast. We loved this aspect of New York, and breakfast became a highlight of the day. The service was fantastic; none of that 'If it's not on the menu, you can't have it' crap, like we usually put up with in our very British way in England's cafés and service stations. Brian's diner excepted; Gloria was fine with whatever you wanted.

There were many fantastic diners dotting the streets of the city with vintage and futuristic interiors straight out of *The Jetsons*. Also, I must mention the delis on every corner with sandwiches piled inches high with whatever you liked. I was used to sandwiches being simply two pieces of white bread spread with marge, a Kraft slice, Dairylea or beef paste spread thin. It was another mind-blower. It must have been like when the Yanks turned up for the Second World War with fags, chocolate and gum, while the Brits had been living on bully beef and one egg a week.

The next day we had to go to Warner's offices at Rockefeller Plaza. We had interviews and photo sessions lined up, so there was little time for exploring. I hated doing these press things; I was a moody sod with a bad attitude, not realising it's all part of the job. It was most annoying when we got to an interview, and all the questions were directed at Mac, like he was the only one capable of answering their questions. The record company people came across as false, and I never took to them; all that 'have a nice day' crap got on my wick. It's fair to say it took me some time to warm to the Yanks; I felt their taste was slightly off. Kids would come up at gigs and say stuff like, 'I like all the New Wave bands, Gang of Four, the Fall and Duran Duran.' I don't know about you, but I can spot the odd one out. They would drop in the name of some other pop shite that was desperately clambering onto the post-punk bandwagon and getting it all wrong. How could they put such bands together? It was hard for me to digest it.

And the tag New Wave was not what we considered the band to be for a start, buster. The British version of punk and the American version of punk are entirely different beasts. Was Television punk? Were Talking Heads punk? Not really. The Ramones were one of the first bands to be self-proclaimed punk. So, I suppose they qualify.

In the afternoon, after the press shit, with jet lag taking hold again, Les, Big Bill, me and Butty get out and wander around. We had been told to venture to the electronics stores near Times Square. We were tipped off that you can barter with the shopkeepers. Unfortunately, my bartering skills were not up to much, and I was sure I'd pay full price for the Walkman that sat on the counter as the salesman said, 'OK, buddy, what do you want to pay?'

A Walkman was the latest thing on everyone's wish list. Still much cheaper than in England. So, we all came out of these glittering wonderlands of technology with bags stuffed with the latest models and accessories. The exchange rate was around $2 for every pound. And the prices of things were roughly the same in dollars as in pounds, so a pair of Levi's would be £20 in the UK and $20 in the USA, only costing us £10. It was the same for everything; it was crazy in a good way for us anyway. We headed down to Canal Jeans and bought Levi's 501s. Big Bill bought a black combat jacket. It became part of him along with his donkey jacket, faded Levi's, Doc Martens and Wrangler jacket. We grabbed packets of Fruit of the Loom boxer shorts. I had not seen boxer shorts in the shops back home. There must have been some shops selling them because, in every sitcom on the telly, it was always boxer shorts if there was a scene with someone in their underwear. This type of atrocious British farce was all over the telly throughout the seventies and eighties. Brian Rix was a foremost exponent of the befuddled character who gets locked out of his hotel room in his boxer shorts; in fact, we started to call these undies Brian Rixes. No wonder *The Young Ones* was a big hit; the shit that was on the telly back then was nearly as bad as the shit they have on now.

Our first gig is on 1 April in Yonkers, only fifteen miles north of Manhattan. The venue is called the Left Bank. I'm sure this gig, so close to Manhattan, is added as a warm-up for the tour. Conveniently low-key and slightly away from the city, any fuck-ups are out of the sight of the New York press, who will surely be coming to scrutinise us at the Ritz gig. It is a strange time: America has become obsessed with the British bands, and many American bands are getting pissed off. They aren't getting radio play on the college stations now dominated by anything coming out of the UK and Ireland; of course, U2 saw to that.

We are hot property; the press coverage, gig reviews and *Crocodile*'s positive reception have all helped build up the hype. Sire Records in New York have been no slouches, and an intensive poster campaign has been going on for weeks before our arrival. Plastered all over the city are posters proclaiming that the 'Sound of the Echo' is coming. No other information is on the poster. It's all an attempt to create an underground buzz. The people who know what it means are part of a secret society and feel special that they are in on this subversive marketing ploy.

The day of the Ritz gig arrives. It is New York, so it's wall-to-wall trendies that are there, just to be seen, but it is a great gig, and we have two more in the same venue.

A woman everyone knows in the New York music scene, Ruth Polsky, is a band booker and promoter, and is known as a kind of New York mover and shaker. She has been onto the new UK bands from the get-go, and was the one that had booked Joy Division to come to New York before Ian Curtis tragically died in May 1980. She's good friends with New Order, especially Hooky. Polsky is involved with a club called the Danceteria and we are invited to a drinks party on the roof. It's full of people desperate to be seen at this thing. I sit back and observe the hipsters being hipsters. Ruth keeps pushing us to play an after-show at the club Hurrahs. We are not keen, mainly because she is so pushy. If she had played it differently, we might have done it. We don't like being pushed; if we are, we tend to push back. It is just how we are. It's a kind of inbuilt mistrust, and this stance contributes a lot to our shooting ourselves in the foot over the years.

Earlier, in 1980, Ruth had got The Teardrop Explodes to come over to New York to play at Hurrahs. She wanted both Zoo Bands to play, the Teardrops and us. Ruth would call Big

Bill often in Liverpool to try to make it happen. We weren't against the idea, but we were still recording, and so the Teardrops went by themselves. Ruth played a significant part in promoting the bands that later became known as post-punk; she opened the door and then was forgotten, with the bigger promotors taking over. We did do some after-shows at the Peppermint Lounge for a bloke called Sal, Sol or even Saul; take your pick. I'm sure someone out there knows who I'm talking about. The after-show sets were fantastic; we generally only did half a dozen songs. Word would go around and the fans would all follow us down to the Pep, as we called it. It was a good place to have a drink and hang out and chat with fans.

I can remember a beautiful girl that came to the gigs; she dressed and looked like a pixie; she really did. She had cultivated the look and spent time on it. The full Tinkerbell but with a bit of New York sassiness. She wore green tights, a scalloped suede skirt, green jacket that a real pixie might wear and pointed pixie boots. The hairstyle was like Mia Farrow's when she was in the film *Rosemary's Baby*. It was a strong look, and she stood out, and in New York, it is hard to stand out as everyone is trying so very hard to stand out. I fancied that pixie girl but was way too shy, self-conscious and rubbish at talking to girls. I did not know the first thing about how to bag off with a human, never mind a pixie. I never knew her name and she vanished, as all sprites do.

The city was still a dangerous place. Every time you left the hotel's safety, especially at night, it was like you had just stepped into a real-life version of *Serpico* or *The Warriors*, passing dark alleys that always seemed to have some shifty characters lurking near them. Fear and crime were rife in the city. Central Park was a mugger's paradise and, essentially, a no-go area when it got dark. Blocks and blocks were dedicated to wall-to-wall porno theatres. Up in lights 'Sex Constant Sex', 'the very best X films', 'Sexsational show', 'School for Sex' and 'Best XXX Porn in town'. Twenty-four-hour sex shops cast light onto the wet streets' glow as enthusiastic wankers scurried into the Peep-O-Rama. All tastes catered for. Time Square wasn't the plush, expensive place it is now, that is for sure.

After the gigs, we would head out and would not know where the hell we would end up; this was all part of the fun of the city. It was magical and scary in equal measure. Officially everything closed at 2 a.m., but unofficially New York was still open if you knew where to look. We didn't, but the people we met did, so we got taken to after-hours clubs.

After one of the gigs, some friendly New Yorkers take us to the 'latest' club, called the World, hidden on the upper reaches of a brick warehouse in the East Village, not far from the East River. The fans, me and Les jump out of the taxi in a very dark and desolate area of New York. We get led to a large building that looks like a warehouse, without any indication of what is happening inside.

Through a door, then ushered into a lift. Not the plush type that you see in hotels with muzak piped in, this was a scatty service lift with those metal concertina-style doors that close with a clang. As we ascend, you can see the brickwork of the lift shaft. After climbing past several floors, the lift stops with a spongy twang. The doors slide open, and the clattering metal door is flung back.

We are confronted with a large, open room. In the gloom, people are milling around. Loud music is playing. Odd bits of furniture, old-fashioned seats, tatty couches, everything is thrift-store fresh. Not much in the way of lighting. A few standard lamps are dotted about. Over in a corner, a skinny bloke is illuminated behind a drinks fridge selling cans of Budweiser. Standing with his back to us is the instantly recognisable David Byrne. He is chatting happily with his friends. Wandering around, it's just a hang – somewhere to go after the clubs. It's a prominent dance place, but I never notice anyone dancing, only people huddled in dark corners in conversation or something a little more intimate.

I feel cool, though, like I had penetrated a secret world, which it is really. It feels like it's haunted by the ghost of Warhol's Factory set; those immortal ghosts will never die. (Yes, they are immortal; that's because they are bloody ghosts, you knob.)

We also visited a bar called Berlin and the Mudd Club, plus the already mentioned Danceteria, Peppermint Lounge and

Me wandering around Rockfield farm

Hurrahs. We walked up to the Berlin bar one night, and Keith Richards was sitting in a limo outside. As you would expect, he was swigging from a bottle of Jack Daniel's. I didn't like the look of the place; it looked like the epitome of New Wave. I didn't like the black and white checked tiles on the facade.

We had become friends with a bloke called Stan Bogdansky; he knew his way around the city, though he was from New Jersey. We christened him Top Cat, or TC for short. We thought he sounded just like the cartoon cat of the telly show *Boss Cat*. He had a few mates he was always with. They became regulars at the shows. They were a hip gang, Stan and his friends. I remember a girl called Cindy. She was tall, blonde and very good-looking. They would take us to the coolest bars and clubs after our gigs. All would pile into big yellow taxis. Many of the band, crew and our new mates would be in tow. Crammed in to each cab, three on the back seat and two on the fold-away jump seats. The type of cab that Robert De Niro drives in the film *Taxi Driver* – they are called Checker Taxicabs. The drivers did not hang about. They wove from one lane to the next for what seemed to be no other reason than they liked throwing us about on the back seats. Every time they switched lanes, the smoothed-by-a-million-arses plastic-coated seat provided a slippery surface. We'd slide about and end up crumpled on the left and then to the right. Thundering down the streets and avenues with deep potholes, every time you hit one you'd think your spine would shatter. The streets were absolutely fucked in New York in the eighties, with wrecked roads, trash and old furniture piled high in disused corners of the streets. People would set up impromptu markets on empty corner lots. I bought a toy piano from one of these markets. And still use its clunky chime on solo projects.

Big Bill Drummond compared eighties New York to a

medieval city. I know exactly what he is talking about. The apprehension you feel in the darkness if you stray from the main streets and cut down dimly lit streets. Expecting to be accosted by brigands or disturbed by wandering, random crazies, like a far-out Don Quixote shouting at bins and street signs and challenging them to mortal combat. Sad fuckers are drifting around in rags. Some old fabric is tightly wrapped and taped around stinky feet in place of shoes. Ladies and gentlemen of the night are hanging on street corners waiting for a client to fund another trip to oblivion and away from their reality. Tricksters on the corners aggressively try to entice you to guess where the ball is with the classic three-cup trick. After a few ales, Jake and Pete were always a sucker for this scam and lost a few dollars that way. We didn't know that the ball is never under any cups; it is in his hand until you pick one. Then the crafty git slips the ball under the cup you didn't choose.

Just like back home in Liverpool, New York was on its arse. It was the New York of *Taxi Driver*, *Mean Streets* and *Midnight Cowboy*. The film that most hit the vibe of what it was really like to be in a band in Manhattan and be out at all hours was, for me at any rate, Martin Scorsese's *After Hours*.

CHAPTER 21

Niagara Falls

'Roadrunner' – The Modern Lovers

BRIIIIIINNNG – BRIIIIIINNNG!

It's early morning at the Taft hotel. The incessant hum of the wall-mounted air-conditioning unit and clanking of the pipes are suddenly joined by another even more annoying sound.

BRIIIIIINNNG – BRIIIIIINNNG!

The phone drags me out of my dream.

BRIIIIIINNNG – BRIIIIIINNNG!

My arm reaches over to the receiver on the bedside table.

'This is your seven a.m. early morning wake-up call, sir.'

'Er . . .' Grunt.

Overnight my tongue has been turned into a stubby lump of gritty sandstone. I persuade it to crack and croak a reply.

'Oh yes, thanks, mate.'

'You are welcome. Have a nice day, sir.'

'Ta.'

I squint, my eyes open a tiny fissure. In floods New York's early morning light. My consciousness is being hauled back into the real world and the reality of a hangover.

How can you know that from forty years ago, Will?

You may well ask. The simple answer is it was standard

procedure for me to get, as we used to say, smashed up after the gigs, so I feel pretty confident that a Saturday night out in New York, drifting from club to club, would have resulted in much alcohol being consumed, and I would be suffering from dehydration, headache and all the classic symptoms of a hangover. This is more than possible: it is guaranteed.

'Les, Les, we've got to get up.'

I usually shared a room with Les; we were a duo. We had a lot in common, including going to the same school and being in the same class at that school. Jake and Pete were also a duo. These two lovable toffs both went to private schools and knew about wine and fancy grub, and they were from the mythical land of Down South. And both were partial to the delights of the jazz cigarette. They were well-spoken; and could use posh words. Mac is a proud scouser, and he could also use posh words but with a scouse accent, so they never sounded posh. Mac would share a room with the tour manager or one of the crew or, if he was lucky, have his own room.

All the rest of the Teds . . . Hold on, 'Teds'? Let me explain that. Teds was a phrase Butty had brought up from Bristol via an art-school chum, Jim. Jim was a rocker/Teddy boy who rode a much-coveted Velocette Venom motorbike. He called any group of people 'Teds', for example, 'I hope you Teds haven't forgotten your bicycle chains?' or 'Come on, you Teds, the mods went that way.' That kind of thing.

All the rest of the Teds, the band and crew, still doze in beds up and down the Taft's corridors. Their eyes are cowering behind pink lids, hoping for a few more minutes of kip. It is lovely here in the land of nod, behind our rooms' weird empty-mahogany-bellied doors. The American phones spit aggressive rings that kick their way into fuzzy heads. Desert-dry mouths creak open to try and speak, and then the victims stumble out of bed, searching for the nearest watering hole, this time just for your actual water. If the phone doesn't get you, there is no escape from Harry, the tour manager's knock, and his cheery morning greeting, 'Get up, you idle bastards, downstairs in five minutes.'

Harry Demac in his workshop in Stockport

Teeth, shower, dress, and then the last-minute idiot check. With brains still only firing on one cylinder, we search the room for the stray socks, shirts or brand-spanking-new Sony personal hi-fis that may have slipped behind the pillow or under the bed.

A little late, we roll out of the hotel and then, along with the equipment, we are loaded into a Ford Econoline van. Soon, we are on our way to Boston's Paradise club. It's 200 miles, not that far, but we have to be ready by 8 a.m. because we are travelling with the crew, and they have to load in and set up all the gear.

This will become the daily routine unless we have a day off, which usually turns out to be a travel day anyway. On these, we end up at the hotel as the darkness arrives; after dumping our bags and a quick wash, we are ready to hunt for food and beer. Sometimes we stop over on the long drives at roughly the journey's halfway point. Harry will have booked a hotel by a retail park. After an hour to reconnoitre, we have discovered all there is to see. We will be surrounded by shops and all the usual food chains. These big retail parks are convenient but boring. The only fascinating thing is the gun section of Walmart. Not that we want to buy a gun or anything like that; it's just so odd to see guns in supermarkets like they are hockey sticks, fishing rods or some other sporting tool. I would much rather be in an interesting small town. One where we could go and explore and possibly find some funky corner bar. We usually stay either in the cheap Holiday Inn, even cheaper Howard Johnson's or sometimes even cheaper still independent motels. I like motels; they come ready and equipped with a nice B-movie quality. We get the random knock on the door and the forceful cry of the Exterminator, who enters and sprays DDT or some other pesticide all around the room's boundary. It is an exotic thrill for Les and me but not so much for the cowering cockroaches with whom we have been sharing the room. And after this odd ritual, whenever we knock on any of the other Ted's doors, we always accompany it with the word 'Exterminator' in a bad American accent, as you would expect.

Motels usually have a pool in the courtyard, so days off for the crew and band members are spent by the pool with drinks and club sandwiches delivered at regular intervals. I'm not a big lover of the poolside hang and would rather be out and about looking for record shops and thrift stores. Sometimes the heat of America does drive you into the pool for a cool-off.

As we set off to Paradise – the club, not the religious concept – headphones are plonked on heads, and ears are pricked up and ready to receive the journey's soundtrack. With only a handful of cassettes to listen to, I'm confident Boston's Modern Lovers will be been on the playlist for this journey, along with Pere Ubu's *The Modern Dance*, Television's *Marquee Moon*, Wire's *154*, the Residents' *Fingerprince*, Bowie's *Low*, all the usual suspects.

With the sound of 'Roadrunner' and 'She Cracked' pumping into my ears, we navigate the streets, tunnels and bridges of New York. Exiting the city, we look back and get some incredible views. For me, it's the Chrysler Building that is my favourite.

The 200 miles go by so quickly, and in a few hours, we are driving down Boston's streets flooded with Irish bars and redbrick buildings. Not much time to explore, but I do get to Newbury Comics and buy some Gilbert Shelton comics, *Fat Freddy's Cat* and *The Fabulous Furry Freak Brothers*.

The Boston gig goes smoothly; the next day, we are getting the Harry DeMac treatment again.

'Hurry up, you bleeders. We've got to get going.'

We are going to Canada.

And soon, we are on the treelined highway to Niagara Falls. We stop for a quick look. All jump out of the van and creep up to the edge of the barrier to gaze in terror at the power of the mighty white wall of water flowing over the falls.

At the Canadian border, the guards are even more sullen than the East Germans. After a comprehensive search of the van, they reluctantly let us in. We drive north to Montreal.

Snaps from our USA tour, 1981

Montreal is trying to be France as best as she possibly can. The buildings, cafés and bistros are giving it their best shot, in any case, but the scenery, the nice weather and the enormous sky give the game away. The next day we go to Toronto, which seems a lot more British than the USA and definitely more British than Montreal. You can even get a half-decent cup of tea. It's very modern, with tall buildings and open areas. There are a few cool streets with the usual record shops and punk clothing stores. The day after, we are back at the border again. Unfortunately, the Canadian guards haven't cheered up yet, and they seem glad to see the back of us. The Yanks let us back in with not much fuss. What are we going to smuggle in? Beaver pelts? Maple syrup? It's Detroit next, which sits on the imaginatively named Detroit River.

Detroit is chock full of impressive art deco buildings now slightly past their best, many with windows boarded up with plywood. Acrobatic foliage clings to cracked brickwork near the top floors, while steel fences and barbed wire hammer home the sadness. 'Danger Do Not Enter' signs are fastened to the walls of crumbling ornate theatres. Cinemas are left with doors open and holes in the roof. The motor industry the city is famous for is dying, and you can tell. The wide streets are empty now. They were built for gigantic cars to sail down – cars Detroit used to churn out in the millions. Not much is sailing down them currently.

I might not have the correct order of the gigs, as the lists you find on the web have quite a few contradictions and, unless something odd happened, individual gigs are not retained in my memory. It would be too much information to be crammed into my tiny mind. To carry all that around would send me nuts. All I have is an overall impression that the gigs went well. No doubt the crowd wouldn't even have noticed my usual odd mistake. But these fluffs would have meant a lot to me then; they would have pissed me off until my next fuck-up anyway.

Mac was developing his stage persona away from the UK; he would let loose and launch into curious dances, usually in the improvised freak-out sections of the songs when he was free from the microphone for a few minutes. He would jerk and stumble in an almost acrobatic manner. It reminded me of a touch of Bowie, a pinch of David Byrne, a smattering of Ian Curtis and a lot of pure Mac. I could see him through my fringed hair curtains; he would be in an enchantment. It's as if he had been taken somewhere by the power of the music and the glee of the fans. I was already well aware that the crowd is the crucial component of the gig; they can dictate if it's a good gig. The crowd feeds and elevates us to places and heights we never thought possible. Gigs are always a joint effort.

Me and Mac with the new look, snow camouflage drapes

Down to Pittsburgh, all cramped in the green Ford Econoline, each of us sporting a new Sony Walkman still glued to our ears. We enter a mountain tunnel; the light at the exit blasts our eyes as we emerge into the heavy industrial landscape of the city.

After the gig, Les and I befriend some girls who have a car. They take us to an area near a gigantic steel mill. The blast furnace's glow can be seen from the road up on the hill; steam and smoke are billowing everywhere, picked out and made beautiful by floodlights. It's almost like the smoke-filled stage we have not long vacated back in Detroit at Bookie's Club. The acrid smell of burning metal hangs in the air as we descend into a grubby car park. Gleaming in among dust, smoke and dirt is the classic American polished aluminium diner, complete with a flickering neon sign. The scene could be straight out of a David Lynch film. The steel mill looks like hell, but this beautiful building shines like a chromium diamond – a sanctuary for the workers twenty-four hours a day.

The next day we head south-east; occasionally, we ride high above the rivers on impressive girder bridges, no doubt forged in the steel mills of Pittsburgh; below them, industrial and chemical plants sprawl down the banks. As we go on, the landscape sluggishly changes from industrialised to a swathe of endless farms. Lush corn fields pan past the windows of our little van. Buttery grasslands dotted with cattle sweep off into the distance. We spot farms on ridges or at the end of tracks isolated from the highway. They are all about the giant grain silos and oxide-red barns topped with gambrel roofs. They sit next to wooden, weather-worn, whitewashed houses. Eventually, the vast fields give way to wooded areas. Much of it looks the same as there's not much we can see in the form of hills or mountains.

Every town we pass through is announced in 10-foot-high letters on the side of unique water towers. Some look like whopping big onions, some are flying saucers, and some are the traditional type that looks like a stubby rocket ship. I love these water towers. They have a definite Americana air to them. There is a lot to like about America; it gets inside me the more we go on. And I am slowly coming to terms with the unnecessary optimism that Americans display at every opportunity.

The thrift stores are a revelation, and a sartorial craziness takes over. Because we are far away from home and out of the judgemental gaze of Liverpool, it seems OK to dress in things you would never wear in the UK. I start buying 1950s bow ties and satin or silk kipper ties made in the 1930s. This leads to shirts with collar studs and tie pins. I find a hat I like, a sort of checked trilby, and I buy a sage-green mohair cardigan with a destiny no one would ever predict (more on that later).

On the highway again, the odd passing headcase has shot at some street signs. These pistol-packing mama's potshots have torn ragged holes through the aluminium, reminding us we are in a dangerous, gun-toting country. To hammer this home, some of the highways have signs with the name of a police officer killed on duty – Sergeant XX Memorial Highway. Then followed by the 'Adopt-a-Highway' signs and 'Litter Control Next 2 miles'. All are signs we do not have in the UK, and it's all part of the strangeness of life on the American road.

It's hard to get your head around the vast distances we have to travel in the USA. In England, it's a ball ache to go the ninety miles to Birmingham for a gig. It can seem a hell of a long way when we encounter a ten-mile tailback and have to stand still for an hour on the M6. Ninety miles is chicken feed compared to the distances between gigs in America. The mile markers evaporate the miles a lot quicker than in England. I have a theory that American miles are shorter than British ones. Besides, we don't encounter the same traffic problems until we hit the city outskirts. The miles fly past, but the long journeys can become tedious. I find the best way to deal with the tedium of these drives is to slip into a meditative state. You might call it nodding off and dribbling with my gob wide open so Les can get sneaky photos of me looking like a dead fish.

Our Ford van is not that comfortable; it's small, but we know no better. Our luxurious tour bus days are yet to arrive. We are used to travelling in Les's Ford Transit back home, which never came with the extravagance of many seats. Youth can put up with a lot, and we do because we are all on the same mission; we support each other; we are what I believe to be real friends or even brothers. I imagine it's like the friendships forged in the army, prison, Boy Scouts or a cult. We are the Hole-in-the-Wall Gang; we are in it together, all for one and one for all and all those bollocks. The Over-the-Wall Gang.

As the week goes on in our cramped little metallic green van, the big thrill is the possibility of a stop at the wondrous world of the truck stop. We pull into the gravel car park. Neat lines of parked trucks, all sparkling clean, greet us. Chrome wheel hubs are like fisheye mirrors that reflect an alternative reality of the road. Truckers are out of their cabs and doing daily truck chores. Much elbow grease is required to polish everything with a hint of chrome, as these metal giants are like a chrome showroom. They climb up to reach the windshield to scrape a thick paste of bugs away. These islands of fuel, food and flags fascinate me. In the shop are all manner of tools, and there is always a large selection of lights to adorn the trucks. Chrome accessories are everywhere, CB radios, country and western tapes, with cowboy hats to wear while listening, T-shirts and trucker's caps, all with the obligatory patriotic slogans. The drivers of these trucks are a very proud and patriotic breed, and they adorn their wagons with many Stars and Stripes stickers, most with slogans, like 'All you need is love for guns and your country.' They look after the trucks with an affection otherwise reserved for family. They watch out for each other with Smokey Bear spotting skills and warn fellow speeding travellers over CB radio, and while driving they stave off sleep by feeding themselves Jolt, all the sugar and twice the caffeine. They live in cabs and sleep burrowed in the back in narrow bunks. In their cabs are TVs and all the 12-volt gizmos of the modern bachelor pad. And, of course, they like both types of music: country and western. We sit at the diner's bar alongside these nomads of the road and attract amused looks with our haircuts and strange clothes. However, we have the checked shirt in common with these grits-chomping lone rangers.

After a gig, the band and crew would go together to bars, drink till kicking-out time, then head back to the hotel or motel. During the day, if we had any time while waiting for the soundcheck, Les, Pete and I would be out on adventures. Exploring the town, we would walk for miles searching for food or record stores, comic stores, thrift stores or vintage clothes shops. Pete was always after coffee; he was a big fan of the espresso buzz; coffee is something I never liked much since the days quaffing milky Mellow Birds around at my mate Devo's house. We would take seriously the sport of seeing how long you could keep a Morning Coffee dunker in the hot liquid. The skill was to retrieve the soggy treat just before the integrity of the biscuit collapsed into the steaming buff liquid. Disaster, you would end up with a sweet sludge at the bottom of the cup. This was one of the few sports I excelled at. I could time the dunking ability of many a biscuit finger to the millisecond. I could've been a contender if it had become an Olympic sport.

On days off, generally, small groups would form. Les, Jake, Pete and me. Mac wasn't one for daytime exploring too much; he liked to stay in his motel room. If you go out mob-handed for food, no one can agree on where to go, and we would walk past restaurant after restaurant, always thinking the next one will be the best one. We would keep going until we saw that the next one was closed up. Shit, we would be running out of time.

Some bright spark would then chime in with, 'Let's go back to that first one, that looked good.'

Getting desperate now, we would all agree, so we would turn around and head back, and when we got there, inevitably they would be closing up.

This happened so often on tours that, now, everyone tends to pair up with just one or two people; that way, you generally get fed. It is not an anti-social thing; it is just learning lessons and how to deal with things that happen on the road.

If you simply can't be arsed going or you dilly-dally in the room and don't get to the meet-up in the lobby fast enough, you can be left behind.

It's always the same greeting when they get back: 'Will, you missed out there, mate. We've just been to the best place for food ever.'

CHAPTER 22

Next Stop, Not Hawaii

'The Big Country' – Talking Heads

Hi Los Angeles, Whisky A Go Go, 1981

We have completed the small tour of East Coast, Midwest and
Canadian cities – our first toe in the chilly American waters. But
now we are heading west to paddle in the warmer Pacific Ocean.
If the pilot overshot the runway and decided, fuck it, I need a
holiday, the next American outpost will be Hawaii. I would have
loved to go there, but our trip stops at the Summer of Love hippy
hotspot of San Francisco. I am fascinated by San Francisco. The

happenings, the free festivals. The heads that hang around Haight-Ashbury, the counter-culture. That time when George Harrison was filmed pottering around Golden Gate Park, followed and, to be fair, freaked out by a throng of flower children expecting him to lead them to something, Christ knows what? We don't often see flower children in Liverpool; we don't get the climate for them to bloom, so I'm not surprised. But it still is a fascinating time. Before we see any of that, it's all down to Chicago O'Hare airport and another terrifying flight. I am sitting by the window and can see the topography of America below.

Brown craggy dry mountains poke above the treeline. And not a road or track can be seen from up here. Lots of it seems to be unoccupied. I expect Sasquatch to have a significant foothold in those remote mountainous regions; I hope so, anyway. I insert one of my cassettes into the Walkman; let's have some music to pass the time. I have made a recording of Talking Heads' second album, *More Songs About Buildings and Food*; through the track 'The Big Country', David Byrne has unwittingly agreed to explain to you what I can see out of the window.

As we head west, besides what Mr Byrne has spotted, there are some other curious sights. Large, perfectly round areas of green pop out in the surrounding beige-coloured landscape. They look strange, alien. What are these random flawless circles dotted on the land? Then it becomes clear to me that they are farms. Farmers with plenty of space to play with don't need to stick to the rectangular field patchwork like everywhere else. This is an efficient way of growing. The farms have a central water supply with arms stretching to the circle's circumference. These arms are supported on wheels and have a powered rotating irrigation system that only waters the areas with the crops on. It still looks odd, though, like the farms they may have one day on Mars. I won't hold my breath for the TV broadcast of that mission, though; on Mars, on the other hand, you would have to hold your breath because of the poisonous carbon dioxide–rich atmosphere. Plus, it is so thin that the blood in your body boils. Not a lot to do with the story, but pretty interesting to a space cadet like me. Luckily the atmosphere on Planet Bunnymen is yet to be poisoned.

I can see the land change below. We are above Utah; it's a flat landscape, a dirty white down there, not with snow but salt. We must be near the Bonneville Salt Flats where a glut of speed freaks and nutjobs have tried to beat velocity records for donkey's years. I flick to the back of the Trans World Airlines inflight magazine, to the pages that detail the TWA flight paths. I recognise the names of several places, towns and cities we might have flown near on our long hop from Chicago. Durango, Milwaukee, Cheyenne, Santa Fe, Denver, Salt Lake City, Gallup, Boulder and the town that should have been twinned with Kirkby, the brilliantly named Dodge City. I shouldn't know the names of these towns, but I do because of all the Wild West TV shows we were fed as kids in the 1960s and 1970s. *Bonanza*, *The High Chaparral*, *Alias Smith and Jones*. All can't-miss TV for a budding cowpoke with a Colt 45 cap gun in his plastic holster and a silver sheriff's badge pinned on a faded Wrangler jacket.

The plane suddenly banks hard, and the no smoking and seat-belt signs are illuminated with a pinging chime. Then comes the captain's distorted voice crackling over the terrible speakers; he says something about landing soon.

In those days, it was permitted to smoke on board and, as a non-smoker, I was looking forward to some fresh air. How we put up with that stinky shit for all those years without much of

American views, 1981

a complaint was nuts. Now, I can't imagine travelling with smelly smokers constantly lighting up and inflicting their stupidity on me. Unfortunately, back then that was precisely what I had to look forward to for the next few decades. Most of the band and crew smoked constantly. Only me and Les did not smoke. I wanted to be out there in the fresh air so badly.

The window reveals the Pacific Ocean's tantalisingly clean air and pale blue water glistening in the sunlight, and it is dazzling. The plane is not so much descending as dropping now in stomach-churning, bumpy free falls. I hope I make it without throwing up on the bloke beside me. I'm clutching the air-sickness bag on standby. We glimpse the runway ahead. It sits on a peninsula thrust out into the San Francisco Bay. We approach over the water, and quickly the runway meets the wheels with the familiar squeal; we all lunge forward as the air brakes are flipped up, and the low seatbelt bites hard into our bellies. The brakes do their job, and the plane slows down to a reasonable taxiing speed. A quick turn off the runway, and we are heading to the terminal.

After the usual rigmarole at baggage claim, a tidy fellow in a suit greets us with a striking Californian neon grin. Under the smile, he holds a sign that reads 'Echo Tour'. Gathering around with trolleys full of cases and guitars, we are led, as usual, to a couple of vans waiting outside.

It is a short ride, and soon we will be on the city's outskirts. San Francisco's buildings are a mix of old and new. The old ones are from the Victorian and Edwardian periods. The new ones are from *Star Trek* – possibly early Rigel VII. Decorative townhouses rest on ridiculously steep streets. High steps lead to heavy doors at the centre of large bay windows, coated in colours from the pastel palette. The houses have carved patterned barge boards and gables adorned with all styles of wooden finials, like fingers pointing at the sky. Some have glazed turrets pinned to their sides. They are well built, but there is always the fear that an earthquake could soon turn them into matchwood. Row after row of these houses are incredibly gorgeous.

As we climb the steep hills, we see that the bay dominates the city, and across the bay, more hills fade off into the distance, all heaved up by the fidgety fault lines that run deep under California. The wind steadily propels a damp chilling vapour into the lower streets as the Golden Gate Bridge, striding across the bay, is lost in the mist. Fog horns blurt a mournful cry over shark-infested waters that the now disused and rotting Alcatraz Federal Penitentiary bathes in.

In our downtime, Jake and I decided to track down the Residents. I have been a fan of the Residents since I first heard them on the BBC John Peel show. It must have been in 1977. I have been buying records via mail order from the band for a few years; hence I know that their studio and HQ are at 444 Grove Street. Like some trainee stalkers, we get in a taxi and set off.

The building is brick with roller shutters. It looks like a regular place, nothing weird about the exterior. What was I expecting? An avant-garde eyeball structure? Well, yes, I was.

I knock on the door, and it opens. Slightly awkwardly, I say, 'Hi, we are Residents fans from England.'

The guy is possibly a member of the Residents; we will never know.

'Oh, OK, cool, you can come in then.'

We enter through a corridor, off which there are a couple of offices with people doing office-like things. The guy that let us in says, 'Do you want a tour to have a look around?'

We both reply like two star-struck girls outside Donny Osmond's stage door: 'Yes, that would be great.'

The two most famous things about the Residents are that nobody knows who the band members are and they wear eyeball heads to conceal their identity. Rumours circulate that they have something to do with the Beatles or have other well-known group members. I've even heard the ridiculous suggestion that I am in the Residents.

I find the whole theory of obscurity a fascinating concept. They are true artists. The art is what matters, not the personalities behind the art, though, somehow, a big personality shines through, and the videos and performances carry that. We are led down into the inner sanctum of the band. The corridors are

Me as a Resident

far from ordinary: they are lined with black plastic bin liners. We are shown a large industrial racking area with all the Residents' records neatly stacked up and ready to be shipped to all corners of the globe.

The Residents guy leads us down another corridor with black plastic pinned to the walls. We emerge in another space in the complex. He points to a darker area and says, 'This is where the videos are made.'

We are overwhelmed and quiet; we don't ask any questions. I am full of questions, but it seems so secretive that they could not or would not answer them anyway. He takes us into the studio, and we are surrounded by a jumble of tape recorders and odd bits of equipment; it's nothing like a studio I've been in before. It's small, and the sound equipment is stacked on shelves that fill the walls. The guy showing us around leaves us to nose about. Then we hear a small commotion down the end of the corridor.

'Get them out of there; you know they don't like anyone going in the studio.'

Our poke around this legendary place is cut short. We are left in a side office. An old picture of a girl in a circular frame is on the wall. I recognise it from the 'Perfect Love' video. Also in the room is one of the famous eyeball heads. When our chaperone leaves for a moment to get us water, I point at the head and whisper to Jake, 'Quick, Jake, while he's not looking.'

Jake instantly knows what I'm up to and takes my Kodak Instamatic as I put the eyeball head on. Jake clicks the shutter for a quick snap. I quickly remove the eyeball, and we make out as if nothing has happened. I'm sure they would have said no if I had asked to try on the eyeball head. They were freaked out enough by us looking at a few tape recorders unsupervised. To a Residents nutjob like me, it's like slapping on a bit of magnolia emulsion with Picasso's favourite paintbrush or pointing at someone with Ken Dodd's tickling stick and saying, 'What a lovely day, missus, for sitting on the bog in Elvis's jumpsuit.'

We tell the people there we are playing at the Old Waldorf. They have never heard of the band. No surprise – we are brand-new to the Yanks. We offer to put them on the guest list, but all are reluctant to give us their names. This makes me think the blokes we meet are a couple of the elusive members of the Residents. We will never know. One thing for sure, none of them was one of the remaining three Beatles.

So, we are playing at the Old Waldorf on Battery Street. It sounds fancier than it is. That's just how I like gigs. I want a bit of scuzziness. I can't be doing with punters confined to seats and ushers taking on the role of Hitler's henchmen and preventing anyone from moving. In my opinion, we are not the sort of band that should be playing in seated places, and even though the Old Waldorf sounds like it will be seated, it isn't.

The stage is relatively low and has been home to many new bands from the post-punk musical landscape. The San Francisco crowd are open-minded and not in the slightest bit self-conscious; they like a good old-fashioned freak-out, and we are trying our best to provide one. The West Coast is so different to the East that they are essentially two separate countries: the hurried East and the mellow West. It must be the weather; everyone cheers up in the sun. Well, they do in England, anyway. If the sun comes out, so do the smiles and helpful shop assis-tants. I like both sides of the country and the people. I like the straightforward approach myself, as well as the shiny-happy types. It is just what comes over as fake that I don't like. The overly friendly people we meet, the ones at the record label, are trying to get us to do what I consider uncool. I am on my guard against them. I think we all are, not just me. We come across as difficult and complex, and this is probably deliberate. It's stupid,

I genuinely am excited to be in America, but the hipster chip in my brain won't let me embrace the atmosphere that comes with it.

Over the years of going back and forth to America, I have become used to the ways of Americans. I have many American mates. I like the place and even miss it when we don't return for a while. I've even started going to America on holiday.

It's at least a five-hour drive to LA, and we have a gig the next day. The road eventually brings us to Sunset Boulevard; I am impressed by massive billboards that ride high above the traffic on spotlight-illuminated heavy metal structures. There is traffic everywhere but no people walking anywhere. The bright sunlight makes everything glow. It all looks too perfect in the sunshine, transient and fake. Like a film set, but that could be because it has been the backdrop to numerous films.

We have three days at the Whisky a Go Go. This is where the Doors kicked off and worked as the house band. To my way of thinking, it was like their version of the Beatles' intense stint in Hamburg. They will have improved by playing many nights and honing their sound, stage presence and passion. They improvise the infamous Oedipus complex section in the song 'The End' at the Whisky. Bewildered go-go dancers in cages try and frug out as Morrison's cries, 'Father, I want to kill you, Mother, I want to fuck you.' Rude.

We do five gigs, including two matinees for all ages. The age to get into a bar in the States is twenty-one. Everyone has to show ID with no exceptions, including us. These strict doormen have surely been trained by the same mob that does the borders and the airports. We always carry our passports for this purpose. If you forget the passport, it is back in a taxi to the hotel to retrieve it. Generally, it only happens once per person per tour.

We check into the legendary Tropicana Motel on Santa Monica Boulevard. We are told Iggy Pop lives in the motel, but though we are most vigilant, we never spot Mr Pop. Many rockers have lived or stayed there, including my youthful favourite Led Zeppelin; Tom Waits had a permanent base there and was often seen using the payphone by the motel's adjoining diner. Tom had bailed in 1979, so we've just missed him. Pity, Pete is a big fan. I'm sure they would have got on like a house on fire. I can imagine the two of them sinking bourbon and chatting till dusk.

Most mornings of this stint in LA, we would congregate in Duke's diner adjoining the motel. After eggs over easy, hash browns and myriad other fried items, similar to but not quite as good as a full English, we would head off to Melrose Avenue, the road with all the groovy shops. We walk there, even though no one walks in LA, even on Melrose; they drive up and down to the shops they want to visit. You can always tell the English in LA: they are the ones who are walking up and down the baking-hot roads. The only other people walking up and down the boulevards in LA are the homeless and the deranged. It's a real mad dogs and Englishmen scene.

Our patch in LA is limited to Sunset Strip, Santa Monica Boulevard and Melrose Avenue. We never really stray outside of these areas. We go to the Rainbow Rooms on Sunset for a drink. I am so up my own arse I leave because some of Rod Stewart's gang are in there.

God, I was turning into a right prick. I like the Faces and Rod's early work, but I was so tied up in the quest to kick out

Pete, Les and Harry, USA tour, 1981

all the old-school bands that I was bothered by his recent rather naff output; what a div.

We have a few nights in Barney's Beanery where Les shows the locals how to play pool by whipping the asses of all comers. Just around the corner from Barney's is the Alta Cienega motel. This is where Jim Morrison was holed up for a while; I make a short pilgrimage to gawp at his doorway, number 32. God knows why; it's just a stupid fan thing to do.

A few years later, Jake, Les and I go and gawp at where Jim is permanently holed up now: his grave in Père Lachaise Cemetery in Paris. We forewent the moronic practice of leaving some shit like a beer bottle or, the latest thing, sticking chewing gum to a tree; so bizarre. Around the corner, Oscar Wilde's gaff is adorned with lipstick kisses. Very unhygienic, I reckon.

We are enjoying our stay at the Tropicana. It's nice to be in one place for more than a day. The kidney pool is in the centre of the horseshoe-shaped motel, with rooms flanking the pool, and there are chairs and tables for hanging around in a jungle of tropical gardens. Palm and banana trees fit in well with its Tropicana name. The Tropicana has a reputation for not being very clean, and legend has it that the pool was painted black so the dirt wouldn't show. I don't notice much muck – it looks acceptable to me. Les and I have ground-floor rooms with doors that open onto the pool area. The sun is cracking the flags; the sky never changes until dusk creeps up and darkness quickly descends. It's like someone has turned down the dimmers. Then the motel becomes a much-altered place; it attracts a unique set of passers-by, junkies, hookers and random crazies. They are probably all there in the daytime, too, but as it tends to do, the darkness adds a new level of threat that is not present in the blazing sunshine. And you become aware of things going on in the shadows.

There has been no shortage of casualties of the Hollywood fame game. California dreamers, youthful starlets and people who came to live a fantasy become old or used up and end up in a nightmare. We constantly see women and men past their sell-by date, now with too much makeup and too much surgery, strutting up and down the aisles of Thrifty, still believing they will be spotted, land a significant part and become famous.

It's all about fame. This fame stuff is unpleasantly addictive. I have always tried my best to avoid it. Am I getting caught up? After all, here I am writing a memoir shouting out, 'Oi! Look at me; I'm over here; don't forget me; look what I've done.'

We are invited onto a radio show, *Rodney on the ROQ*. The radio station is called KROQ, and Rodney Bingenheimer has been playing the Bunnymen records for a couple of years. We learn that Rodney is a fan of all English music; in the seventies, he had a discothèque called Rodney Bingenheimer's English Disco, which was a very trendy hangout. It became a glam-rock destination and Rodney was host to all the visiting British groovers such as Marc Bolan and David Bowie, to name but two.

Rodney is a slight fellow, quiet and kind of a bit kookie. But when the on-air light flicks on, he comes alive and is brimming with confidence. Rodney has done his research, and he knows it's no secret that the New York band Television is one of my favourites and has influenced me. After the interview on KROQ, he presents me with Television's first single on the little record label Ork, 'Little Johnny Jewel'.

Rodney tells me, 'I have two copies and thought you might like one; there are only a few hundred.'

It's a record I will treasure for all my life.

At one of the shows at the Whisky, we are all in the graffitied and battered dressing room. Will bands ever get fed up of drawing cocks on dressing-room walls? It's that weird no-man's-land period after the soundcheck but before the gig. The usual apprehension is in the air, and tension crackles about the sparse dressing room. I have a hollow feeling in my stomach. The churning is saying let's get on with it. There comes a knock on the door. In comes a tall, side-parted, fair-haired bloke in glasses. Mac is lying on the floor with a white towel around his head. He has washed his hair; this is all part of his spiked hairstyle ritual. The resulting barnet would make David Bowie jealous. He would surely have given his left bollock, the one that occasionally popped out of the kabuki theatre one-legged jumpsuit, to achieve that spikey-top look.

The tall bloke bends down and offers his hand in the traditional gesture of shaking hands. Mac glances up at him and he continues to lie there.

The tall bloke says, 'Hi, Ray Manzarek from the Doors.'

Mac remains on the deck and glances up at Ray again.

Ray follows with, 'Hey, man, that's OK. Don't get up.'

I'm unsure if Ray is being sarcastic because Mac has given no indication that he would get up anyway.

Now realising who this is, Mac then says, 'Oh yeah, er . . . Will likes you a lot.'

With a wave of his slender hand, like he is dismissing one of his minions, Mac gestures towards me on the other side of the room. I knew exactly who it was as soon as he entered the room. It's all a bit awkward, so I offer Ray a beer, which he takes.

He hangs around for a stilted moment or two and then eventually says, 'OK, I'll leave you guys to get ready. Have a great show.'

And with that, Ray leaves the room. It seems that word had got back to Ray that we are a little bit like the Doors, and he wanted to check us out. It must be Mac's low voice or Les's bass lines because I sure as hell can't play as well as the Doors guitarist Robby Krieger.

A year or so later, Ray was suggested by the label as a possible producer for the next record, but nothing came of it. We eventually worked with Ray on the Doors song 'People Are Strange' for the *Lost Boys* soundtrack a few years later. We all find Ray to be a brilliant fella, so laid-back, so mellow. To hang with him is a joy. Mac becomes very friendly with him and even introduces him to the delights of a pint of mild. Ray seems to get a taste for it and takes to this particularly northern beer like a duck to water, or perhaps he was just being polite.

CHAPTER 23

Tony the Truck in Hibernation

'Holidays in the Sun' – Sex Pistols

Pete, Les and the crew get into camouflage chic

We landed back in England, back to Melling, back to my tiny bed in my freezing bedroom. The house is as grim as ever. The eye-opening tour of the USA and being away from home for a time have expanded my world and mind. The village feels so small now. And this has got me thinking about moving out of 15 Station

Road. I have now turned twenty-three, and I could do with some space. My friend Paul Simpson has had a flat for ages, and he manages it. Why not me? I won't be in Melling for long this time anyway; we have a UK and European tour starting very soon.

It seems assassination season is upon us in 1981. In the USA in March, President Ronald Reagan was shot and wounded by some nutter obsessed with the film *Taxi Driver* and determined to impress the young actress Jodie Foster by, er, killing the president; it used to be a box of Milk Tray and maybe some flowers from the garage forecourt in my day. He was convinced the Travis Bickle approach was the sure way to a lesbian's heart; however, I'm not sure he knew that part of the story. Poor sod was on a hiding to nothing from the get-go. Then six weeks later someone tried to assassinate John Paul II, and an ex-monk hijacked an Aer Lingus flight from Dublin to London because he wanted to find out everything the Virgin Mary told some kiddies in Fatima back in 1917.

Things were a bit weird in 1981.

Meanwhile, we are up and down the country on tour. We are visiting all the usual places, including the Liverpool Empire. This place is the poshest venue that Liverpool has to offer. I have seen many bands there, including Queen, Pink Floyd, Dr Feelgood, 10cc, Emerson, Lake and Palmer, Roxy Music, Nazareth, Genesis, the Sensational Alex Harvey Band – all before punk rock, of course. If you were into music, this is who we all followed. So please don't deny it. I have no shame or regret about this.

I would prefer to play someplace other than the Empire, not because Nazareth wigged out there, but because, as I've mentioned, I don't like playing in places with seats. In short, it's a pretty shit vibe from the stage. I have come to rock and not to make you feel comfortable in your plush padded armchair, sucking on overpriced wine gums. We only play a few seated venues on this tour. That's a bonus to me.

The tour kicks off at Rock City in Nottingham. It's a great venue, friendly and scuzzy, how I like them. We are bringing the Blue Orchids on tour with us this time. This is Martin Bramah and Una Baines's new band. Both Martin and Una were in the Fall and we are all big Fall fans, so we're trying to help them somehow. I'm not sure the tour does much for them, however.

Being a support act is difficult, and only sometimes does it get you on to the next rung of the slippery ladder. We had supported the Fall a couple of times. Once Pete de Freitas had joined, we decided not to do any more support slots, even if it meant carrying on in smaller venues for a time. We wanted them to be our gigs and thought being a support band would depreciate our power somehow.

I would watch how Martin Bramah played with his high-toned scratchy, spiky and sparkling melodies. Along with Tom Verlaine and Richard Lloyd from Television, Martin significantly influenced me when I first tried to learn guitar. I would always have the Telecaster's pickup selector on the bridge pickup. And in the studio, it took much pushing for me to alter this setup. Mark E. Smith wasn't the only significant member of the Fall, not by a long chalk; Martin was just as important to us as fans. Mark E. himself may have disagreed. Over the years, Smith's tyranny grew more robust, and his curmudgeonly persona was good for column inches in the music press. So many members came and went that it was hard to keep up. As the frontman and the one constant element, he became the Fall. Like he famously said, 'If it's me and your Granny on bongos, it's the Fall.'

As fans, we all loved the weird shit that Smith pulled on stage, but it was easy for us from a distance; we weren't in the Fall, so we weren't dealing with him sacking members mid-gig and wandering around the stage while showing no interest to the crowd. I remember when my mate Steve saw the Fall in Liverpool, Smith did the whole gig with his back to the audience while retrieving beer cans from a plastic carrier bag. I would have loved to have witnessed that act of defiance. He was forever fucking around with the settings on the band's amplifiers. If anyone had tried that shit in the Bunnymen, he would have been decked. Mark was a great and genuinely eccentric frontman, that is for sure. It seems he wilfully had no designs on pop stardom. The notion of it is ridiculous. This coloured my way of thinking as well. I was in a constant battle, squaring things I thought were cheesy with my desire for the band to get a more significant following.

We have a sleeper coach now; it's a top-notch state-of-the-art converted Magical Mystery Tour-style coach, with an area for beds at the back and seats at the front. Essential kettle, fridge and microwave. We've also acquired an articulated lorry to carry our

Pete, Big Bill Drummond and Les on the bus

massive PA equipment and lighting rig. Our truck driver is called Tony; this becomes shortened to, er . . . Tony the Truck. And the word is that he is a Hells Angel. He undeniably looks the part. A large chap, he has those Charles Manson eyes poking out from a face forested with a whopping black bushy beard; he could easily be a cult leader or part-time guru. He has a curious taste in booze: Calvados. It's apple brandy. I've never heard of it before; not much call for it in the BICC social club in Melling, but it is guaranteed to get you out of your mind. If I went anywhere near a couple of those, I'd be genuinely smashed up. Plus, to top it off, he has a tidy heroin habit.

On the UK leg of the tour, on the way to Scotland, we are happily trundling up the piss-wet A1 when, through the rain-soaked bus window, we spot what looks like Tony's truck parked up in a layby.

'No, it can't be, can it?'

We nervously laugh at this even though he's supposed to be in Edinburgh much earlier, so the humpers and the crew can unload and get set up. We pull into the layby and climb the steps to Tony's cab. He is uncomfortably slumped in the driver's seat.

'Tony! Tony!'

The rain is not helping us see through the windows; it's hard to tell if he's even breathing.

We are shouting and banging on the locked truck door. Nothing. Oh shit. We are now starting to have the idea that he may be dead. The laughing at this latest lark has stopped, and we are now increasingly worried. Les tries to open the passenger door. It opens, and he clambers in.

Les shouts out, 'He's OK; he's snoring.'

Les gives him a good shake and slowly, like a massive black bear coming out of hibernation, Tony opens his eyes and gives us his trademark menacing smile.

'Fuck, Tony, we thought you were dead.'

Tony comes back with, 'Was just having a kip, no problem.'

There is a problem. Time is a problem. The gig should all be set up by now. No one is prepared to have a go at him; he's a big unit. After a coffee brewed in the tour bus galley, we get back on the road. Keeping an eye on him, we drive convoy style. It's tight, but the crew work like crazy and the gig is fine. We manage to stick to the old showbiz saying . . . 'The show must go on!'

We finish the UK leg on 9 May 1981 at the Hammersmith Odeon – it's a shame because it's another seated venue. The American tour has boosted Mac's confidence; he does his best to get the crowd on their feet, inviting them down to the front to the dismay of the bouncers, and by the end, the place is rocking, so we finish on a high.

Next on the ever-lengthening agenda is the European leg of the tour, starting in Brussels. We pick up our old Belgique friends, Annik Honoré and Bert Bertrand, who travel with us for a few of the shows. We go into Holland, with the flatter-than-a-billiard-table panorama of the lowlands sliced by canals, dams, dikes and ditches. You can see for miles, well kilometres (when in Rome and all that). The tallest things on the horizon are windmills, some still used to pump out the water from the land and back into the sea. It's been nice having Annik and Bert with us. Annik tells us more about Jacques Brel, and Bert teaches me to say some antiquated French sayings such as 'Mon brave homme' and 'Nom d'une pipe!', which are like coming out with 'Cor blimey' or

'Flipping heck.' I suppose you had to be there, but it cracked him up when I would use it in shops or restaurants. Annik bails out after our final Dutch show in Nijmegen and returns to Brussels on the train. Burt stays with us all the way to Italy. He is constantly writing in his journal. Bert has the tiniest and neatest writing I have ever clapped my eyes on. I would have loved to know what he was putting in his diary. We would have to get it translated and probably have to use a magnifying glass to read it.

At the beginning of June 1981, it's our first time in the Scandinavian countries, Stockholm in Sweden, and then Norway, with Fredrikstad, Skien and Oslo all lined up in Norway. (Online, there are many contradictions about the exact tour dates, and sometimes we are logged down as being in two cities on the same day. Nice trick if you can pull it off.)

After the Stockholm gig, we are soon on the bus and are ready to drive through the night as usual. It is not too long till we are out of the city and we set off to the west, winding through the pitch-black Swedish countryside. After a few hours in the bunk, I am up early and sitting up at the front with Ted, the driver. We have just crossed the Norwegian border. It's getting towards dawn, and there is one of those soft summer mists hanging above the fields. One of the best things about touring is watching from the bus windows as strange lands drift past. From my front seat, I have a panoramic view through the huge windscreen. We crawl past distant red-painted barns and whitewashed wooden houses. The roads are unlit and tiny; they wind the way through the hills. A window is open and the draught holds that lovely early morning chill; the air is fresher here. Farms and houses are sparsely dotted about. I'm taking it all in, all the rolling hills and . . . I'll resist saying the Norwegian wood. It's more like the Norwegian forest. The scenery is exceptionally verdant; the farmlands are almost too lush for my brain to handle.

As the light increases, we pass a field of green corn. Tall, healthy stalks rise up motionless, and then, suddenly, my eye is drawn to some movement, a wave in the stillness of the corn. A moose is lolloping across the field like it owns the place, and I suppose it does. The mist shrouds the creature's head. I had never seen a moose before, not even in a zoo. The moose is one of the weirdest critters I have ever seen. It is massive for a start. It is well over six feet at the shoulder. Add that crazy elongated head with the velvet tangle of antlers plonked on top, and it is getting on for eight feet tall. I will always remember the sight of him as he nonchalantly tore his way through the corn.

We turn up in the Norwegian town of Fredrikstad for a gig in a little hall, possibly a church hall. I'm not sure how it got booked. Big Bill is in charge of booking the gigs, so we just go where we are told. The place is small, really small. We arrive with a coach and a mammoth articulated lorry packed with equipment. It can hardly get through the narrow lanes of Fredrikstad.

We go into the venue, but there is no way the PA will fit in there. Well, not with an audience as well, at any rate. It looks like we won't be able to do the gig. Too much stuff, too many complications. A young kid has booked the gig. He is tall, as lots of them are over in Scandinavia for some reason. (I can't remember his name, so I'll call him Olaf the Lofty after the tall court inventor from *Noggin the Nog*.) Olaf is looking worried and a bit out of his depth. We want to do the gig; we hate cancelling gigs. It's not fair to people that have bought tickets, and to come all that way not to do a gig is beyond moronic. But just one of the massive speaker cabinets our soundman Harry has built would fill most of the place up. Then Harry has an idea: we can use the much smaller foldback speakers as a PA for the gig. It's a good idea. I will just use one amp and a few effects pedals. Harry, Jake and Butter-Free Dave all swing into action and start to get the stripped-down version of the equipment in.

At eight o'clock, the hall is packed out with probably only about one hundred kids. There isn't much of a stage, and we're on the same level as the punters, but it all works out well. We do the gig and everybody is happy – especially Olaf the Lofty, the young Norwegian music fan who's laid it on.

'You must come for breakfast in the morning to my mum's house,' says Olaf.

The next morning, it's getting on for 8 a.m. and the rest of the band are still asleep in the coach. I'm up and having a cuppa when a knock comes on the door. It is Olaf from the gig. Dazed and confused, we start to emerge from the bus. Olaf leads us past colourful wooden houses and a boatbuilder's yard. It looks like we are in a fishing village on the river. We arrive at the very neat house of the young promoter's mum. It has that clean Scandinavian look that is all the go nowadays. Olaf's ma has really pushed the longboat out. She has laid on a really good feast of eggs, ham and various breads, sliced meats, cheeses and buns.

It was so nice to have a glimpse into a Norwegian home. It was a small thing, but it is one that has stuck with me. It made the difficulties of the gig with only half of our usual stuff even more special.

★ ★ ★

We are supposed to have a day off during this little Scandinavian jaunt. Truthfully, when we are on tour, I don't like days off. I would prefer to be playing a gig. I am looking forward to having the night off, though, because we are in a new and interesting place. On most of our days off, we are parked up in dumps by the side of a road out of the towns or in the middle of nowhere. It's not easy to park a bus anywhere.

We have all been looking forward to a day off. And I am set on exploring, going out on the town, getting smashed up, etc. Back in London, the Korova label is getting ready to release the single 'A Promise', taken from the *Heaven Up Here* album, but we need a B-side fast so, suddenly, the day off and scooting around Norway on the lash is just another faded dream. Big Bill has somehow found a studio about sixty miles from Oslo in a place called Tistedal.

Our coach driver, Ted, has been christened Turn Around Ted for his uncanny knack for overshooting the gig venues and heading down the wrong roads, getting stuck in the city-centre one-way systems and squeezing down alleyways that are only suitable for a donkey cart to get through. We are forever backing out of tight spots, holding up traffic while irate locals have their hatred of the English validated. When we get to the studio, it's down a steep gravel path, and there is no way our coach driver is going down there in his bus. Even Turn Around Ted knows that's a non-starter.

'You have got no chance. I'll never get out again on that gravel stuff.'

He parks his coach high on the main road.

The engineer from the Tistedal studio, Claes Neeb, is expecting us and drags a trolley up to the coach. We start with much slipping and sliding to ferry the equipment down the gravel slope and into the studio. It's a job to keep the amps and drums from falling off the trolley, it's so sheer. We set up the equipment, and Claes mics everything up. We have nothing planned, and we are just going to wing it. I have a magical little device called an EBow. It creates a magnetic pulse that vibrates the guitar's strings when it's positioned correctly, using the adjacent strings as little tracks for the gizmo to run on. It's half electronic wizardry and half real wizardry. The notes can be played indefinitely or at least till the battery runs out. If you have heard 'Heroes' by David Bowie, you have heard an EBow in action as Robert Fripp uses one on that track.

Les pipes up, 'Eh, Will, can I have a go on the EBow?'

'Sure.'

At first, Les has some difficulty keeping the EBow in place. The strings are too wide apart to rest the EBow comfortably in the correct position, but he soon gets the hang of hovering it over the much thicker bass strings. The EBow vibrates the bass notes and has a deep cello-like quality. Les starts to create a circular pattern of notes. Pete sticks mainly to the bass drum with occasional incendiary snare bursts. Our collective instincts kick in and, out of nowhere, the song, which will be called 'Broke My Neck', is starting to become something. It's more experimental than a chart-bothering pop hit. Mac and I play off each other in a stabbing rhythmic battle. Pete builds up the drums. It's time for me to go full-on asymmetric Andy Gill from the Gang of Four. Once the backing track is done, Mac enters the vocal booth and adds the lyrics he's been magically conjuring up.

I liked doing B-sides like this, going into the studio and seeing what happens. There was no pressure to make a commercial tune or even stick to a conventional song format or anything like that. We could be as experimental as we liked. The label was not interested in the B-sides; understandably, it was all about the A-sides for them. At that time, working in the studio was my favourite part of being in a band; to be fair, most elements of band life are brilliant, and playing live is the greatest buzz you can have. It is the best job in the world as long as the personalities are all gelling and have a common purpose.

We keep advancing: now on to Berlin. Back on the transit corridor, which has the same weird vibe as the first time without the snow. And this time, the vehicle is not spinning around on the icy autobahn, and there's no acid-tripping fun that formed a prominent part of our previous Berlin escapade.

After the gig, Les and I are cooling off at the end of an alley at the side of the Kant Kino. We are chatting with a lad from Manchester, Mark Reeder, and his mate Alistair Gray, both from the band Die Unbekannten. Mark came to Berlin in 1978 looking to buy records and liked it; he befriended some squatters, so he stayed. It was that simple. It's strange to hear his Manchester accent in Berlin while the city is still the front line in the Cold War.

All of a sudden, out of nowhere, a skinny German appears. He is wearing a battered brown leather jacket and light military-style trousers, his blond hair is thinning, and his side parting is not quite what you would call a comb-over, but it is doing an excellent job at hiding the bald part of his bonce. He's a good ten to fifteen years our senior. He is very drunk and is unstable on his feet. He is thrusting a tin of lager at Alistair and telling him to drink.

Mark Reeder, Manchester boy in Berlin

'Trinken, trinken.'

Not knowing how to react, Les and I are just looking at this bloke; we assume he has been at the gig. Alistair is getting pissed off, and we are all giving him the *We wish you would fuck off, pal* look.

'Were you at the gig, mate?' says Alistair.

His head is swaying around, and the eyes in his head are wobbling around. 'Trinken, trinken.'

Alistair was getting more cheesed off now and tells him, 'Ich will keinen Drink.'

This bloke is proper out of it.

We go back to chatting, hoping the drunk fellow will get the message and just fuck off. But he is still insisting Alistair drink the lager, at which point Alistair tells him to fuck right off in German.

'Verpiss dich.'

He doesn't, as requested, fuck off. He stays put, reaches into his leather jacket and pulls out an old revolver. This isn't a Luger, as one would expect a random crazy to be brandishing in post-war Germany. In my opinion, the Luger is the best-looking wartime handgun. It was the star of many wartime films and espionage TV shows, so when we were kids playing war, the toy Luger was the gun me and my junior schoolmates coveted the most (along with the Johnny Seven toy machine gun).

This thing the drunkard clutches has a dirty wooden handle. The gun itself is relatively small and looks a bit knackered, and the gunmetal is marked with scratches, scuffs and dents; the ancient pistol seems to have seen some action, probably in the war years. His head is swaying, his eyes are rolling, and now he is holding a gun. Small or not, I don't fancy having another hole drilled through my body. He is randomly waving it around and then points it at Alistair and tries once more to get him to drink the lager. God knows why. He starts to rant in German about something; we have no clue what he is going on about, and the increasingly erratic gun movements are making me even more nervous.

Les just happens to have a bottle of red wine in his coat pocket. He offers the wine to the guy, who promptly puts the gun back in his pocket and takes the wine. The imminent threat of death by drunken gunman is swerved.

'Les, come on, let's go.'

Me and Mark waste no time heading down the alley and back into the safety of the gig venue, but Les doesn't seem to think there's any rush, and Alistair isn't the slightest bit arsed. He must have encountered this sort of thing before in Berlin. It is a frontier town, after all. They take their time and eventually trot back into the venue as cool as a pair of cucumbers straight out of the ice box.

Mark was good friends with Joy Division and promoted their show at Kant Kino in January 1980. He's been in Berlin long enough to know his way around and often visits the East, telling us that we could go to Friedrichstraße station and get a day visa to visit East Berlin. We have already climbed one or two wooden viewing platforms dotted along the Wall, and peered over into the killing zones. We've seen the guards on the other side watching us through binoculars from their watchtowers, and seen them patrolling the fences. East Berlin seems so weird and intriguing that we really want to go and have a look.

We have a rare day off so, the next day, Jake and I are up early to get the train to the checkpoint; it is only a couple of stops, no distance at all. We rattle past dimly lit *Geisterbahnhöfe* – the ghost

A Berlin wall (not that one). Still wrecked by WWII, 1981

stations. These are the unfortunate stations that happen to lie beneath the wall's footprint area called the death strip. Above are attack dogs and killing zones, and the SM-70 anti-personnel mines – the self-killing machines – are positioned at various vantage points. They are triggered via tripwires, ready to spray a wide arc of shrapnel designed to kill or maim anyone trying to get across the Wall, otherwise known by the East German spin doctors' snappy tag of the *Antifaschistischer Shutzwall* (Anti-Fascist Protection Rampart).

We arrive at the station and head to the checkpoint. It is a wooden-sided box painted in a nasty cream gloss. There is no queue, and we are the only people trying to get into East Berlin. Everywhere is dull and foreboding, including the uniformed sentry in the box. There is a glass panel with a small opening on the countertop to slide documents and cash under. The guard in his sage-grey uniform sits high on a stool behind the glass. We have to pay a few Deutschmarks for the visa, and we are also obliged to change at least twenty-five Deutschmarks into East German DDR marks before we are allowed to go in. The passport is stamped, and we are free to enter the East.

We emerge into a very different Berlin. It is quiet, hushed. We can see the futurist East Berlin TV tower with the metallic ball structure rising above the old, battered buildings like a giant pin. The buildings are war weary, with bits blasted off by Soviet tanks and still needing repair. It looks like not much has changed since Adolf and Eva's wedding day. We have no map, so we just wander about. There seem to be no shops or at least no signs of shops but, eventually, we see a bookshop. Just then, a red Ferrari appears on the cobbled street. A Russian general gets out and he dons his distinctive peaked cap with a broad red band; a beautiful girl in a fur coat is with him. They head towards the bookshop but keep walking past. It's a strange sight among the little Trabants and Ladas. Yes, some are definitely more equal than others here.

The bookshop is very old-fashioned, but they do have some interesting items. I buy a cast-iron statue of Lenin as a seventeen-year-old boy. I also fork out a few pfennigs for a bust of the older hairless revolutionary that we all recognise. We purchase some Soviet-style posters, too.

Then I hit the mother lode. In a record rack, among the stacks of Red Army choir records, revolutionary operas and balalaika music, there are a few Western records: compilations of the Doors, Rolling Stones, Led Zeppelin and David Bowie, all on the Soviet state record label Melodiya. It looks to me like they are from a box set that has been split up, as they are all numbered. Led Zeppelin is number six, and Bowie is number ten. To buy this Soviet vinyl booty, it's a complicated affair of picking what you want and then being issued a ticket to take to the cashier; after payment, you are issued another receipt and then head back to the counter to present the proof of payment, by which time the items have been wrapped and bagged up ready.

They cost very little, and with paper carrier bags clutched, we are soon out of there and back pottering around the streets. We stumble upon a café attached to the state opera house. This is the Operncafé on the wide Unter den Linden; we head in and sit down. It's an impressive building, but the once-plush interior looks a little shabby. A band is playing in the corner: drums, bass, guitar and accordion. They are pretty bad, and me and Jake have to stifle laughs as we listen. We are no virtuosos, but this lot sound like they have just been selected randomly, whether they could play anything or not.

'You on accordion, you can be bass, you are on guitar.'

'But comrade, I can't play the guitar.'

'OK, salt mines then.'

'Oh, did you say guitar? Sorry, comrade, I misheard; yes, I can play the guitar very well and have been playing since I was a little boy.'

'Next, drums.'

All the hands go up.

We order some food. Jake has a vague idea that he recognises the word for egg, *ei*, so we order what we think might be egg sandwiches. He's hit the jackpot, and our boiled egg mixed with salad cream is pretty good too. We have coffee; I would not risk the teapot in this place.

After all this excitement, we head back to the station. We have hardly used up any of the DDR marks and, on the way out, we give the ones we have left to the East German border guard. He says nothing and sticks to the customary blank expression.

CHAPTER 24

Michelangelo's *David*
Waiting for the Bus

Easy Rider soundtrack – Steppenwolf et al.

Me wearing a Residents Ralph Records T-shirt in Florence

Our epic European tour continues on, and on we go. We travel through Switzerland, then France, including gigs in Lyon, Paris and Clermont-Ferrand, which stands out partly because of the town's smell. No, not French onion soup, duck a l'orange or Chanel No. 5. This is where Michelin tyres are manufactured. A vast factory belches a distinct whiff of rubber into the air. It's like France's version of Akron, Ohio, in the United States, aka Rubber City. I only know this because of *The Akron Compilation* released in 1978 on Stiff Records, complete with a scratch-and-sniff sleeve. Who said collecting records isn't educational? Akron was the home of sci-fi mutant boogie boys Devo, who had become the biggest band to come from Akron. So, like record companies worldwide, Stiff go on the sniff for more Devos, way after the horse has bolted. The Stiffs do come home with a reasonable compilation of bands from the city, though.

Back in Clermont-Ferrand, we are on our way out of the town. It's been a hot day. We hope for some relief to be delivered by the cool night air. The sun sinks below the horizon, but the temperature drop does not arrive. The summer sun has concentrated heat on the dead centre of France. Inside the bus, it is unbearably hot. Air conditioning? It is an English bus; forget it. Not in those days, non-existent. The night is just as hot as the day. We must stop so our driver, Turn Around Ted, can catch up on his sleep. We will be off on the long road to Italy in the morning. We have gigs in Milan, Florence and Naples. After a short drive, Ted swings the bus into the hills, and we have been swallowed up by a densely wooded area. Ted has found a secluded woodland track just off the road. Inside the bus, we are all doing what Brits do best: moaning about the heat.

'Fucking hell, I can't stand this.'

Jake decides to sleep outside the bus. He gets the mattress from his bunk and lays it on the floor close to the bus. Me, Les, Kit the artist, Butter-Free Dave and Pete all think this looks fun, and we decide to do the same. The ground is thick with leaves and pine needles, giving the mattresses an added level of comfort that the bus lacks. We sleep in the open air with mattresses lined up beside each other, all snoring away like sleepy sardines. I dream of a family of brown bears ridden by mischievous garden gnomes, you know, the little chaps that sit still by ponds until you are not looking. As soon as your back is turned, they get up to all kinds of evil shenanigans. The bears emerge from the French fairy-tale woodland. Curiously they come, a-sniffing and a-snuffling. The bears are confused by this line of sleeping humans. They don't like it, and they become scared as this is an unusual scenario for the woods. Now unsettled, it's time to quietly flee back into the trees, back to the safety of the caressing darkness of the forest. This is not a trip; it is just a really good dream.

The following day, we awake with dew-wet faces and a chill that can only be cured with cups of piping hot tea and buttered toast with lashings of Marmite from the bus's galley.

Meanwhile, in London, Bill Butt has teamed up with Martyn Atkins, our record-sleeve designer. They are pulling on leather pants and jackets, helmets, boots and gloves. They are getting dressed for a long motorbike ride: Martyn has just taken possession of a brand-new BMW R100, and he and Bill are preparing to put one thousand miles on the clock. They are riding across Europe to join us at our Italian destination, Florence. On the way, they will film the trip with a Super 8 camera, documenting the journey across France and then into Italy. All from the back of the bike.

Butty and Martyn will be taking turns on handlebar duties. The BMW's parallel twin will throb its way through French lanes flanked by poplar and silver birch trees. Then, as the temperature increases, cypress trees and olive groves. They will fly past trains, cement factories, rivers, lakes, electricity pylons, churches, forests, villages and towns. Winding the bike up into

Martyn Atkins and Bill Butt on the road to Italy

the Tuscan hills, Bill and Martyn try to outdo each other. Who can bank the bike the lowest through the tight, snaking bends? As they are weaving up through the mountainous landscape, Butty banks the Beemer so low the protruding engine pot hits the road surface, and they are flung off the bike. Now, they are skidding along the tarmac on leather-clad arses. Luckily the speed was low, and they are only moderately injured.

In the coach, we are a day or so ahead of them on the same roads. All roads lead to Rome; well, in our case, eventually right past Rome and onto Naples. The coach has a happy atmosphere; we are messing around with plastic saxophones we picked up at a French service station. At the same time, Turn Around Ted had been stocking up on cartons of cigarettes. It becomes clear why Ted, a non-smoker, needs all these fags when we get to the Italian border. Just like in the films, the Italian cops wear what must be part of the uniform issue: mirrored aviator sunglasses. They approach the driver's window. Ted hands them a couple of packets of ciggies, and they are now asking for T-shirts; it's a routine procedure to get through Italy with as little hassle as possible. Ted is an old hand at this lark and has been down these roads many times. You won't be going anywhere fast until you give them something, anything. As we go further into Italy, at any point we expect to be followed by a dull green Fiat Polizia car, always piloted by two mirror-shaded coppers; it is only a matter of time till they pull in front of the coach, flick on the blue light, and stop us. The British coach is a dead giveaway; they know we are easy pickings. We get pulled over several times; yet more cigarettes are dished out.

When we get to Florence, it is an outdoor show but it feels enclosed and like an indoor show. It is in the stunning Piazza della Signoria, the square by the Uffizi Gallery in the heart of the city. It is beyond magnificent, grand buildings surrounding the square peppered with statues. It's almost unbelievable that we can play in such a beautiful place. It's only a stone's throw away from the Ponte Vecchio. And just at the top of the square is a replica of Michelangelo's *David*. He's been standing there like he's waiting for the bus for over one hundred years now, with his big, worried head, tidy ball bag and flaccid tackle on display. Maybe he knows what's coming, and the worried look is out of fear that the volume of the sonic attack about to be unleashed on his marble winkle, all those bad vibrations, might be enough to tremble it right off.

The original *David* is kept safely indoors to stop it from being damaged by the weather, bird shit or post-punk onslaughts. We are unaware that the gig is for the benefit of the local Communist Party and is a free event; around two thousand people are expected to show up. (In Italy back then, politics looked very black and white, either communist or fascist, with no real middle ground. I didn't give a monkeys who it was to benefit. I was glad to be there and experience such a brilliant day.)

Me riding Martyn's BMW

Around about eleven, the muffled chatter of the locals is joined by a new sound: Butty and Martyn arrive on the rumbling BMW. It's still a few hours before the soundcheck, and the sun is still high in the Italian sky. They park the bike and set about filming in the square. They film the band mooching about individually, the crew setting up, people going about the day, bemused at what's happening in their backyard. Butty films Tony the Truck as he stares into the camera and seems to be doing his best Charlie Manson impersonation. Our new tour manager John Martin is conferring with some official-looking Italians – God knows what that's about.

Night falls, and the square is full right to the back. The Gregorian chants are popped into the cassette player, and the gig begins. As the gig progresses, Mac wrestles with a spotlight at the front of the stage, pulls it from the gaffer-tape anchors and aims it at the crowd. No mean feat: these things get hot. It's pure theatre, and Bill captures it all on the Super 8 camera.

Kit has been trained by Butty to take over lighting duties. The theatrical lightshow casts shadows all around the square.

Giant Bunnymen effigies leap and dance on the Uffizi's walls. And all too soon, the gig is over.

It's time to pack down and go for a drink. We could have done with some local knowledge; nothing seems to be open. But at least tonight we have a night in a hotel. I am sharing with Les; I have a photo of him casting shadows on the sparse room's wall.

We are off to Naples next, so the following day, after a light continental breakfast, we are back in the coach and heading south. The promoter has warned Bill that things might get sketchier in the south.

Florence soundcheck: Kit Edwardes, Martyn Atkins and Pete

'It's Mafia country, they are running everything, and they will ultimately be putting the gig on. So be careful and don't expect to be paid.'

Bill never told us any of this; not surprising, really, and we would have gone anyway.

Eventually, we arrive in a dusty town. Two metal gates open

up into a football pitch. The bus and Tony's truck are driven in. We are not worried about ruining the grass; there isn't any; it's a sandy surface, totally dry. The heat down here would have burned off any grass that might have been optimistically sown there years ago. Now it's a dust bowl. A wooden stage has been constructed at one end of the pitch. It must have been some effort to build, and it looks sturdy.

Harry, the soundman, needs to know where the power supply is. The stage is up against the wall with no sign of electricity.

'Bill, where's the fucking power?'

'Hold on, Harry, I'll find out.'

Bill finds someone who can speak English. 'Can you ask whoever is in charge where the electric source is?'

John Martin, the tour manager, comes over to help. Bill says, 'That geezer says there is a socket over there by the toilets.'

Harry goes over to the toilets to have a look. He is kicking off now. Shouting is heard around the pitch.

'That's no fucking good, you fucking prick; we need three-phase power.'

The Italians are looking on, confused.

'You do not bring electricity with you?' says one of the English-speaking Italians.

'No, we don't bring electricity with us, for fuck's sake.'

'We get the stage near the electricity?'

A van enters the arena and ropes are tied around the stage's legs. The Italians think that by dragging the stage closer to the one power outlet, we might be able to do something. The van starts to move forward. The stage creaks and cracks and is beginning to buckle.

'Stop, stop!' the shout goes out.

A big man in a dark suit turns up; he adds an authoritarian presence to the situation. I glimpse a small black badge on his lapel. We speculate that he is a Fascist Party leader or possibly that he is Mafia. Mr Black Suit observes with a face like thunder as John, the tour manager, and Big Bill figure out what to do. The Bunnymen camp has already recognised the gig is off; there would be no way to power an entire PA rig from a single plug-hole providing just 120 volts.

Band, crew and various others shove the wooden stage to the
other end of the footy pitch

Punters are starting to turn up, and the organisers are letting them in. They know nothing about the power problem and wonder why no gear is set up on the stage. They are probably thinking we've just decided not to do the gig on a whim, or we don't consider their stadium to be good enough. Either way, we are starting to feel uncomfortable. We want to get out of there; the atmosphere has turned sour. There is now a definite tension as the Italians grasp the situation. They will have a couple of thousand fans turning up soon, to be told, 'There will be no gig.' They will be asking for a refund but are unlikely to get one; things could get nasty. We have already accepted that we won't be getting paid, and we are keen to leave the place now.

As the afternoon wears on, we all line up to try and push the stage the 100 metres or so to the other end of the pitch. This works way better than I would have expected or wanted. It's a pointless exercise, anyway. We are worried that we will get lynched by a baying mob. A decision is made. Discreetly, we are instructed by John: 'OK, keep it quiet; we are gonna get on the coach and leave; we need to get out of here before it all kicks off.'

And this is what we do. Nothing had been unloaded from the truck, so we give Tony the Truck the news. He has been fast asleep in his cab and unaware of any of the shit that has been going on. It's getting dark now. We start the bus and edge our way through the crowd that has now built up into quite a throng. As we leave, the punters realise there will be no show here tonight. Things are getting thrown at the bus and kids are banging on the windows and sides. Around the football pitch, there is a warren of tiny streets that must be navigated. We all hope Turn Around Ted can remember the way out and back to the main road. This is deffo a time we don't want him to live up to his name. It is slow progress; the crowd are still following us, banging on the sides of the bus and shouting abuse in Italian with the occasional 'Fuck you' helpfully shouted in English. Tony in his truck and Martyn on his bike slowly follow us through the small streets. Martyn is getting the worst of it, with stones and tin cans getting lobbed at him as he rides. He has to stick with us as he doesn't know where we are going. Butty is on the bus with us, filming the mayhem out of the back window.

As we get towards bigger roads, we can increase the speed, and we are breaking free of the gauntlet we have been running, but a few kids are still with us. Les has the window open and is trying to explain with pidgin Italian and hand gestures why we couldn't do the gig, but it's no use.

One young kid shouts out, 'I have been waiting thirty years for this.'

He obviously means three years. We have only been a band for three years.

The convoy carries on till we eventually pull into a service station. Butty rejoins Martyn on the BMW and we all set off north, into the night.

CHAPTER 25

A Cloud of Blackness Emerges
from Under the Bridge

'This Perfect Day' – The Saints

Back in Liverpool, it's excellent news, well, for me anyway, I've lost my virginity to a real live girl. I had liked her from a distance for a long time. She is one of our Eric's friends. We have a lot in common; we are both woolly-backs who live in council houses in rural villages. She comes from Lydiate, which is near Melling. I'm not sure how I managed to pull her. From the distance of time, I don't think she liked me that much, so God knows why or how it happened. They say you always remember your first time well; I'm afraid I don't. I don't even remember where it happened, so it must have been a pretty perfunctory effort, definitely on my part. I'm sure the words hair and trigger would be appropriate. I was like an elastic band stretched and ready to break. I was only a trainee shagger, after all. The going-out-together situation didn't last long.

But at last, almost a decade behind just about everyone else in Liverpool, I'm out of the starting gate; you shall go to the ball!

I had been determined to move on from Melling, and I finally did that too, so I was finally making my way in the world of adult things. In May 1981, before we had gone to Europe, I had a couple of weeks off, and I got out of Station Road and moved in with Ian Broudie. Brod had a flat in Toxteth, right in Liverpool 8.

He had heard on the grapevine that I was seeking a place and he offered me his spare bedroom. It was a small room at the back, with a window providing a panoramic view of the bins. But it was clean and, above all, available for a few quid a week. It was on the ground floor of a big Edwardian apartment building on a wide double-carriageway street.

I worried about telling my dad I was about to bail out. He was in his sixties, and now he would be alone. One by one, everyone had steadily left him. I was the only one to stick around. I felt guilty, unsure why he had never been arsed about us as a family. I put it off, but I had to let Brod know one way or the other soon.

Liverpool Football Club are riding high; they have won the league. So maybe Dad is, er . . . happy? A perfect time to tell him I was leaving.

It was all quite odd, considering he never showed any emotion . . . or not precisely that. I mean any feeling. Anger is an emotion. Johnny Rotten keeps banging on that anger is an energy. Maybe; I know it takes too much energy to be angry nowadays.

'Dad, I'm getting a flat with a mate.'

My revelation did not precisely mortify my dad, though I thought I could see he was a little upset. The reality of a future life of loneliness seeped into him. I had realised by then that his going to the pub every night was an attempt to combat deep loneliness and depression. It was more than just the appeal of the booze. A sympathetic molecule sparked inside me as I spread these thoughts around my mind.

He comes back with, 'He's not on fucking drugs, is he?'

'Er . . . no.'

I'm thinking, *Fucking hell, ha, that's a laugh. Ian Broudie on drugs? He won't even take paracetamol.*

'Are you on drugs?'

'No, I'm bloody not.'

That was not the complete truth, but I didn't consider myself that arsed about drugs to the detriment of all other aspects of my existence. I'd had that go on LSD in Berlin, and that coke that was doled out in Brussels, but it had been a one-off. I never saw the point of that crap. You might be surprised by this statement, with my fascination with psychedelic records, the sixties, hippies and happenings in San Francisco, the clubs in London, UFO (pronounced You-Fo, by the way), Middle Earth and Syd's Pink Floyd, etc., but I never got that arsed by or into the drug scene. It seemed to be against punk-rock ethics or something, even though by this point I realised that punk groups were all out of it on speed and coke, and some of the druggy-hippie stuff appeared to have made it into the punk scene. Worse, heroin had crept in, in the shitty way it always does. I liked being an outsider to all that. I had started to think that finding answers in booze or drugs was a fundamental weakness. And it was so fucking boring for everyone around it. Though I was not telling my dad any of that: he would never understand.

Instead, I said, 'I'm just getting a flat in town. It's no big deal.' Followed by, 'I'll come and see you every week, when I'm home, that is.'

Though I wasn't lying, and I would come and see him, I knew visits would be few and far between.

Did I see a glimmer of upset in his stony eyes? Or was I imagining it? I tried to soften the blow.

'You will probably see me more than you do now. I'll visit you on a Sunday.'

Now I was lying, but I was trying to make him feel better. Even when things were difficult, he was still my dad and, underneath the cold chill of the Sergeants' demeanour, there was a tiny ember of affection yet to be extinguished. My mum, brother and sister's embers had long since been extinguished.

The move went smoothly with the help of Les and his trusty Transit van. I didn't have that much to take anyway; it all fitted in the van and took just one journey. My four-track TEAC tape recorder was by far the heaviest item, and nearly did our backs in lifting it. I had bin bags full of clothes, records and hi-fi equipment. I got settled in and set up my hi-fi. With a few trips to Liverpool's Rapid Hardware, the one-stop shop for all your bedsit needs, this was the most critical job.

My room in Ian Broudie's flat. Princess Avenue, Liverpool

I loved the road we were on, Princess Boulevard. To my woolly-back eyes, it had the romance of Paris without the obligatory sausage dogs trotting along and shitting everywhere. Only one hundred years ago, Victorian gentlefolk would spend their weekends perambulating up and down the boulevard. Ladies with lace-gloved hands would have been holding on to Mary Poppins-style parasols. And they would act coyly while knowingly flashing their ankles at cocky scouse lads parading in their Sunday best. They'd doff their boaters and puff on pipes through the brambles of handlebar moustaches as trams glided past on their way to Aigburth.

A hundred years later, in 1981, Princess Boulevard has seen better days. The large houses and apartments have been converted into bedsits. Some buildings are in such bad repair that they are due for demolition. This once-affluent area is now cheap bedsit-ter land. It's chock-a-block with students and popular with arty types, hipsters, punks and dropouts. And with individuals like me who believe they have all four characteristics. You can't move without bumping into the latest crop of post-punk bands. Yes, Toxteth is the place to be. Paul Simpson has a basement flat over the road, and Julian Cope lives on Devonshire Road, at the end of the boulevard, just by the park. Big Bill's assistant at the Zoo office, the super-efficient and adorable Pam, has her flat almost opposite Ian Broudie's place. Big Bill would have been lost without Pam's organising skills; she never forgot anything and was always willing to help with any problem; everybody loved Pam.

I even managed to get myself a girlfriend who lived across the road, Laura. She was blonde and very pretty. We were getting a lift back to the boulevard in the back seat of Ian Broudie's Datsun

Pam Young and Pete Buxton

when the proximity of our bodies triggered a passionate snog-ging session; we ended up being an item, as they say on telly, for about a year or two.

It's now October 1981, we are back on tour, and for the second time in a year, we are heading to the USA, this time starting in Austin, Texas. We have a few days off in a hotel to get acclimatised. The hotel is very close to the Congress Avenue Bridge. We are mooching about looking for food. At the side of the hotel is a river walk that we are just pootling along with the warmth of the day receding nicely and the dusk appearing like God has turned down the lighting via his celestial dimmer switch. A cloud of blackness emerges from under the bridge.

Accompanying the expanding dirty smudge streaking through the air is a sound like a million pairs of leathery wings flapping. That is because a million pairs of leathery wings are flapping. Over a million bats are taking flight. The stripe of bats stretches out across the steadily darkening sky and continues for some time. They head along the Colorado River and out over the reservoir of Lady Bird Lake. We climb up to the bridge and get a better view. Quite a few people have gathered to watch. This is a regular thing around 8 p.m. The bats are off for dinner, and Lady Bird Lake has a million reservations.

After our Texas gig, we are going overnight to Atlanta next, this time behind the shiny aluminium, fully air-conditioned bodywork of an American Eagle tour bus. We will be snug as a dozen corpses in coffin-sized bunks, two lounges and a kitchen area. It is a lot better than the van. I take up my usual position. I sit beside the driver, generally a redneck into country music. They have the obligatory gun in the glovebox. And a tummy tuck under their cowboy shirt. They are usually a pretty unfriendly bunch and get extremely pissed off by the state that the bus can get into over a long drive. They usually don't want to know us limeys. And they hate the music we play. Not much chat is back and forth, but it's worth sitting in the quiet atmosphere to be able to concentrate on the horizon as we head towards it but never quite get there.

Firstly, through desert areas of Texas. In the headlights of approaching night-time truckers, all we can see are shadows of the distinctive shapes of cacti as they patrol the sides of the freeway. The road is eaten up in 100-mile mouthfuls. The dawn appears for another day; the sun's rays reflect off the polished chrome of our American Eagle, dazzling the sensitive eyes of real American eagles circling high above. The aluminium skin heats up to egg-frying temperature but the air-con is on max, and it's not too bad until the overworked units freeze up and fail, and we begin to cook. The miles continue to be sucked up and spat out by the bus. The landscape changes and, by late morning, we are in a much greener belt.

With the lush foliage comes more humid air, which we only find out when we reach a truck stop and step out of the air conditioning and into a wall of humidity. We don't get this kind of moist air in England more than maybe once or twice a year, just before a thunderstorm. And as soon as the rain comes, the heavy air is gone; everywhere is cleansed with a lovely ozone freshness.

In Atlanta, we glean local knowledge and head to the hip area, Little Five Points. There are fantastic shops. I descend on all this American stuff like a cultural locust. Comic and record shops, vintage clothing stores. It's all still new and exciting to me.

And so it goes like all tours in a bus; we voyage along the quiet roads by night, and the relentless progress is broken up with the odd truck stop or day off spent in a hotel. On the bus, we go to bed in one state and wake up in another. And I don't mean pissed and then sober, but yes, that does frequently happen. On the morning of 16 October we wake up in the state of New York. We have two gigs at the Ritz (now known as Webster Hall) on 11th Street. Backstage talk is still about Johnny Rotten's antics in the post-Sex Pistols outfit Public Image Ltd, when they had played behind the Ritz's video screen. Not sure if it was faulty or PiL had thought, *Fuck it, the screen can stay down*, triggering a full-on riot.

We would never orchestrate a riot; it's not our style. We prefer the music to create tension. And who wants to be hit on the head with a flying bottle? Not me, that's for sure. The Madness gig had taught us that.

The stage is decked out in the latest incarnation of camo netting: snow camo. We may have given up the jungle camouflage clothing and returned to civvies, but a vestige of our military looks remains in white netting; it's perfect for picking up the coloured lighting effects and the oil wheel projectors we have time-travelled back and borrowed from the sixties. Globules of orange, blue, red and green lights are created by oils of different viscosity that cannot mix and are trapped between two circular glass discs with a sealed edge. We add this effect on the slim chance you didn't think the music is psychedelic enough.

The gig takes its usual course, and we are heading towards the last dying breath of our encore, 'Do It Clean' as usual. The band is swirling into a hallucinogenic maelstrom of sound or, as we still call them, freak-outs. Sections of the songs are left open to improvisation. As the final crescendo inevitably approaches, Mac signals to us vocally to get ready for the last chorus.

He belts out, 'Do it clean, know what I meaaaaan . . . I mean.'

We all reach the vinegar stroke with one last thunderous clanging stab at the mighty E chord that signals we are all done. It blasts through the speaker stack and I lift my guitar high into the air in some sort of 'look at me, I'm such an excellent fellow' pose. I should have known better.

I have never been one for over-the-top gestures on stage. You won't find me with my tongue out of my gob and flicking like a cobra in time with the wanky solo I'm inflicting on you. Like all those heavy hair bands that weirdly are getting popular at the same time as we are. On this occasion, I may have had a little too much pre-match lubricant in the form of the band's latest tipple of choice, the rock 'n' roller's staple stage juice, Jack Daniel's and Coke.

Pride comes before a fall; the guitar machine heads become entangled in our new white camo netting that Butty and Kit had stretched across the stage, giving us somewhere to feel safe in a smoke-filled bunker of lights and mayhem. I extract myself from the guitar strap, and the Telecaster hangs in the netting, squealing like a pig at dinnertime. It appears to float in mid-air.

As we leave the stage to the right, I turn and look at the scene from the wings. Smoke is billowing everywhere and my guitar is dangling like an inedible fruit through the fog of sonic war. It screams until Jake begins to clear the stage equipment. He puts it out of its misery by unceremoniously whipping out the jack plug like Baron Vladimir Harkonnen plucking out the heart plug of some poor minion. (If you have seen David Lynch's film *Dune*, you will know what I'm on about. If not, why not? The spice must flow.)

We end the tour in San Francisco. Then we are off for our first time in Australia.

Tea up

We have made Sydney our base. The first six gigs are in the outlying districts of the city, and we are staying in the Cosmopolitan Hotel right on Bondi Beach. Wait a minute, let me just run that past myself again . . . I am in Australia now. This is crazy; how the hell did I end up on the other side of planet Earth? I should be washing spuds or scooping up dead rats in a scabby kitchen down some Liverpudlian back street, but by some weird, fickle finger of punk-rock fate and a love of music, I am in bloody Australia. Home of TV gold, such as *Skippy the Bush Kangaroo*, *Chopper Squad*, *The Flying Doctor* and *Ryan*, though I mainly watched *Ryan* for the chance of seeing Pamela Stephenson in thigh boots and a miniskirt. This would keep a fifteen-year-old full of testosterone happy for several seconds.

Australia is home to every type of deadly animal and insect God could think of for his own amusement on that Sunday off he gave himself. Or it could just be evolution, survival of the fittest and all that.

In the hotel, we have suites with a cooker and pans; everything you need to make food is in the cupboards. We decide to make a Sunday roast, a bit of home-from-home time. After all, it's only midsummer and in the low hundreds outside. What better way to cool off than a shitload of roast spuds piping hot from the oven? Just around the corner are some shops. It's very much like England – obviously not the weather, but a strip of small shops selling vegetables, a laundrette, a general store and a butcher's. While we are in the butcher's, a little kid is hanging around outside, must be about seven or eight; when we come out with a leg of lamb in our bag, the kid looks us up and down and says, 'Pommie bastards.'

Pete and a fan, Antipodean tour (basically not sure if this was
Australia or New Zealand)

We find this hilarious. Our milk-bottle-white legs must have
given us away. We chuckle all the way back to the hotel. A
couple of hours later, we have a roast dinner in the middle of a
baking hot Bondi Beach.

The next day, before going to the gig, we met in the hotel
bar. Simple Minds were also in the bar; we don't talk to them,
nor do they speak to us. It was a strange rivalry kind of thing.
We sat at the bar not more than ten feet away, without acknowl-
edging each other. We drank our beers. A very odd way to
behave, I must say. To go all that way, to be in the same line of
business in the same hotel bar, and to blank each other is such
a funny carry-on. The same thing happened in London's
King's Road once. The Jesus and Mary Chain were walking

towards us. We clocked them, and they clocked us, and we just walked past each other, staring at the ground. I can't explain it. It was like we were rival gangs or mortal enemies, but we were just bands trying to out-cool each other. Pretty pathetic, really.

In some downtime, we hang about on Bondi Beach. I am burning my face to bits in the midsummer sun. I have brought my warmest clothes to Australia. My Harris tweed jacket is a particularly bad idea. I had no real idea of how hot it would be Down Under, as the locals like to call it. I really never thought it through.

Les is swimming about fifty feet from where the sea meets the sand. He looks like he's having a great time. In reality, he is trying to get back to dry land. He is pumping his legs and arms as hard as he can. He is getting nowhere. The beach at Bondi suddenly drops, so as the waves are coming in, they don't just dissipate on the beach. They roll down deep and head out again, creating an undercurrent. Les is caught in the pull of the returning waves. He struggles to try to reach the beach, but the breakers have him and are dragging him further out. And now he is getting tired. A girl on the beach recognises what's going on and runs to where the waves are crashing. She is shouting and gesturing for Les to swim sideways towards the left of the beach. She knows the drop-off isn't as severe on that side and the waves will lose their grip on Les's tired legs. Les sees her and begins to edge toward the left. After fifty metres or so, he can head towards the beach.

'I couldn't go back; I was getting dragged out to sea,' he says, exhausted.

The girl who saved him explains the situation with the

undercurrent and the steep drop-off. Les could easily have drowned that day.

After our gigs around the Sydney area, we are playing at a fantastic dance hall in Brisbane next called Cloudland. It's 13 November 1981. The building has a seaside take on an art deco feel. Lots of white-painted concrete. Inside is a beautiful sprung dancefloor. It's a bit tatty now, but you can see it has been a fantastic venue in the past. All the great Australian bands have played there, from AC/DC to the Saints. It sits high on top of a hill in the Bowen Hills area of Brisbane. We have great views of the surrounding countryside and can see the Brisbane cityscape below. A large arched entrance dominates the frontage.

After the gig, we are outside chatting with the support band, Scapa Flow; I enjoyed their set; they have definitely nailed their colours to the post-punk, er . . . post. And they sound a little like the Cure, with a touch of Joy Division thrown in for good measure. As we chat, we notice off to the left that there are clouds in the distance; we must be higher than the clouds. It feels like we are looking down on them, but it could be because they are far away in the distance. Above us, the sky is clear, and the moon is bright. The distant blanket of clouds is constantly flashing. A violent tropical storm is kicking off along the coast. The clouds are lighting up like there are strobe lights hidden in giant balls of cotton wool. The display is like nothing we have seen before. The silence makes the whole thing even weirder. Not even a rumble can be heard; no sound of thunder reaches our lofty viewpoint.

After the Australian leg, we go to New Zealand; well, it would be rude not to after coming all that way. After a

harrowing landing at Wellington airport, we fly to one of the
shows in a commercial seaplane. I must say it's an odd thing to
take off and land from the water.

Big Bill Drummond, Antipodean tour

We had a night off in New Zealand and headed to a party not
far from our hotel in Wellington. We walked down a few neat
roads and into an estate of bungalows. We must have been quite
near the coast as it was sandy underfoot. Not sure how we got
invited. We must have met some fans after the gig. The party
was in a typical housing estate – rows of houses, each with a car
parked up the driveway.

We are drinking a few beers, and it's a surreal feeling with all
our travelling; suddenly, we are in the home of a random person.
When a bike gang turns up and gatecrashes the party, things

start to take a darker turn. The gang take the furniture out of the house and build a bonfire in the front garden. Things are getting heavy fast. We decide to sneak off. There are too many to get into a rumble, and I learned what a shit fighter I am back in Belgium. We can't just walk past these bikers and risk getting a kicking for our clothes and hairstyles, so we opt for the safer option, the coward's way out. We go to the bog and climb out of the window, sneak around the back of the house, and then join the road out of the eyeline of the wild bunch. We watch as they throw another wardrobe on the fire.

CHAPTER 26

Brod, the Pool Hall Kingbird

'My White Bicycle' – Tomorrow

Back in Liverpool, it was the same faces in the clubs and bars around town. You would inevitably bump into someone from a band when walking up Bold Street. It was like, that's all they ever do, constantly walking up and down Bold Street. I felt uneasy that the Bunnymen had given me a way out, and my mates in other bands were struggling to get somewhere; they were still doing the same old things. I seldom talked about the good things that had opened up to us. I felt guilty that I didn't deserve all this good fortune.

'All right, Will, you've been to America, haven't you? How did it go?'

I would look awkwardly down to the ground and say, 'Yes, er . . . it was good,' when it was way better than good, it was fucking amazing. A mind-blowing situation. So, I kept it low key and, even then, I felt like I was bragging or rubbing it in, showing off that the band was getting somewhere. I always play down our achievements. It was almost as if I was ashamed that we were earning recognition. I suppose it's part of the deep imposter syndrome engrained in me.

★　　★　　★

January 1982, we are again back at Maida Vale Studios, London, recording another session for Peel's show. This time, we only have three songs. The ideas are not exactly drying up, but with all the touring we have been doing, we have had very little time to nurture new songs. We always go on tour intending to try and write new songs. It's a good idea in theory, but it never pans out like that; in the real world, time is short. Once the soundcheck is over, we must get off the stage quickly so the support band can set up. And writing on the tour bus like the Partridge Family jamming away at the back of the bus would be mayhem. Mac hasn't got the correct hairstyle to be the next David Cassidy.

The three songs we do at the Peel session are still very much in the development stage, and two have working titles: 'Taking Advantage', which will become 'The Back of Love', and 'An Equation', which becomes 'Higher Hell'. The song 'No Hands' is purely a Peel show one-off. We all sit in a circle and do this thigh-slapping rhythm, and we build the song around that. We don't think it's good enough to pursue on the next record, probably a bit too weird even for me.

It's decided that rechristened 'The Back of Love' will be the next single. Les and I are not keen on having a song with 'Love' in the title. It just instinctively feels odd for the Bunnymen. A bit too commercial for us. Mac is trying to convince us it's OK.

'Yes, but this is the *back* of love,' he says. 'The back! Of love.'

He's pointing out the problems of being in love. It is not all a wine and roses deal. You have to get through issues and work on love. I get it now, of course, and it all seems silly, but we were so paranoid about being seen as a sell-out in any way. It was more important to me than anything else.

We are booked in at Trident Studios in London's Soho; this is quite a buzz for us as Bowie recorded many of his classic albums at Trident. We are all happy that Brod is back in the producer's role. We trust him and his judgement. This time he has adopted the name Kingbird; it has been given to him by one of his mates back in Liverpool.

We run through the song a few times, and somehow it gets decided to speed the track up quite a lot; it was something like 130 beats per minute, and we whack it right up to 145 bpm. It's a fast and furious speed to keep up with. I'm on intro duties, so I have to be spot on; it needs a few takes. It's a radical decision, but the track comes alive with this speed kick up the arse.

Brod has the idea of giving the song the emotional intensity of a Jacques Brel recording; Brod and Mac have listened to many of the Brel recordings. The way he sang with raw emotion is what Brod sees for the track. He convinces Mac to really roll his Rs and spit out the words vigorously.

In the breakdown section, Mac is snarling out the lyrics; it is almost primaeval and is magnificent in its fury.

We hire three cello players; Brod hums the parts to the musicians and instructs them to dig deep into the instrument; he wants to hear the rasping growl of the bow on the strings. Hunting in the studio, we find a percussion box; all studios have one. Inside we find some of those kids' corrugated plastic pipe toys. When spun around, the pipes produce an eerie hollow tone of a trapped spirit, a warbling mythical creature. The four of us go into the recording room. The juxtaposition of this studio scenario doesn't go unnoticed by me: as we don the headphones, we form a circle around a very posh and ridiculously expensive German microphone while clutching the cheapo kids' toys held above our heads. We are ready to spin.

Mac getting funky on the rhythm guitar in Dundee

From the control room, Brod plays the track, routed to our headphones. At the designated point in the song, we all whip the pipes around our heads like cowboys about to rope a feisty cowgirl in an episode of *Bonanza*. I am careful not to thrash the delicate mic or even more delicate bandmate beside me. We are whirling the colourful pipes like crazy. The faster we spin, the higher the note goes. The tuning isn't spot on, so we have a go at speeding up or slowing down the tape machine, but in the end we just decide the discordant quality adds to the overall anarchy of the section. All the pipes have a slightly different pitch, generally around the note of E, which is good enough for jazz, as the old saying goes.

As we emerge from the drop, Brod asks the cello players to emulate the high, vicious scream of the strings from Bernard Herrmann's soundtrack for *Psycho*. You know, the horrendous shower scene where Janet Leigh gets stabbed up by a crazed Anthony Perkins in drag, and the black blood swirls around the plughole.

Rob Dickins at the label and Bill Drummond universally hate the track. We are despondent, and Mac tells Big Bill to fuck off out of the studio. Which he duly does.

It's agreed to give it a remix at Air Studios, which isn't far from Trident in Soho, just down the road on Oxford Street. Oxford Street is known for being the centre of shopping in London – also, the centre of street-corner geezers selling watches, nasty jewellery and fake perfume from stocked-up suitcases. An accomplice feigns great interest in the case's contents while keeping one eye out for the Old Bill.

Behind door 214, the hustle and bustle of shoppers are muted by the soundproof walls, and we enter the serenity of George Martin's studio. George, tall with that posh voice, is pottering about; he welcomes us in and gives the impression of being unflappable in a crisis. I immediately think that he is perfect officer material. And it turns out he was a second lieutenant in the war, flying spotter planes. John Lennon is said to have hilariously and sarcastically christened him Biggles.

Brod sets about the mix with an Air Studios engineer called Colin Fairley, and while we're hanging around in the games room, Paul McCartney pops in and says, 'Oh, so you are the Bunnymen from Liverpool, are ya? Nice to meet you.'

We look on with broad smiles.

My God, Paul knows our name and seems to know who we are.

He sticks around for a brew and I play a video game with him. It's either *Asteroids* or *Tank Commander*, one of the latest video game crazes.

Macca was in the studio adding a few bits to one of his songs. I'm pretty sure he was working with his old mate Biggles, er . . . I mean George Martin. Paul was exactly like you see him on the telly when he is getting interviewed, a lovely fellow, still down to earth and quite prepared to be friendly to us young upstarts and have a cup of tea and a chat with us. I think our Liverpool connection also helped with the musical camaraderie. Sorry for name dropping, but it's Paul McCartney, for fuck's sake. I have a deep respect for Paul, the experimenter in the Beatles, the one member who I think pushed the psychedelic boundaries of their records. As I see it, Paul always sought new sounds and influences to throw into the Beatles' pot.

Mixing does involve a hell of a lot of hanging around for the band. You don't want to be in the control room if you are not directly involved, getting in the way and slowing things down all the time. They definitely don't want me chiming up from the couch at the back every two minutes. Les and I decided to jump ship for a while. We headed out for a short walk among the throng of shoppers and pushed our way through a plethora of spivs. We managed to avoid buying the shitty sovereign rings on offer and carried on till we spotted a cinema just up the street. The film title shimmering in two-foot letters backlit by the fluorescent glow of the Picture House's marquee was Andrei Tarkovsky's *Stalker*. It's a real mindblower that one. It's long and very slow by today's standards. Modern viewers with zero attention spans will have to try hard to relax. If you just let the sumptuous, ramshackle, industrial Soviet decay flow over you, it's a wonder of filmmaking. We both loved it. Les and I both like photography, and every frame of *Stalker* is a masterpiece of photographic art. Just saying.

Brod and Colin were working on the sound for the complicated drum patterns Pete had created. It was particularly complex because it involved Pete crossing his hands and playing the low tom with what, technically speaking, was the wrong hand. It was an incredibly awkward situation. To get a powerful hit on the tom drum would take great strength. Pete, of course, had power in spades, so not a problem, and he managed to beat the shit out of the drums anyway. This arse-over-tit technique was the only way for him to do it, and it highlights the incredible way Pete played the drums; he had no boundaries and would always find a way to do what he wanted.

After Brod and Colin's mix was finished, Big Bill was back in the studio. This time, he loved it, and the record label was moderately happy too. So were the public, and it became our biggest hit up to that point.

The flat back in Liverpool I had with Brod was going well. My dad and I had built a bed on stilts to optimise the high ceiling and the space of my small room. I had my TEAC four-track reel-to-reel machine, some bits and bobs of random equipment to play with, and the effects I had been collecting. I had not long since bought an excellent Electro-Harmonix pedal called Attack Decay that could emulate a reverse guitar sound. I was obsessed with the sound of a backwards guitar. I would love to add it to my armoury of effects, but this would be tricky without a time machine and a way of reversing the Earth's rotation, especially in a live set. So, I settled for the Attack Decay pedal, a close second. In the studio, it was possible to reverse the tape, play something and listen with the tape playing forward. This was always an exciting prospect and one of my favourite things to do. You never knew what it would sound like; the brain would have to untangle the sweeping fade in and out of the guitar into hopefully a recognisable and pleasing combination of notes. Anything trippy was OK by me. And often, I would have to be reined in by the band or the producer, or the whole bloody song would have been backwards. My favourite track featuring backwards sounds is 'My White Bicycle' by Tomorrow. If you haven't got a clue what the hell I've been chuntering on about for the last paragraphs, you can search it out.

After Brod had produced a couple of songs for the Bunnymen, he looked like he was heading inevitably to become a producer, but he told me he wanted to write songs and have a band. He is brilliant at songwriting and arranging, and can play the guitar a lot better than me, that's for sure.

Brod had bought the latest piece of home recording technology: the TASCAM Portastudio four-track recorder. This cassette-based machine ran at twice the speed of a regular cassette, and this speed increase helped with the quality of the recorded sound. It was like a sketch pad for songwriting; you could quickly get ideas down in a basic form. Quite a few bands had them; they were fun and a handy tool. Now and then, Brod would ask me to help him record some of his songs by operating the Portastudio. One such piece was called 'Tall Ships', and I think Brod had been playing the H. P. Lovecraft song 'The White Ship' and adopted the ship part of the title. Nowt wrong with that; that's how inspiration works. We had been playing H. P. Lovecraft, an American band named after the sci-fi and horror writer, in the flat quite often. It was the first time I'd heard them. In 1983, Brod's demo song got used by the band he started with Paul Simpson, Care, and became 'My Boyish Days'.

Brod recorded another tune using my four-track and Roland Drumatix drum machine and a few other bits of equipment I had lying about. And it was called 'What Kind of World?' In answer, I suggest 'Another Green One.' By the sound of it, it was a triumphant homage to Eno's *Another Green World* record.

Brod has an encyclopaedic knowledge of music and likes many of the bands I like. It was exciting living with him. He introduced me to the great mod band the Creation. Their guitarist Eddie Phillips was the first to use a violin bow on the guitar. And I'm sure that led me down many a strange path trying to eke out other-worldly sounds from the guitar. I would bow the guitar strings with various bits of metal, screwdrivers and scissors over the years.

After Brod had tried on just about every pair of keks, shirt, jacket, shoes and jumper, we would eventually go into town. I would leave him at Kirkland's, where he would dominate the pool table, and I would go deeper into the centre with my girlfriend Laura. On the way back, we would call into Kirkland's and there he would still be beating everyone on the pool table. We'd scoop him up and drift up the hill to the Everyman on Hope Street; we would be heading in the right direction and getting closer to Toxteth via every pub or bar on the route home. Inevitably, we would all end up in Casablanca. Then, at closing time, it was just a matter of stumbling the half-mile back to Princess Avenue.

One day I was in the flat, and there came a knock on the door; it was the bloke from across the corridor; he was asking, 'Do you want to buy a watch?'

I didn't. He showed me the watch. It was a beauty, for sure, silver with gold inlay around the bezel. A Longines pocket watch from the 1920s. He told me it had been valued at £800, and even showed me a certificate that confirms it's worth that much. And he only wanted £40. Come again? I thought it must have been robbed or dodgy somehow.

It turned out this bloke next door was heavily into gambling, and he needed the cash to get himself out of some shit he had got himself into; he was desperate, so I gave him the forty quid and I've still got the watch.

Laura and I did go with him and his girlfriend to a casino one night to see what it was all about. It was like an adventure into the nightlife world of older people. The place was full of tidy gents and women wearing too much makeup. I suspect they weren't there for the gambling. We got fifteen quid's worth of chips. Yes, I know, the last of the high rollers. We won thirty-five quid, and then we stopped. We doubled our money, and that was it. We went home and left him and his girl to gamble away all night. It was a short but interesting glimpse into a world out of our comfort zone, but normality for the late-night denizens from the flat next door. We only went the once; even with the winnings, I couldn't see the point of it.

We are getting a good following now. We could be playing in bigger venues. But we are always looking for someplace unusual to play.

Big Bill is Scottish, very Scottish. He is hatching a plot, always looking for an excuse to fly north and visit his homeland. He reckons that to progress the band, we must go north, almost to the tip of the British Isles, and I reckon he thinks we've got lots of new material to work with. The problem is that we only have four new pieces to add to the setlist; one of them has already been recorded, and another is destined to be the B-side. Bill still wants us to play up in Scotland. I'm convinced he just fancies a trip to John o' Groats.

At the Zoo office:

'All right, Bill, what have you got planned for our next gigs? Manchester Apollo? The Royal Court in Liverpool?'

'Er, not quite,' he replies in his soft Scottish accent, somewhere between little Jimmy Krankie and James Bond – the real one, that is, Connery, Sean Connery.

'I think you should play in Wick.'

'Wick? Where the fuck is Wick?' we ask.

I chime in, 'I know I get on your wick.' I'm trying to be funny.

'Wick is near John o' Groats.'

'What, the John o' Groats right at the top of Scotland? The most northerly point of mainland Britain? Let's get this straight. You think we should go to the top of Scotland to do a gig?'

'Aye, a few gigs.'

'OK, when do we go?'

He sets to work and finds some small venues in the highlands. The tour is called the 'Wee Scottish Tour'. Brod is producing the record, so he's coming with us. It's taken some persuading to get him to agree to work with us again. As we need to get cracking on writing, maybe we could jam some things together on the short tour? Brod will also be employed as a rhythm guitarist and even keep an ear on the sound mix from the stage. As we will be playing a few new songs, the tour's meant to be a pre-production thing for the next album but ends up as fun gigs in unusual places. At least Brod can suggest changes or ideas for songs where something's lacking – there's nothing like playing live to make you realise what is not working in a piece.

We are taking our very expensive (at the time) Bose PA setup purely for the vocals, marimba, drum machine and my little Casio keyboard. These are small halls; we won't need a big PA for our minimal setup – you might say it's 'compact and bijou'. *Yes, you might say that, if you are a pretentious turd.* Yeah, you might. *You just did.*

We need some lighting for the stage. I head to St John's Precinct, the building next to that naff concrete tower called St John's Beacon, the one the sixties planners let slip through their hay-burning taste net.

With a fist full of band funds, I go to Habitat – paper lampshades, colourful crockery, and beanbags (it was like a hippie IKEA). I nab half a dozen Anglepoise lamps. These little lights will be the only lighting on the stage. No flashing lights or psychedelic effects on this tour, I'm afraid. We will have to be an unadulterated rocking unit.

The day comes, we load up and off we go. First, we skirt past the Lake District and pass Carlisle on the empty M6. As we continue north through the border at Gretna Green, the M6 merges into the A74 and swings to the north-east. Getting up to Edinburgh takes bloody ages in the van at fifty miles per hour. The A74 turns into the A73. As we sweep through the outskirts of Scotland's capital, we cross the Firth of Forth via the Forth Road Bridge. On our right are the red girders of the glorious mess of steel known as the Forth Rail Bridge. Stretched across the cold water of the Firth of Forth, it appears to leap like a robotic metal hare to the far bank. If Edinburgh were Liverpool, Dunfermline would be McBirkenhead. After a few miles, we are at the Glen Pavilion for the first gig on the Wee Scottish Tour.

There is one hiccup when in Dunfermline. After we set everything up on the stage, my Roland JC-160 amp decides to pack in. Jake is dispatched to find me a replacement amp and heads to the local music shop in the town, Sound Control. In the shop is a kid. His dad is buying his first amp, a Roland JC-50. The young lad offers up the amp.

'You can use this if you like?'

Jake doesn't wait to be asked twice. He brings the amp back and it gets set up for me.

Me, Dundee gig

The lights go down and we head onto the stage; each of us flicks on the switch of an Anglepoise lamp, and we start the set. We have been starting with the brand-new track called 'Fuel'. We had recorded it in Brod's flat in my back room, under my new bed on stilts, on my four-track machine, and it got used for the B-side of the twelve-inch of 'The Back of Love'.

I use the young kid's amp, but it's not the same sound and I am pissed off.

After the gig, the kid comes up to me and asks, 'Was the amp OK? It's mine.'

'No, it was fucking shite.'

The kid is mortified he had let me use his brand-new amp, and I'm ungratefully telling him it was shit. The lad goes home with the amp, apparently walking six miles back to his village.

I still feel bad about this. It was unforgivable, twatty behaviour on my part. The weird thing is that the same kid, called Michael, became my roadie in the mid-eighties. By this time, he had grown up a bit and now looked like Curly Watts from *Coronation Street*, so he became Curly; in fact, Michael became known as Curly McCable. He then became the band's production manager, as well as a close friend. After working for us, he went on to do Jane's Addiction, and was one of the team that started up Lollapalooza festivals in the USA. Or, as he called it, Line up of Losers. The other odd thing is that Curly is the kid brother of Richard Jobson from the Skids – the one who shouted, 'Run away! Run away!' at the fisticuffs in the square in Leuven. It's a weird and wonderful world where coincidences happen all the time. Curly is still my good friend, but he loves to remind me of when I was a total cunt. And I cringe with embarrassment. Sorry, Curl.

The next day, the van chugs up to higher ground, and the scenery changes into vast open moorlands, forests, hills and mountains as we head north-west; we get to Aviemore, climbing up into the real honest-to-goodness highlands now. The gig is in a sports centre so we spend some time before the soundcheck watching curling on the ice rink. Never seen that before; well, seen it on the telly. Funny watching the sweepers going at the ice like crazy with a brush.

The next show is in the town of Wick. Perched high on the north-east coast of Scotland, it's a one-horse town, but someone left the stable door open and the horse has bolted long ago. As Big Bill had said, it is very close to John o' Groats. The van seems to be causing some commotion in the town. Heads turn on both sides of the street as the rusty Transit heads up Francis Street. People pop out of shops, with mouths flopping open as we go backwards and forwards between the hotel and gig. Les flicks on the hazard warning lights. He starts flashing his full-beam head-lights, beeping the horn and waving. Locals are even more curi-ous now at this vanload of outsiders. Vacant looks on their faces. It is undoubtedly the most excitement this town has seen since the Vikings came a-raping and a-pillaging. I want to melt into the seat with embarrassment, but this makes it more fun for Les; he really is a bastard, a funny one, but a bastard all the same.

Big Bill's idea was that we could work the songs out live and get them into better shape, away from the eyes and ears of the press, so if it's a big fuck-up, it won't be noticed too much. The problem is that it is so unusual for a band to play in such small towns as Wick and Tain that it does precisely the opposite and draws the press to follow us. Also, many Scottish fans from Glasgow and Edinburgh are taken by the adventurous nature of the Bunnymen gigs and follow us. Some bring sleeping bags and are bedding down in doorways; others are kipping in vans and cars.

All in all, it worked out well. We didn't fuck up, and the gigs were ace. The low-key style warmed us to our fans, and we would chat with them and be the opposite of rock stars. The vibe on the stage was great, and the crowd could see we were having a good time, which helped. And it was brilliant to have Brod along. The press was impressed that we could do such a tour, and we started to get this reputation of an intrepid and adventurous band that would play out-of-the-way places just for the vibe. Bill got what he wanted, and we even managed a trip in the van to see John o' Groats before heading down south back to the north.

★　　★　　★

When we came home to the flat in Toxteth, spring was in full swing, and two new girls seemed to be everywhere we went in town. Courtney and Robin, exotic creatures, Americans? That's odd; what the hell were they doing in Liverpool? The Courtney in question was seventeen-year-old Courtney Love. Why were they in Liverpool, a depressed northern town with not much going for it except the gritty people and the scouse humour, or so we were told? You need a good sense of humour to live there, blah, blah. This is in the days before the Albert Dock had been developed; even the Beatles' legacy hadn't been cashed in on. So, what brought these girls here? The simple reason was they had seen The Teardrop Explodes in Dublin, or at least Courtney had; Robin, her friend from Portland, joined her after a short time. They became fans of the band and even followed them on tour to London, where they stayed for a while.

Julian Cope, 'Copey', suggested they should visit Liverpool and they could live in his vacant flat. He had already offered it to Pete de Freitas and Paul Simpson, who had moved in purely so it wouldn't be left empty and vulnerable. Pete and Paul were unaware of this arrangement between Cope, Courtney and Robin, but when the two girls knocked on the door and gave the Copey story, it all rang true. It was precisely the kind of thing Copey would do. Reluctantly, they let them in. I'm sure Pete would never have turned them away. Pete was too kind a fellow to see these two wandering around Liverpool with nowhere to go.

Courtney was blonde with a thin, tight bone structure. Robin was dark-haired, had bright red lips and had a Siouxsie Sioux look about her. They just seemed to have materialised from nowhere and suddenly were everywhere. Courtney was definitely the louder of the two and would assault you like a hurricane; she was extremely effervescent, the fizziest girl I had met. And it freaked me out, to be honest. If I spotted them on the other side of the road, I would say, 'Oh god, look, there are those fucking crazy American girls. Quick, hide.' And we would try and fade into the background, which was no easy task with my hair; that mushroom head of mine can be spotted at two hundred paces.

Courtney Love, me, our friend Tina, my girlfriend Laura and
Courtney's friend Robin. At the Hacienda, Manchester 1982

Eventually, we did become friends with Courtney and Robin, and would hang out with them in the bars, pubs and clubs. I kept a low profile and would take it all in from my usual spot in the shadows, but they became particularly good friends with my girlfriend, Laura. I still speak with Courtney occasionally, and she reminded me that I taught her how to play the riff from 'Rescue' on her guitar, a Gibson Melody Maker. She also asked me to give her guitar lessons. That's a laugh. I could barely play myself, so who was going to teach me first? I have no recollection of this, though I believe her; it's totally possible. She told me the conversation went something like this:

'Hey, Will, can you give me guitar lessons?'
'Nope.'

So here we are in spring 1982. We have existed for only three short years. We have made two full-length long-playing records. Both have been critically acclaimed in the music press. We have even been bothering the outer reaches of the charts. Our following is growing, and we can play where we like, when we like. We have inventive and maverick management in Big Bill Drummond. We have been to the USA twice. We have played in quite a few European countries. Blasted up and down the UK reasonably extensively. We have learned on the job and have become a tight-rocking entity. We have even been to the other side of the Earth to Australia and New Zealand. All that way to hang vibrations in the hot Antipodean air. I have had some moments of arrogant prick-ery but so far I've managed not to succumb to the full-on status of total wanker.

EATB first publicity shot

Acknowledgements

A big thank you to these teds.

MARTYN ATKINS
STEVE AVERAGE
DAVE BALFE
HOLLY BLOOD
ROBIN D BRADBURY
BILL BESSANT
IAN BROUDIE
BILL BUTT
PETE BYRNE
ENRICO CADILLAC JR
ANDREAS CAMPOMAR
JON CHILD
BERNIE CONNOR
PAUL (DAVO) DAVENPORT
JAMES DOOHAN
BILL DRUMMOND
PROFESSOR COLIN FALLOWS
LAURA BOWEN GARVIE
PEASY GORDON
BRIAN GRIFFIN

JESS GULLIVER
MATTHEW HAMILTON
MICK HOUGHTON
MICHAEL (CURLY) JOBSON
PHILL KNOX ROBERTS
COURTNEY LOVE
STEVE MURTON
KATH MURTON
DAVID (YORKIE) PALMER
LES PATTINSON
MARK REEDER
ALICE SERGEANT
GRETA SERGEANT
STEPHEN (OUR KID) SERGEANT
PAUL SIMPSON
JULIA TRICE
HOWARD WATSON

Photo Credits